DEBT OF HONOUR

How an Anzac saved the Assyrian people from Genocide.

Sarah Lindenmayer

 A catalogue record for this book is available from the National Library of Australia

Copyright © 2018 Sarah Lindenmayer

All rights reserved worldwide.

No part of the book may be copied or changed in any format, sold, or used in a way other than what is outlined in this book, under any circumstances, without the prior written permission of the publisher.

Publisher:
ASPG (Australian Self Publishing Group)
P.O. Box 159, Calwell, ACT Australia 2905
Email: publishaspg@gmail.com
http://www.inspiringpublishers.com
National Library of Australia Cataloguing-in-Publication entry

Author: Lindenmayer, Sarah

Title: **Debt of Honour**/*Sarah Lindenmayer.*

ISBN: 978-0-6483177-2-2 (print)

Genre: Australian History, World War 1

○ ○ ○

Dedication

In memory of the Assyrian victims of the Sayfo, 1915-1918.
Requiem aeternam dona eis, Domine.

o o o

Contents

Dedication 3
Author's Acknowledgment 7
Assyrian Community Acknowledgment 8
Savige Family Acknowledgment 9
Prologue 10

Part One: Calamity

  1. The Search Party 14

  2. The Council of Chieftains 20

  3. The Siege of Urmiah 24

  4. Year of the Sword 32

  5. Patriarchs and Potentates 42

  6. The Smallest Ally 51

  7. Bethnahrin 58

  8. The Generals' Ruse 70

Part Two: Mission

9. A Great Stunt 78
10. A Pioneer Boy Enlists 87
11. Preparations in Egypt 99
12. Chewing Sand at Suvla Bay 106
13. Gellibrand's Apprentice 122
14. Never a Finer Gathering 137
15. The High Road to Hamedan 142
16. An Alliance of Phantoms 155
17. All the Best in a Fellow 169

Part Three: Homeland

18. Conspicuous Gallantry 188
19. Defeat is an Orphan 198
20. A Knight's Legacy 214
21. Between the Rivers of Paradise 225

Bibliography 234

Endnotes 238

o o o

Author's Acknowledgment

As with all labours of love, this book has been a long time in the making. Since the story was first revealed to me, I felt it compelled me to plunge into the writing with all the energy and determination I could muster.

Of course, without the Assyrian communities of Sydney and Melbourne, for whom this is a deeply personal and emotional subject, it would have been impossible. In particular, my thanks go to Mr Gaby Kiwarkis, who from the beginning has shared his passion, insight and support. I thank Mr Joseph Haweil for his ongoing advice and generous assistance.

I gratefully acknowledge the generosity of the Savige family, which has supported me over several years. I am especially grateful for the precious private letters of General Sir Savige, which have not seen the light of day for 100 years.

My parents, husband and siblings have given their unwavering encouragement and empathy for the Assyrian cause and their respect for the general's legacy. Had I not embraced this gift, I would never have made such wonderful friends and I would not have experienced the rather mysterious ways in which the book itself pressed me onwards during the more shadowy times.

○ ○ ○

Assyrian Community Acknowledgment

This final year of the Centenary of Anzac 2018 is highly significant for the Assyrian community. Not only do we commemorate the Armistice we also commemorate the centenary of Sayfo, during which many thousands of Assyrians were killed.

We are an ancient people, who trace our ancestry directly back to Mesopotamia and the Assyrian Imperial dynasty. In our calendar this is year 6768. For millenia, our people have celebrated and survived the chances and changes of this fleeting world.

The Australian Assyrian community honours the great ANZAC General Sir Stanley Savige, who so valiantly saved over sixty thousand Assyrians from the atrocity committed in Persia in 1918. We are forever indebted to Sir Savige for his courage and compassion and for rescuing our people.

We gratefully acknowledge the devotion of the author Sarah Lindenmayer, who has captured our story with depth and authenticity. Finally it is available for all to read and understand.

This is our history. It is forever linked with General Savige's story. Together, it is a tremendous Australian odyssey.

Let us learn from the past and be humbled by it. Let us take heart and be grateful for what we have been given. This book will be a reason for lost souls to find rest in God's paradise. They will not be forgotten.

Gaby Kiwarkis
Assyrian Levies Association

Savige Family Acknowledgment

Sir Stanley's attitude to life was the same as his attitude to Military Service. In 1938 he said "life itself is worthless without some form of service to the community".

He lived by this statement, which embodied the boy, who from humble beginnings as a Sunday School teacher became a leader of men and a General.

We, his family, are very proud of his life dedicated to service; to his family, to the Army; to the Australian community in the founding of Legacy and his unwavering determination when he saved the Assyrian people from certain travesty in 1918.

His spirit of generosity was felt by all members of his extended family and the community in which he lived. He was known as a kind and generous man, loved and admired by all.

This book is a wonderful tribute to the man and the soldier, Stan Savige, who was brave, benevolent and bold. Sarah Lindenmayer is to be commended for bringing his extraordinary story to life.

The Savige Family

PROLOGUE

The past is an endless string of moments of change. Whether great or terrible, private or collective, they are the points after which nothing remains the same. Here is the story of such a moment.

One evening in August 1918, somewhere in the highlands of North West Persia, an Anzac rode into a campsite milling with Assyrian refugees. He dismounted his horse and collapsed on the ground from sheer exhaustion. Who was he? Who were the Assyrians? And what happened there?

It began with a lust for power. Way back in time, back to the origins of civilisation, the Assyrians emerge with their bloodthirsty drive for dominion over all the kingdoms and riches of the Near East. Over three millennia later at the end of the Great War, Captain Stanley Savige and the Assyrian tribes became entwined in an astounding moment of change—a hell-raising, secret military mission to Persia. Before he came face to face with the Assyrians that afternoon, Captain Savige had never even heard of them. Yet, after a week of mayhem and violence, his courage altered their destiny forever. Today, Savige is acclaimed by the Assyrians as a national hero, but in Australia he remains virtually unknown.

One hundred years after this tragedy unfolded, the Assyrians continue the struggle for survival in their homeland, Iraq. Untold until now, this is the true story of how an Anzac rescued the Assyrian people from certain death at the close of the Great War.

'Gentlemen, are you prepared to undertake a desperate venture which will probably cost you your lives, but if successful, will mean everything at this stage of the war to the British Empire?'[1]

British War Office proposal for mission,
General Birdwood's Field Headquarters,
January 1918

'The stand made by Savige and his eight companions that evening and during half of the next day against hundreds of the enemy... was as fine as any episode known to the present writer in the history of this war.'[2]

Charles W. Bean,
Australian war correspondent, 1918

'The widespread devastation of Assyrian communities, cultural property, and young people with the potential to enlighten and fascinate the entire world was just such an appalling loss to the region and to humanity'.[3]

Hannibal Travis,
International Association of
Genocide Scholars, 2007

'...My parents and the other refugees were fleeing from the Ottoman Empire to escape what would later be known as the 'Armenian, Assyrian and Pontic Greek Genocide'. By the grace of God my parents survived, for the reason they were protected, and protected by none other than an Australian soldier...and I, as the newly elected Liberal member for Smithfield, pay tribute to him today in this House.'[4]

Andrew Rohan,
Honourable Member for Smithfield,
NSW, June 2011

Part One
CALAMITY

o o o

Chapter One
The Search Party

Since the Assyrians are a tiny minority and lie in the path of the Turkish advance, they are probably doomed.
Secret cable from Intelligence Bureau,
Baghdad to British War Cabinet,
London, 12 March 1918

North West Persia, July 1918

Somewhere east of Bijar, in the heart of the Zagros Mountains, Captain Stanley Savige, an Australian officer, lead a small patrol along the rocky goat tracks and caravan trails. Captain Savige was an Anzac joined to a secret British mission to Persia, the most unlikely battleground of the Great War. The men had been trekking throughout the wilderness in the stifling, thin air for several months with little success but overnight their situation had changed. Somewhere in the highlands nearby were unidentified allied forces and Captain Savige's patrol was on the lookout for them.

A few days earlier, on 17 July, Captain Savige had received orders via wireless cable from the British mission headquarters at Hamedan, a few hundred kilometres to the south, in central Persia. His orders read:

1. You will be in charge of the party detailed hereunder proceeding with Major Moore.
2. Instructions as to time of departure, transport, etc will be notified later.
3. You will draw from the Q.M. sufficient ammunition to make up to 200 rounds per N.C.O. and O/R.[5]

Further instructions would be issued only when the search party was well down the track from Bijar. Since the mission had departed Baghdad in March, each man in his patrol had lost almost half his body weight due to illness, heat and hunger. In a letter written in May, he told his cousin that;

> We have been marching continuously for 10 days now...We had a frightful march yesterday, 16 miles. This sticky clay which sticks to ones boots like lead and had only 1 biscuit from 5:30am to 7pm. The people are in far worse health...they are simply dying of starvation.

For weeks, they had been living off dried fruit, wheat biscuits, bully beef and the occasional boiled egg, but now their rations and water were running out.

Dwindling rations were not Captain Savige's only problem. The Turkish Army was on the move in the mountains and there were murmurs of violent clashes taking place, to the north. The remotest parts of the Zagros Mountains had never been chartered officially, therefore Savige had no maps. Neither did he have an interpreter. To avoid any unwanted attention, he relied on a prismatic compass and his instincts as needs be. There was no time to replenish their rations in the local village so the captain decided that while there was still daylight, the search in the highlands around Bijar should continue.

16   Debt of Honour

The whole party now consisted of officers and non-commissioned officers from various imperial and commonwealth regiments and battalions; men from the Cheshires, Norfolks, Yorkshires, Kents, Highlanders, Auckland, Wellington, Canadians and Royal Irish Fusiliers. Major Moore, a political adviser who had joined them from the British General Staff in Baghdad, made up a unit of twenty-three men altogether.

Captain Savige and the party were weighed down by several wooden crates laden with rifles, 100,000 rounds of ammunition and a poultice of Persian silver.[6] This was the currency of negotiation throughout the Persian alps, and it was better than any map. For the time being the party was escorted by a small cavalry unit to protect their cargo. After a long day's ride, they camped in the open air.

Throughout the mission, Captain Savige kept two diaries—a field diary to record the unit's operations and a personal diary for his own reflections, which he scribbled down in the evenings. It was at this point in the mission that he wrote 'after spending so many months together in a far off land and being such a small party, a deep friendship existed between the officers and men, a friendship which people living the humdrum life of the cities of civilised lands, have no conception of...Under our conditions...all the best in a fellow comes to the top.'[7]

Well before sunrise the following morning, the captain roused the party and they had headed off into the hills without knowing exactly what was around the corner.

The object of the mission was finally spelled out in a wireless cable, which Savige read as he sat around an open campfire with the other men, after a full day's trek. He was given the following details:

> deliver the silver and the arms to...the Commander of the Assyrian Army at small outpost village of Sain Qaleh on...23rd July. Our

duty on arrival at Urmiah...Take command of two gunboats... anchored on Lake Urmiah...organise immediately this irregular army and endeavour, if possible, to keep the southern road open to Tabriz in order that we could be reinforced later on.[8]

At first light, the search party pushed off directly northwards from Bijar to Sain Qaleh, a route of about 190 kilometres. Captain Savige was on the lookout for General Agha Petros, Commander of the Assyrian Army. The plan was to join forces with the Assyrians and march back to Urmiah to fight the Turkish army, which had captured the city. The arsenal of light artillery, ammunition and Persian silver would be used to reinforce the Assyrian garrison when they reached Urmiah.

One of the other officers, Captain Scott Olsen, would take charge of the small fleet of armed vessels anchored on the lake. The other men would establish flank posts at vantage points and road junctions on the eastern and western sides of Lake Urmiah to reinstate communications with the mission post at Bijar and Hamedan HQ. They would also undertake surveillance of the main Tabriz–Teheran road to block any attempts by the Turkish army to progress towards the Persian capital Teheran. The whole plan relied on General Petros and the Assyrian forces successfully breaking through the Turkish cordon around Lake Urmiah and reaching Sain Qaleh by 23 July.[9] Failing that the city of Urmiah would be decimated by the Turkish Army.

Captain Savige knew that forced marches were the only way the search party could reach their destination in four days through menacing terrain. He recorded the marches in his field diary: '19th July, Left Bijar, trekked sixteen miles to Punjah—arrived Kizil Bulahk distance sixteen to eighteen miles—arrived Takan Tepe sixteen miles—arrived San Jud twenty-eight miles.' On and on they went around mountains and through ravines and hairpin bends in the blistering heat, men and horses all wasted. As ordered, on the morning of 23rd July, they rode into Sain Qaleh.[10] But Captain Savige's diary entry reads: 'People not there!' Even though they were a day late themselves, there was no sign of the Assyrians; no soldiers, no horses, not a whisper of their whereabouts.

Knowing that the Assyrians were in dire trouble at Urmiah and holding out for reinforcements and supplies, the captain and his men were anxious to make contact with the general but they were also bewildered by their absence. Were the Assyrians lost? Perhaps the Turkish Army had attacked them en route to Sain Qaleh? Was it too late to help anyone in Urmiah? 'Bitterly disappointed' was all Captain Savige wrote in his diary that day.

He decided to wait for the Assyrians at Sain Qaleh for a few days, in case they had been waylaid by fighting or other unforeseen obstacles. In the meantime, they bribed the local Persian telegraph operator to ascertain whether his party's movements had been detected by any Turks present in the area. The Vali (Governor) of Sain Qaleh visited Captain Savige the next morning to give official assurances of his hospitality, but the telegrams intercepted by the operator confirmed that the governor had in fact alerted the nearby Turkish Army commander of their arrival in the town. The Turks were now on their way to Sain Qaleh to disable the search party.

It was too dangerous for Savige and his men to linger in the town any longer. The captain received orders to abort the mission and return to Bijar at once. Captain Savige believed it was wrong to abandon the Assyrians and so, not being easily deterred, he made one final appeal to his senior officers at HQ:

The idea of still being able to reach the Assyrians had not by any means left us and after consulting with the commander of the party, we ascertained that he was quite willing for us to remain at Takan Teppeh, in order to establish a post, with the hope that we would raise a force strong enough to work through to Urmiah, should the Assyrians and the Armenians fail in their breakthrough.[11]

His strategy was approved by the senior officers:

We showed both the Colonel and the Major that the idea could be carried out by travelling along the banks of the stream, which passed Sain Qaleh and flowed into the Lake, and by travelling all night with the stream as a guide there would be little risk of being caught, and as for supplies, we had the men who were prepared to do the job, if need be, on dry rice and water.[12]

Camped on a barren hillside, Captain Savige and his search party staked out the night, guarding their treasury of weapons and silver, and waited for the Assyrian Army.

Chapter Two
The Council of Chieftains

Later that night, 30 July, a ghostly plume of dust rose from the floor of the valley, where the men were encamped. An unknown rider was moving at the gallop around the cliffs waving what appeared to be a handkerchief. He soon charged straight into the search party's campsite, dismounted and handed a piece of paper to the captain. It was a handwritten note from General Agha Petros. At last, the Assyrians had broken through the Turkish blockade at Urmiah and were headed south to join the British scouting party at Sain Qaleh. Turkish forces were 'evacuating the area south of Lake Urmiah' and were not far behind. There were cheers all round at the news of the breakthrough. At the break of dawn on 1 August, Captain Savige and his men packed their camp, saddled their horses and advanced back down the road towards Sain Qaleh to meet the Assyrians.

The search party covered a huge distance that day and pulled up at sundown to camp out of sight, otherwise the Turkish troops would make short work of them. Captain Savige surveyed the valley below with his field glasses. Behind the curtain of fading light, about a mile away, he spotted a band of unrecognisable cavalry. The head rider held up a large, red silken standard with a huge white cross that billowed in front of the horsemen. As they got closer, he could read the words on the standard: Trust God and follow the Cross. It was the advance guard of the Assyrian Army.

The guard dismounted in the middle of the road to scope the foreign camp site on the crest of the hill. Through their field glasses, Captain Savige and the Assyrian guards spied one another for a minute or two. Then Captain Savige shouted down the hillside that they were English. Within moments of the information sinking in a wave of cheering 'in no half hearted manner'—shouting, whistling and air-firing—ricocheted around the valley.[13] There they waited for the main army of mountaineers to follow.

Around the bend, swinging up the valley in flamboyant style was a colonnade of Assyrian cavaliers, many thousands of them, decked out in colourful, tribal uniforms and heraldry, cheering and singing as they went.[14] It took a few hours for the entire cavalcade to assemble but finally, behind the standard bearers and cavaliers, in the midst of the clan chieftains rode their commander, General Agha Petros. The Assyrian Army surrounded Captain Savige and the search party at the hilltop camp site.

The chieftains gathered around the camp fire to discuss the days' events and summoned Captain Savige and his officers to join them for an all-night conference. Firstly, the chieftains explained their late arrival; a few days earlier they had breached the Turkish cordon south of Urmiah, swooped down upon the Turkish headquarters at Suldaz and decimated their enemy in the ambush. They bolted down the road to join the search party at Sain Qaleh as agreed, but they were completely exhausted. They were out-of-pocket and their rations had run dry.[15]

When the chieftains settled down for the night, Captain Savige and Commander Petros commenced their negotiations in private. Petros made it clear that he was exasperated by the size of the so-called British regiment. According to the terms of the agreement he had expected a much larger force of British soldiers and equipment—a handful of officers officers and three field guns verged on an insult. There was nothing the captain could do except reaffirm his commitment to Petros and assisting his cavalier force. The captain and the general eventually settled upon the terms of a new joint operation against the Turkish Army.[16] Captain Savige would lead the combined Assyrian and British force back to Urmiah to rescue the Assyrian civilians from the Turkish siege.

Before they set off, Captain Savige gave a generous portion of the Persian silver to the chieftains in order to purchase food, supplies and ammunitions for the operation. General Petros requested that Captain Savige ride at the head of the column with the other British officers in order to impress the Persian governor and the villagers of Sain Qaleh with a display of military strength and unity, which would spread by word of mouth throughout the province and beyond. It was 5 August when the entire joint mounted regiment departed for Urmiah, escorted by their traditional heralds carrying their banner.

By dusk, on the outskirts of Sain Qaleh, the joint Assyrian British force peeled off the main road to encamp for the night near an orchard. In the fading light, something caught Captain Savige's eye. Strangers were hiding in the grass a short distance away, huddled together quietly under the fruit trees. Their appearance was dishevelled and unfamiliar; the women's faces were not veiled. Captain Savige felt uneasy and was hesitant to approach them.

General Petros sidled up to the captain to find out what the matter was. For a few moments the general stood gaping at the strangers in the orchard. Like an ox, he bellowed from the pit of his stomach: 'My God! Here are my people! What calamity has happened during my absence?'[17]

○ ○ ○

Chapter Three
The Siege of Urmiah

I seem to have left I know not how many homes;
and to leave each was still to leave a portion of mine own heart,
and all I had was regret and a memory.
Christopher Brennan

The women and children hiding in the orchard were Assyrians who had escaped the Turkish siege of Urmiah. They were barefoot, injured and in a state of shock. No one could comprehend how they had made it all the way to Sain Qaleh on foot, a journey of 500 kilometres, without food or protection. Anxious for details, the mountain chieftains questioned the women but they were too exhausted and distressed to provide any useful information about what had happened in the city.

Then one man among them, a doctor, who rode in later that evening, recounted the chain of event chain of events leading up to the evacuation of Urmiah.[18] The Turkish Army overpowered the Russian garrison at the southern end of Lake Urmiah and rushed into the city. A dreadful massacre ensued. The Turkish forces and the Kurdish militia set about wrecking and burning houses, violating women and plunging the whole city into bloody bedlam. Those who were able to get away fled into the mountains and plains, chasing the heels of their patron Agha Petros.[19] The city finally succumbed after years of bloodshed and deprivation.

Urmiah was the capital of Azerbaijan province in northwest Persia, where the borders of Turkey, Persia and Mesopotamia converged. From the Zagros Mountains three rivers flow eastwards across the province into an enormous, forested salt lake; it is thought that Urmiah means 'cradle of water' in Aramaic. Although predominantly Azerbaijani, the province was also home to a large, Christian minority that comprised around 45 per cent of the population—approximately 76,000 Assyrians, 50,000 Armenians, and a small community of 1,000 Jews. Kurdish tribes mainly inhabited the surrounding highlands. Assyrians had lived there for centuries, as sharecropper peasants, in compact farming settlements along the rivers, the plains of Urmiah and Salmas and the uplands of Tergarwar, Mergawar and Baradost. Of the estimated 300 villages scattered throughout the plains and uplands, 60 were exclusively Assyrian.[20]

Before the war, this northern territory of Persia had been in Russian hands, but since the first winter of the Great War, it had twice been overtaken by Ottoman forces, as they battled for control of the Caucuses. Living conditions in Urmiah had deteriorated drastically during three years of conflict. In July 1918, the American Ambassador to Persia cabled a report on the state of affairs there:

> Urmiah is now completely isolated being surrounded on all sides by Turkish forces. There are from four to eight thousand (As)syrian Christians under arms in that region who claim so far to have been victorious in one of about a score of encounters with the Turks. They are nearly out of funds and ammunition and

their condition is serious…It is alleged that Turks have stated in Tabriz that if they succeed in taking Urmiah they will massacre every Christian in Azerbaijan province, but such allegations are incapable of proof.[21]

Three years earlier, in the winter of 1915, the population of Urmiah had swelled with many thousands of Assyrians and Armenians from outlying districts of both northern Persia and eastern Turkey, who were trying to escape the onslaught of the Ottoman Army. The Persian Government did little to protect the citizens of Urmiah from attack because it was preoccupied with its own turbulent domestic affairs. Likewise, the Persian Army turned a blind eye to the siege, leaving the Assyrian mountaineers and Armenians to fend for themselves against the Turkish invasion of the city.

Persia had declared its neutrality to the rest of the world in the national parliament in Teheran on 1 November 1914 and remained neutral throughout the Great War. In reality, the country was in a fragile, highly conflicted state. Political rebellions were rife, tribal allegiances were fluid, ethnic tensions were on the boil, communications were unreliable and danger lurked in every corner. Tribal clans—such as the Baluchis, Azeris, Kurds, Turki, Lashanis, Jangalis, Senjabis, Bakhtiaris, Kashqais—fought each other for political influence, while religious minorities—such as Jews, Cossacks, Armenians and Assyrians—struggled for status and security.

Persian institutions were corrupt and dysfunctional, having been usurped by foreign governments and armies for decades prior to the Great War.[22] The Persian Government had little capacity to manage its unruly borders with India, Afghanistan, Russian Turkestan, Russian Azerbaijan and Mesopotamia.[23] The country was also crawling with spies and double agents.

Added to these domestic pressures, the Turkish Army was on the warpath. Local sources claim that the Ottoman governor of Van, Cevdet Bey Pasha, gave orders for the killing of civilian minorities to commence in his province, which borders onto north west Persia. The Turkish infantry set to work burning and sacking houses and barns, violating women and girls and ruining crops, barns and irrigation works. Thirty Assyrian villages were decimated and approximately 20,000 civilians were murdered in the pogrom. Around 13,000 people fled in one direction onto the Salmas Plains, and in the other direction, scores of thousands more Assyrians and Armenians fled on foot to the Caspian seaports, hoping to squeeze onto Russian navy boats and merchant steamers.

Similar atrocities were perpetrated in the Assyrian centres of Mardin and Diyarbakir. Another 30,000 or so destitute Assyrian refugees headed for Urmiah seeking refuge with European expatriates, church missions and consular houses.[24] The director of the American mission in Urmiah, Reverend Dr Shedd described the crisis, as he watched the refugees pouring into his compound:

> The retreat of the Russians put all Christians in peril. The Salmas Christians, except about eight hundred, most of the Christians of Tabriz and eight to ten thousand from Urmiah, fled with the retreating Russians. They left on the shortest notice, without preparation...Many perished by the way...This party of fugitives increased in number by several thousands from regions in Turkey between Khoi and Van...This flight left some 25,000 Christians in Urmiah. All of these sought shelter from the massacre...The French Roman Catholic Mission sheltered about 3000 and the American Presbyterian Mission about 17,000.[25]

In May 1915, the Turkish Army, lead by Halil Bey, suffered a terrible defeat at the hands of the Russian Army on the Salmas Plains. During their retreat through the Assyrian tribal upland of Gawar, the Turkish forces decimated the villages of Gagoran, Pirzalan, Maskhudawa, Mamikan, Diza and Zezan, which left around 1,000 villagers dead.[26] Despite the Russian victory and the retreat of the Turks, the Russian Army withdrew unexpectedly from the eastern provinces of Turkey and northern Persia, due to the burgeoning revolution at home.

Overnight, Russian garrisons were abandoned and occupied towns were evacuated. Hundreds of Armenian and Assyrian villages dotted throughout the region were left without protection. Once word of the Russian retreat had spread, panic erupted like like a brushfire through the Christian areas of Persia and eastern Turkey, from house to house, village to village, north western the Zagros and Hakkari mountain ranges and down to the Salmas and Nineveh Plains. One American eyewitness, Reverend Labaree, who worked at the Tabriz mission, described the mayhem:

> The whole northern section of the Urmiah plains learned of the departure of the Russian troops about ten o'clock on the night of Saturday, the 2nd January. By midnight the terrible exodus had begun, and by morning the Christian villages…were practically deserted. People left their cattle in the stables and all their household goods, just as they were and hurried to save their lives…and the vast majority of men and women and children were on foot. Before the seven days' hard walking through the slush and mud to the Russian border…all encumbrances were cast aside, quilts, extra clothing, and even bread, for it became a question with the poor, tired struggling crowd which they would carry—their bedding or their babies.[27]

The missionaries were overwhelmed with the sick and the wounded. Day and night they baked bread by the ton to feed the refugees, and in the morning they dug graves over every square inch of ground in the backyards of the mission compounds. Despite their efforts 'not less than four thousand' refugees succumbed to starvation, typhoid and tuberculosis during the endless winter siege of 1915. Almost overnight, the beautiful lakeside city had become a ghetto. One of the eyewitnesses, a Swiss missionary named Miss Shauffler Platt, described what happened inside the compound on the night 11 January, 1915:

> Several families from Degala are camped in our parlour...an old woman had just come in who didn't seem able to answer anything...we had absolutely no place but a stone floor for her, but we took up a carpet from my bedroom, rolled her up in it...and she went to sleep...she had escaped barefooted, almost naked and without food. She died a day or two later. One poor woman, who had both her husband and son killed has gone crazy and we haven't any place to put her but a dark closet under the stairway. At midnight I was awakened by her pounding on the door. She was nursing a baby...she died two days later...We have not been able to take the dead from our yards, so we are burying them in the little yard by the side of the church—twenty seven so far.[28]

One year on, the siege of Urmiah was lifted lifted when the Russian Army reoccupied north-western Persia but the residents were too frightened and weak to return to their village homes. In 1917, when the Bolsheviks took control of the Russian Army and abducted the Tsar's family, General Agha Petros was so incensed that he resigned from his commission with the Russian Army, refusing to take orders from revolutionaries. He immediately took command of the Assyrian

Army, an autonomous force of 15,000 cavaliers, and established his headquarters in Urmiah.[29]

After changing hands a few times between Russian and Kurdish control, Ottoman forces again laid siege to Urmiah in February 1918, where they encamped around the perimeter of Lake Urmiah. The Assyrian Army had been defending their city against several Turkish battalions without supply or reinforcements for more than six months. Ammunition and rations were near empty and their communication system was out of order. The mountaineers and the civilians were at the point of collapse. General Petros had been waiting for several weeks for news of backup promised by the French, British and Russian commands, but the materiel never arrived. The Assyrians were unable to hold out much longer when another wave of Turkish and Kurdish forces swept through the area.

The siege of Urmiah continued. Lifeless bodies lay upright on doorsteps, and others were strewn in the streets like leaf litter. By July 1918, although scores of thousands had perished from disease and starvation since 1915, approximately 130,000 Assyrians and a cohort of Armenians were still trapped inside the city walls. The only thing preventing the Turkish forces from inundating the city was a remnant of Tsarist Russians and Armenian loyalists who held the garrison at Lake Urmiah. But when they learned that General Petros and the Assyrian mountaineers had crushed the Ottoman troops at Suldaz, at the southern end of the lake, they realised the way was clear to return to Russia, and they immediately abandoned their posts.

Upon the collapse of the lakeside garrisons, the Turkish forces and the Kurdish militia began butchering Assyrian and Armenian residents and refugees. It happened in a flash, and a stampede ensued.[30] The city gates were choked with people trying to escape the massacre. Those who got out of Urmiah tried to catch up with General Petros who they knew was somewhere in the mountains, on his way to join forces with the British Army near Sain Qaleh. As they fled the city, Turkish and Kurdish troops stole their belongings and abducted women and young girls as payment.[31]

The news of the siege distressed the General Petros and his tribal chiefs. For Captain Savige and his search party, it raised more questions than answers about the Assyrians and what had caused the deadly mayhem at Urmiah. At that late hour there was nothing General Petros or Captain Savige could do for the fugitives in the orchard, let alone the people left behind in the city. There were a few days of hard riding ahead them, so they turned in for the night. The knowledge of the task ahead no doubt weighed heavily on each of them.

Chapter Four
Year of the Sword

When sorrows come, they come not single spies, but in battalions.
Shakespeare, Hamlet, Act IV

Turkish agents arrived uninvited at Qudshanis, a sleepy hamlet perched in a rugged valley of the Hakkari mountains of eastern Turkey, in late autumn, 1914. The Turks brought large quantities of gold bullion with them to blackmail the Assyrian patriarch, Mar Binyamin Shimmun, but they were too late. Agents and emissaries of various imperial quarters had already approached the patriarch with their shady promises and double-edged deals when the Great War began in the summer.

The agents seized a narrow window of opportunity left open just after the Russians declared war on Germany and just before the Ottomans declared war on Russia. War had made a risky situation even more dangerous for the Assyrians. Depending on which side of three borders they resided, the Assyrians were either citizens of the Ottoman Empire in Turkey or Mesopotamia which were allied to the Central Powers, or they were citizens of neutral Persia. In the Russian-occupied zones of Persia, Tsar Nicholas Romanov, as head of the Russian Orthodox Church, provided nominal protection for Assyrian and Armenian Christians. The Ottoman Government had long suspected that the Assyrian patriarch would join his formidable army of 15,000 cavaliers with the Tsar's army, and had entreated him to remain neutral. In the Persian highlands, however, allegiances were fluid. In a place where the enemy of one's enemy was not necessarily one's ally, reliable friends could be hard to come by. However, the mountain Assyrians' stalwart allegiance rested with their patriarch.

Binyamin Shahmir was born at Qudshanis in 1887 into the Shimmunite patriarchal family, one of six siblings. His mother had fasted from meat during her pregnancy in order to consecrate her son for a life of service and sacrifice. He became a wise, gentle-hearted and gracious young man with dark eyes and a serene presence. At age 16, Binyamin was coronated as His Holiness Patriarch Mar Shimmun XXI on Palm Sunday, 1903. It took place at the church in Qudshanis, which had been the throne of the Patriarchal See of the Assyrian Church of the East since the mid seventeenth century.

Mar Binyamin Shimmun was adored by the people, who called upon him for all manner of duties; to appoint their tribal chiefs, to settle legal disputes, to conduct religious feasts and instruction, to collect the Koranic based millet taxes, to negotiate with all manner of domestic and foreign authorities, to lead the tribal army and nurture the spiritual welfare of his mountain flock.[32] Qudshanis lay to the west of Urmiah on the other side of the Hakkari ranges, making the patriarch and mountain tribes Turkish subjects. Youthful and innocent though he was, Mar Binyamin would guide his people through a watershed in Assyrian history.

When the Turkish agents appeared in Qudshanis in October 1914 to offer Mar Binyamin an ultimatum, they did not realise that the Russians had jumped the gun. Months earlier, Russian officials from Urmiah, possibly in negotiation with General Agha Petros, had already promised to arm the Assyrian mountaineers with 25,000 rifles and some small artillery in return for the Assyrian patriarch's loyalty and the service of his mountaineers.[33] Mar Binyamin had much to weigh up. The Turkish offer was very tempting; the gold bullion would go a long way in alleviating the dire poverty of his community. But the offer was laced with treachery. The patriarch would have to guarantee that the Assyrians would remain neutral during the war.

Relations between the Russians and the Assyrians had improved over the preceding decades since 1889, when about 15,000 Assyrians had converted to Orthodoxy. In 1906, the Russian Vice-Consul in Urmiah met Mar Binyamin Shimmun to discuss a compact between them in the event of hostilities and, in 1910, cordial ties were formally established. In 1913, the Mar Shimmun's decision to unite with the Russian Orthodox Church was delayed due to the outbreak of war.

On 3 August 1914, Mar Binyamin was summoned by the Ottoman governor of Van, to persuade the Assyrians to stay neutral but within a month the Russians had formed a local brigade of Assyrian mountaineers.[34] When the Russian Army vacated their garrison at Lake Urmiah, the Assyrians were run over by the invading Turkish forces.

Then German agents appeared in Qudshanis with another ultimatum for Mar Binyamin to consider. The German consul in Mosul, Mesopotamia, had dispatched a squad of secret agents to convey an unambiguous message to Mar Binyamin—that every Assyrian man, woman and child throughout the Ottoman Empire would be guaranteed personal protection in return for the patriarch's neutrality during the war. But before Mar Binyamin could give his final answer, the guns of August 1914 fired up on the Western Front.

Before the Great War had officially begun, Turkish military authorities commenced a general mobilisation in Mesopotamia. They reinforced the port city of Basrah and dispatched around 10,000 troops from Bagdad to Mosul.[35] The British Admiralty scrambled to secure their oilfields and infrastructure in the Persian Gulf, and to protect over 130 miles of pipeline between Basrah and Mosul.[36] On 1 November, the Turkish Government declared their alliance with the Central Powers, Germany and Austria, against the Entente Powers of Britain, France and Russia. Four days later, Great Britain declared war on Turkey and invaded Mesopotamia the very next day, on 6 November. Turkey declared war on Britain on 11 November.[37]

While all eyes were on western Europe, a holy war was announced by the Sheikh-ul-Islam, Commander of all Believers, in Istanbul on 14 November against the armies of Russia, France, Britain and Serbia. The Sheikh declared; [38]

> Take them and kill them whenever you find them. He who kills even one unbeliever among those who rule over us, whether he does it secretly or openly shall be rewarded by God. And let every Muslim, in whatever part of the world he may be, swear a solemn oath to kill at least three or four of the infidels who rule over him.[39]

The injunction to jihad was disseminated in mosques and newspapers throughout the Ottoman Empire, and in neighbouring Muslim nations such as Persia. It was music to the ears of the Germans because it heaped the coals of religious sanction onto smouldering political trouble in countries where the British were most invested—India, Afghanistan and the Near East. Within days of joining the Central Powers, the Turkish Minister of War, Enver Pasha, ordered sea mines to be laid in the Dardanelles. Soon German personnel, matériel and 15 million marks worth of gold began flowing into Constantinople.[40]

That's when the knife twisted in Mar Binyamin's back. As added security and to expedite his decision, the German agents informed the Mar Shimmun that his younger brother Hormuzd had been abducted and was being held to ransom by Turkish authorities in Mosul: 'Your brother is in my hands, and unless you and your nation will lay down your arms, that brother shall die.'[41] Mar Binyamin agonised over his answer but there was no sufferable solution:

> It is impossible for me to surrender after seeing the atrocities done to my Assyrian people by your government; my people are my charge, and they are many. How can I give them up for the sake of one, even if that one be my own brother?[42]

The patriarch was helpless to prevent the onslaught against the Assyrian community. During the first winter of the war, innumerable massacres and pogroms were perpetrated against the Assyrian and Armenian Christians who lived throughout the valleys and highlands of eastern Turkey and northern Persia, sparking upheaval and terror within their communities. People abandoned their villages, farms, churches and houses en masse to escape the vengeance of the Turkish and Kurdish military forces.

The old and sick were left behind; livestock were left in their stalls. Tens of thousands of Assyrians fled on foot from the surrounding Hakkari ranges and the Salmas plains to larger towns and cities such as Mosul, Khoi, Van, Dilman, Tabriz, Diyarbakir, Siirt, Erivan and Urmiah. Hundreds and thousands of Assyrians and Armenians made a dash for the Mediterranean and the Caspian Sea ports, clambering onto overcrowded boats and ferries in the hope of making a sea crossing to safety. Over 30,000 Christians crammed into the American, French and Russian mission compounds in Urmiah until they were bursting.

In April 1915, Mar Binyamin Shimmun summoned a council of the Assyrian tribes to make a final decision. The chieftains of the Baz, Jilu, Tyari, Tkhuma, Diz and Baktiari tribes assembled to decide on a survival strategy. Should they side with the Turks for protection against the Kurds? Mar Binyamin's mind boiled; he must surely have been plagued by awful scenarios: 'The war will soon be over and at least, without any reason to doubt our loyalty to the Sultan, my brother's life will be spared.' On the other hand, if the Assyrian mountaineers allied themselves to the European Entente powers they would be supplied with Russian arms for the duration of the conflict: 'The Tsar will surely be victorious against the Turks and then finally, if the Russians keep their word, our people can look forward to autonomy in this land.'

Then again, if the Assyrians sided with the Entente Powers, a German victory would bring a devastating revenge by the Turks: 'Oh dear brothers! We are trapped like doves in a cage. If we remain neutral we forfeit the promise of independence. If we take sides we may be wiped off the face of the earth. Lord show us a way out.'[43]

Meanwhile the Ottoman Governor of Mosul, Rashid Pasha, corralled a force of 7,000 troops with 15,000 Kurdish militia reinforcements and light field artillery along the banks of the Great Zab River in north-eastern Mesopotamia, ready to fight the Assyrians.[44] Russian troops continued retreating from the region leaving their little ally to fend for themselves in the Hakkari mountains. The tribesmen were armed with 20,000 French rifles and 400 Cossack reinforcements. The promised delivery of Russian and British military back up and ammunition never arrived.

On 10 May 1915, Mar Binyamin Shimmun and the Council of the tribal chieftains called the Assyrian nation to arms against Turkey.

The Assyrian Army rode into the highlands singing their traditional war song:[45]

> Forth we go to battle, raging o'er the mountains;
> Hearts all yearning forward to Mosul's fertile plains.
> Nineveh's fair city summons back her children.
> Forth we go to battle in thy name, O Mar Shimmun.
>
> On the Tigris' banks lies Nineveh the holy;
> Her old walls shall be to us a diadem and crown.
> There alone, Assyrians, can our race be established.
> Forth we go to battle in thy name, O Mar Shimmun.[46]

On 21 June, Turkish forces opened fire on the Assyrians. The sight of the Turkish troops and the hammering, deafening sound of the light artillery—heard for the first time by the terrified villagers of Sarispedo, Asheta, Geramon, Arosh, Halmon, Zaweta, Minyanish, Zarni, Shimchadjian — and sent them scattering down the valleys and highland passes.[47] It was about this time that Mar Binyamin Shimmun learned that his brother had been tortured to death in a prison at Mosul. He also learned that his patriarchal home and library at Qudshanis—a treasure trove of ancient liturgical texts and vessels, embroidered vestments and heirlooms—had been desecrated and burnt down by the Kurdish forces. One by one farmsteads were sacked, churches torched and people butchered.

Some 30,000 survivors—men, women and children from 12 different tribes—came together with their goods and chattels into one gigantic camp, communal camp at the headwaters of the Tal and Tkhuma gorges at the northern edge of the Hakkari mountains. In the midst of the clans sat the patriarch, Binyamin Shimmun, surrounded by his family and the tribal chiefs.[48]

For weeks the fugitive families lived off sheep's milk and maize, and although meat and water were in good supply, without any salt or shelter they began to weaken and succumb to illness. By late September 1915, the temperature plunged and snow started drifting over the higher peaks. Mar Binyamin could see that his people were going to die in one of two ways—slowly by starvation, or suddenly by the edge of the sword.

Mar Binyamin conferred with the chiefs; there were few options left. He decided to make a mercy dash to the Russian garrison at Bashqala, lying at the bottom of the plateau thousands of feet below. It might be the last thing he ever did for them. With 40 of his fittest mountaineers, Mar Binyamin took off into the night through the rugged tracks under enemy surveillance. When they made it to the Bashqala garrison, they found the Russian forces in position, waiting for the Turkish Army to attack. The patriarch pleaded with the Russian commander to come back with him and help the people to retreat from the mountain-top camp, but the commander warned them to stay at the garrison, urging the patriarch not to sacrifice his life by going back.[49]

There was no one to save them. Their highland home had become a trap. Surrounded and outnumbered, by what means could Mar Binyamin extricate his people, all 30,000 of them? Even if it were possible, where should he lead them to safety when the world was at war? Mar Binyamin rode back up to the camp with empty hands and a leaden heart.

In the half-light of dawn, Kurdish forces encircled the camp and got their machine guns into position. Then they opened fire on the people as they slept on the ground. Some hid behind rocks, others lay petrified. Gunfire continued in deafening bursts for several minutes, followed by shrieking and wailing.

Five hundred people were dead, hundreds more were injured and dazed.

As quickly as they had appeared, the Kurdish cavalry retreated into the crooks of the mountains and down the valley, carrying away dozens of women and children who had survived the ambush.[50] By noonday, rumours had reached the chieftains of another massacre of 2,000 Tkhuma and Tyari clan folk in an adjacent valley. Once more, the clan chiefs assembled around the patriarch, this time knowing for certain that there was no one to help and nowhere to hide. It was a night of dread, a night of lament.

Mar Binyamin must have stared into the darkness for hours. Did it seem to him as though time itself had turned against the Assyrians? Would he have imagined that his people's past and future would be devoured in one gulp? It was inconceivable that they had come to such a pitiful end; it reflected nothing of their glorious past. It spoke nothing of their faith or resilience. Again and again the Assyrians had appealed for assistance, pleading for protection from the intermittent skirmishes and pogroms, imploring authorities for clemency. The missionaries had been their only source of support.

Somehow, the patriarch smuggled his people off the mountain. It is likely, after a night spent in supplication that at first light Mar Binyamin dressed in his cassock, hung the patriarchal cross around his neck, and turned towards his people, blessing them as they lay strewn across the ground like washing lost on a windy day. He may have prayed over them in the ancient words of the Assyrian church: 'O Desired One of the nations, who binds two into one, who appeared to Moses on Mount Sinai help us. O Dayspring, reaching from beginning to end, come save us who dwell in the shadow of death, Lord our God!'

Mar Binyamin Shimmun gathered the Assyrian clans together and led them off the mountain into the valley below. Down through the stony paths they marched, beneath pinnacles, across footbridges, passing by their ransacked villages, staring into the ravines, asking 'when shall I ever drink the waters of Qudshanis again?'[51] In a few days, the clans made it to Urmiah. There they piled in with thousands of other Assyrian families who had already sought asylum inside the overcrowded, unsanitary compounds of the American and Russian missions, during the winter siege of 1915.

The Assyrian calamity was the first of its kind in the twentieth century, or perhaps the first that came to the attention of Western powers. It is estimated that between half to two thirds of the Assyrian population that dwelled in the mountain regions of Ottoman Turkey and northern Persia was annihilated.[52] The term 'genocide' was first coined to describe these atrocities. Under the banner of what is now known as the Armenian Genocide, the ethnic cleansing of the Assyrians by Ottoman government forces is rarely acknowledged because their true identity as a unique ethnic and religious minority distinct from the Armenians was never properly understood or reported by foreign authorities. This misconception continues today and has serious ramifications for the Assyrian people.

The Assyrian term for genocide is Sayfo, meaning the Year of the Sword. 1915 was the bloody culmination of a long campaign of persecution and ethnic cleansing aimed at exterminating the Christian population of the Ottoman territories. The seeds of this violence germinated decades earlier and so it seemed at the outset of the Great War that the Assyrians had succumbed to their fate.

As winter drifted over the alpine peaks and valleys of the Hakkari Ranges, Mar Binyamin Shimmun and the Assyrian clans departed their ancestral homeland, never to return.

o o o

Chapter Five
Patriarchs and Potentates

*What are kings, when regiment is gone,
but perfect shadows in a sunshine day?*

Christopher Marlowe

In the midsummer of 1842, Reverend George Percy Badger disembarked at Constantinople's chaotic wharves in a swathe of perspiration. The briny air rose from the Bosphorus Sea and mingled with the smells of fish, spices and overripe vegetables, perhaps leaving Father Badger with the sensation of wading into a tub of seafood broth. Tucked away with his personal belongings was a letter bearing the official seal of the Archbishop of Canterbury and the Lord Bishop of London that spelled out the terms of his official visit. He was to establish contact with the Assyrian Christians in the Ottoman provinces and report back to the Archbishop as soon as possible. Father Badger intended to deliver the Archbishop's letter in person to the Assyrian Patriarch at Qudshanis.[53]

The Archbishop of Canterbury sent Father Badger to Constantinople in response to a written plea he had received some months earlier from the Assyrian Patriarch, Mar Abraham Shimmun. In his letter, Mar Abraham had implored the Church of England to help protect his forlorn congregation by whatever means possible.[54] He described how, after centuries of deprivation and persecution, the once mighty Assyrian Church of the East had shrivelled into a network of destitute parishes, scattered throughout the mountains of Turkey and Persia. Without outside aid, Assyrian Christians faced a bleak future.

The patriarch's letter caused a sensation in church circles. In the English imagination, even to those classically educated clerics of Oxford and Cambridge who studied ancient history and theology, Assyria was the name of a wicked, fallen empire that had taken the Jews into exile in Babylon as described in the Holy Bible. Aside from that, the wild borders of the Ottoman Caliphate were far beyond the grasp of the British Empire. Now this intriguing letter from the Near East had brought the Assyrians leaping back to life off the pages of the Old Testament and into the drawing room of the Archbishop's palace in London.

Before long, the Church of England parishioners had raised funds for a mission to the Assyrian Church in Kurdistan, but the Archbishop needed an envoy, someone of sound character to represent him at the Sultan's court and robust enough to see the mission through from start to finish. George Percy Badger was just the man. Twenty-seven years old and newly ordained in the Church of England he was also a brilliant Orientalist—fluent in Arabic and a walking lexicon of Eastern affairs.[55]

George grew up in Malta and had spent his childhood beetling around the island's medieval streets and fishing villages until he felt rather more Maltese than English. His family never had the means for him to attend university, but that didn't prevent him from pursuing his passion for history and languages. At 20, George left home to study Arabic in Beirut and returned to Malta to work as a translator with the Church Missionary Society until 1840, when he married Maria Wilcox at the governor's palace at Valetta. It seems that George and Maria spent their honeymoon on a sea crossing to England, and within a year of arriving he was ordained as a minister.[56]

Having arrived in Istanbul, Father Badger needed a *ferman*, the official travel visa, which would guarantee him a safe, hospitable passage through Ottoman territories to Qudshanis. While he waited for his papers to be stamped at the Sublime Porte, the gatehouse of the Sultan's palace, he also waited for Maria, who would soon join him on the mission. At a time when Naples and Venice were perceived by the English as exotic destinations, Istanbul must have seemed to the young couple like another world. When the Sultan's visa was finally granted three months later, the Badgers departed in search of Qudshanis.

Their first stop was the Black Sea where they hired a local guide and a few horses for the uncomfortable trek south to the Hakkari ranges. They made note of the Assyrian villages and churches and monasteries that they saw along the way: 'on entering the city walls we found ourselves amidst a heap of ruins, and it was some time before we could convince ourselves the place was not deserted. The streets are narrow and filthy in the extreme, and the inhabitants look wretched and woebegone'.[57] Just as they were about to descend the mountains of eastern Turkey into Mesopotamia, they were struck down by a virus that brought them 'to the brink of the grave'. They reached Mosul in one piece but it took four months to fully recuperate.

Father Badger's fondness for the Assyrian priests and bishops and parishioners in Mosul and Baghdad grew at the same rate as his disdain for the interference of Western missionaries with whom he refused to associate, saying 'they may succeed in the spreading abroad a vast amount of secular knowledge through the medium of their schools...but the good if any, will rest here'.[58]

Large, influential missions were established in Mesopotamia by the Roman Catholic and the Orthodox Churches in the sixteenth century, when envoys from Rome, Paris and St Petersburg first travelled to Constantinople and Baghdad. Many Assyrians in Mesopotamia gradually shifted their allegiance to the Pope and became known by the Vatican as the Chaldeans. Protestant denominations arrived in the Ottoman territories much later. In 1820, the Boston-based American Board of Foreign Missions established centres at Mosul, Mardin and Urmiah. During the latter half of the century Swiss, German, American and French missionaries were busy at Urfa, Van, Khoi and Urmiah, building and running new schools, teaching colleges and seminaries, establishing printing presses, translating bibles, publishing books and dictionaries as well as managing orphanages, hospices and almshouses in remote communities.[59]

When the Badgers arrived in Mosul there were approximately 12 Assyrian dioceses in Mesopotamia. The patriarch of the western rite Chaldean Church was based in Baghdad and the patriarch of the eastern rite, the Mar Shimmun, was based in Qudshanis, in the Hakkari mountains of Kurdistan. Each diocese was served by dozens of bishops and thousands of monks and parish priests throughout the region. All Christians who lived in the provinces of the Ottoman Empire, such as Mesopotamia, were subjects of the Sultan. At various times, Assyrians amongst other religious minorities would convert to Islam or migrate to escape persecution by the Ottoman Government in the hope of protection from Western authorities. Father Badger would report that the Assyrian Christians of the Near East had numerous foes—foreign interference, poverty, heresy, religious persecution, illiteracy, corruption and conversion. But his mission was far from complete.

One brisk morning in February 1843, having farewelled Maria, Father Badger set out to cross the River Tigris with three mules and his guide, Daoud. Within a few days they reached the foothills of the Hakkari ranges where "mountains upon mountains rose before and around us, and I could scarcely realise that I was travelling to an hospitable part of the world."[60] As snowdrifts covered the passes and the biting wind enveloped him, he may have felt relieved that Maria had stayed behind. It was possible to lose one's way at any turn. However, they arrived safely in Qudshanis, the seat of the Patriarch of the Assyrian Church of the East, the Mar Abraham Shimmun. Here the two men were able to discuss at length the needs of local people and the purpose of the Archbishop of Canterbury's mission. Father Badger took leave of the patriarch and returned to Mosul just before Easter 1843.

Several weeks later, on the Feast of the Ascension, the Kurdish Emirs Ismael Pasha, Tatar Khan Agha and Badr Khan Bey instigated a rash of small town massacres across Kurdistan. Badr Khan invaded the tribal district of the Assyrian Tiyari clan with his cavalry, torching houses, fields and orchards, looting and demolishing churches and abducting women and girls, who were enslaved or given away as gifts. Upwards of 10,000 Assyrian villagers were murdered in cold blood that week.[61] Mar Abraham Shimmun fled with the highland clans down the mountains onto the Nineveh Plains of Mesopotamia. They didn't stop until they could see the Tigris River. However, word of their plight had already arrived ahead of them and parishes made preparations for an influx of Christian refugees from the mountains.

When the Mar Abraham arrived in Mosul, he stayed with the Badgers, and he fell silent in grief.

After a while, the patriarch was able to tell the Badgers what had taken place:

> They pursued us in the mountains and in the wilderness did they lay in wait for us. Mine eyes are dimmed with tears, my bowels are troubled, my glory is poured out upon the earth for the destruction of my people; because the women and children and sucklings have been sold as slaves in the towns and villages.[62]

The bloodletting and the destruction was outrageous, yet even the most powerful cleric in the British Empire, the Archbishop of Canterbury, who had the ear of the Queen of England, could not have prevented the massacre with only pen and paper. Not long after the Ascension Day massacre, the renowned British archaeologist Austin Henry Layard, who was travelling through the region, came upon the site of the massacre.[63] Layard wrote:

> It was near Lizan that occurred one of the most terrible incidents of the massacre...we found ourselves at the foot of an almost perpendicular detritus of loose stones terminated...by a wall of lofty rocks. We soon saw evidences of the slaughter. At first a solitary skull rolling down with the rubbish; then heaps of blanched bones; further up fragments of rotting garments...skeletons still hung to the dwarf shrubs...the declivity became covered with bones, mingled with the long plaited tresses of the women, shreds of discoloured linen and well-worn shoes. There were skulls of all ages, from the child unborn to the toothless old man. [64]

What caused this hellish violence to erupt? Were not the Assyrian Christian community subjects under the protection of the Sultan himself? To outsiders the brutality and regularity of such attacks on the Assyrians were a criminal matter for which the perpetrators should be held to account. But for the locals, it was rarely that straightforward. The Zagros and Hakkari Mountains are a place of ancestral agonies. Assyrian and Kurdish tribes had lived for centuries in a tangle of allegiances, blood oaths - and internecine vendettas handed down from father to son, from mother to daughter, like a family heirloom. Neither the Shah of Persia nor the Sultan of Turkey held much sway in the ranges; government officials visited the lawless region at their own risk.

The Kurdish emirs and maliks were the standover merchants of the highlands and although they were in charge, they and the Assyrian mountain patriarchs held positions of aristocratic authority within their respective communities. The Mar Shimmun is appointed by hereditary succession for the term of his natural life, passing from uncle to nephew, generation after generation—a kind of spiritual dynasty. Occasionally emirs, maliks and patriarchs even consulted one another about the choice of heir, as was the case with Kurdish Prince Nurallah and his nephew Suleyman. When the two men had reached a stalemate over who was the rightful heir, the Assyrian patriarch weighed in and vouched for Suleyman. In doing so he made a lifelong enemy of the prince.

Added to these complex cultural relationships was the encroachment of foreign church missions. While these aided the spiritual and material needs of the Assyrian millet, their presence also disrupted local power balances within the Ottoman provinces. The Muslim Kurdish tribes had good reason to believe that the growing Western presence was eroding their lucrative, feudal authority. The Kurds opposed the central authority of the Ottoman Turks and used the political tension to establish a free

Kurdish state, Kurdistan, but their aims were thwarted when Badr Khan was deposed in 1847.[65]

Father Badger and Austin Henry Layard, the priest and the archaeologist, both filed official reports of the Ascension Day massacres from Mosul with the British ambassador, Lord Stratford Canning, in Constantinople. Canning insisted that the Ottoman Sultan should bring sanctions against the Kurdish chieftains. After much lobbying by the British Foreign Office at the Sublime Porte the massacres came to an end and the release of many Assyrian slaves was secured[66] and the Emir was banished.[67] In 1852, nine years after the massacre, the Assyrian Patriarch was granted official millet status for the Assyrian Church of the East.

At the end of his mission in 1852, Father Badger published a two-volume report about the conditions of the Assyrian Christians in the Ottoman territories. He and Maria returned home and continued a life of service in the Church of England, undertaking British civil service appointments in India and Africa. Before he passed away in 1887, George Percy Badger was made a Knight of the Gleaming Star by the Sultan of Zanzibar for services rendered to his kingdom. Mar Abraham Shimmun's letter to the Archbishop of Canterbury nevertheless, amounted to nothing; the promises of support never materialised and he passed away in anguish.

In 1867, Mar Abraham's nephew, Ruwil XVIII, succeeded him as the patriarch. Mar Ruwil Shimmun wrote another letter to the next Archbishop of Canterbury calling again on the Church of England for moral and material add:

> To the most revered and zealous Fathers, the elect of the Holy Ghost...the holy ministers, elect primates, orthodox patriarchs, watchful shepherds, the Archbishop of Canterbury and the

Right Reverend the Bishop of London...We desire to represent to you our abject condition, our spiritual destitution and our lack of the means of instruction, trusting that you may condescend to listen to the appeal...In so doing, we take the liberty of submitting to you the four principal causes which have reduced our community to its present low condition and which moreover threaten its existence...Our ancient books have been destroyed and we have no scribes or printing presses to replace them; no schools wherein to educate our youth. Our seminaries have...become the resort of the vain and the wicked. The learned have perished from amongst us...beseeching you to compassionate the condition of our people, who are wandering over our mountains like sheep without a shepherd.[68]

The florid expression belies Mar Ruwil's despair because nothing much had changed since Father Badger's mission 25 years earlier. If anything, life for the Assyrians had become harsher. They lived like pariahs in their own country—illiterate, malnourished, impoverished by the Caliph's taxes, exploited by Turkish and Kurdish landowners and with a medieval life expectancy. Mar Ruwil's desperate words must have appealed to Queen Victoria because soon afterwards the British Government and the Church of England had announced official ties with the patriarch and the Assyrian Church of the East.

o o o

Chapter Six
The Smallest Ally

In the country of the blind, the one-eyed man is king.
       Desiderius Erasmus

Thus had the Assyrians become Great Britain's smallest ally in the Near East when the Great War began. Cordial at best, suspicious at worst, theirs was a relationship born of circumstance rather than mutual trust and understanding. The English had enjoyed an unparalleled status in Persia ever since the East India Company struck a deal with the Shah in 1622.[69]

By the middle of the nineteenth century, British foreign policy in the Middle East was resolutely focused on the security of British imperial assets in the region.[70] The gateway to the colonial coffers of India and Afghanistan was via Persia, and these were to be protected at all costs. Her Majesty's government guarded its business relations with the Persians as a lioness guards her cubs, and any foreign interference was deemed unwelcome.

Despite the failure of the Archbishop of Canterbury's mission it did raise awareness and sympathy among the English for the plight of Christians in the Ottoman Empire. By 1870 the population of the Assyrian Church of the East was comprised of approximately 16,000 extended families inhabiting the region between Mesopotamia, eastern Turkey and north west Persia, or between 100,000 and 150,000 individuals. Twenty years later, according to a French scholar, half the population lived in towns and cities and the other half lived in mountain tribal villages.[71] Five volumes of correspondence flowed between Downing Street, London and the British Consul stationed at Diyarbakir, Turkey over the three proceeding decades, revealing growing concern for vulnerable Christian millets of the Ottoman Empire and the creeping intrusion by the Russians into Assyrian affairs. It had become politically prudent for the British to protect the Assyrians from other spheres of influence.[72]

British fears of foreign intervention were based neither on conspiracy theory nor paranoia. At the close of the nineteenth century, British companies owned around 70 per cent of the world's commercial shipping and the pound sterling ruled world markets, buying five American dollars and 19 German deutschmarks respectively.[73] This did not sit well with Germany which, as the most powerful nation on the European continent, entertained great aspirations. Germany's Mitteleuropa policy asserted its plans to 'divert the Levantine, Indian and Far Eastern trade from the sea lanes to London over to the Reich'.[74]

In 1878, the German Chancellor, Otto von Bismarck hosted the Congress of Berlin in the wake of the Turko–Russian War. Aside from some realignment of borders and declarations of independence, the British used their platform to influence the Ottoman Government's reform agenda. Britain bartered with the Ottomans for increased security of the Christian millets, the Armenian and Assyrian communities in Turkey.

The Mar Shimun was allowed to establish a consultative council that addressed taxes and other community grievances, thereby making the Mar Shimun the official rapporteur between the Christian millet and the Ottoman government. These changes alarmed the Kurdish leaders who were anxious about the new privileges awarded to the millet subjects by the Sultanate. Their feudal grip was being undermined and trouble began to brew. Two years after the Congress of Berlin, Kurdish Sheik Ubaidulla Shamsdinan led a rebellion against the Ottoman Government, attacking the Assyrian tribal districts of Berwar and Tergawar, and occupying Urmiah. The uprising eventually failed, and the Sultan exiled the rebel sheik to Mecca.[75]

When the vindictive, paranoid Sultan Abdul Hamid II came to power, life for the Assyrians took a turn for the worse. The sultan manipulated the Kurdish emirs and sheiks into a power struggle against the Turkish pashas (governors) for his favour.[76] In 1890, the Sultan formed the Hamidiye, the Lightning Troops. These irregular Kurdish cavalry regiments were the blight of Armenian and Assyrian communities. For almost two decades, the Hamidiye carried out the Sultan's ruthless orders with impunity.[77] The Sultan's reign ended in 1908, when the ultranationalist Young Turks' Party (CUP), lead by Mustafa Kemal, staged a coup d'etat against the Sultan and seized control of the Ottoman Empire.[78]

British authorities had long been aware of the persecution of Christian civilians by the Ottoman Sultanate, and subsequently by the Turkish Government of Mustafa Kemal. As far back as 1844, British and American press agencies had reported on the extermination of religious minorities by Ottoman forces, including articles in the London and New York *Times*, *The Washington Post* and the *Wall Street Journal*. Reports of massacres and ethnic cleansing continued throughout the First World War into the postwar era.[79] The British began collecting evidence in earnest when the Caucuses campaign commenced.

One of the most authoritative sources of evidence regarding the massacres of Assyrian and Armenian people in the Ottoman provinces during the Great War is known as the *Blue Book*, presented to the British House of Lords by the British Foreign Office in 1916.[80] It contains detailed, primary source evidence of widespread Turkish military atrocities, according to which the British Government intended to hold Turkey to account once the war was over.[81]

This, and similar official documents, reveal a glaring miscomprehension regarding the identity of Christian minorities in the Near East. Frequent references are made to 'Armenians' as an umbrella term incorporating all Christian minorities leading to confusion and inaccurate reporting by foreign authorities. This was mainly due to a lack of expertise and engagement within foreign offices. The tyranny of distance certainly played a part in the lack of understanding about Assyrian ethnic and linguistic identity. Assyrians, are ethnically, religiously and linguistically unique people, distinct from the Armenians and any other minority in the region.

At the turn of the century, ethnic tensions and civil unrest were widespread in Europe, Russia and the Middle East. It was a time when treaties and pacts between old empires and new nations, and minorities and governments were tested and recalibrated. Just as the tensions and violence peaked, the Russian army invaded Persia. With a nose that could sniff insurgency from a thousand miles, the Tsar's government stacked eight infantry battalions and one Cossack division at the Turkish–Persian frontier cities of Tabriz and Urmiah.[82] Within a few years, the Russians had not only army garrisons around Urmiah, but a large consulate, an imperial bank and an impressive mission house as well. But this was nothing out of the blue for the Persians.

Tsar Peter the Great invaded Persia in 1723 via the Caucasus Mountains to occupy Baku on the Caspian Sea, and ever since then the Russian Empire had been on the march southwards.[83] Out of the devastation of the Napoleonic Wars, the Muscovites gradually expanded the Tsarist Empire in every direction and bells started ringing in London, Vienna and Constantinople. Within a few generations the Caspian Sea and the Black Sea were transformed into Russian lagoons.

In 1898, Tsar Alexander III approved the establishment of the last Russian Orthodox mission to the Assyrians at Urmiah. One Assyrian bishop realised that this was an opportunity to secure his diocese and forged an alliance with the patriarchate of St Petersburg, which placed many thousands of Persian Assyrians under the protection of the Tsar.[84] The Armenian and Assyrian Christian communities were sometimes referred to as 'Little Russia' by Ottoman and Persian authorities. Not being short of rivals, the Persians observed the Russian encroachment from Teheran with a bloodless eye.

As the Ottoman Empire weakened, European bureaucrats and businessmen scrambled to shore up alliances and resources in Persia and Mesopotamia with which to fund and fuel the new generation of military hardware—tanks, submarines, zeppelins and dreadnoughts. In 1901, the British struck a profitable concession with Shah Mozzaffar al-Din Qajar to conduct an oil search over an area spanning 1,200,000 square kilometres.[85] The deal was funded by an Australian gold mining magnate, W.K. D'Arcy, with exclusive privileges 'to search for, obtain, exploit, develop, render suitable for trade, carry away and sell natural gas, petroleum, asphalte and ozokerite throughout the whole extent of the Persian Empire for a term of 60 years'.[86] After several failed attempts, oil was struck in 1908 and a refinery was hastily built on Abadan Island in the Persian Gulf.[87]

A year before the oil was sourced, without the prior knowledge or consent of the Shah, the Russian and British governments partitioned Persia into three zones under the St Petersburg Convention. It created a Russian zone in the north around Transcaucasia, a British zone in the south and the remainder in a neutral zone along the Mesopotamian frontier. The convention stripped Persia of its sovereignty and its revenue.[88] In 1910, the American consul in Baghdad reported that 'about 90,000 rifles and pistols and about 12,500,000 rounds of ammunition were shipped into the Persian Gulf', bearing English manufacture marks. Perhaps this provocative dump of weapons was meant to further unsettle tribal relations in Persia and the disintegrating Ottoman Empire.[89]

Persian authorities could tolerate the meddling no longer. After decades of foreign profiteering and political interference, there came fierce reactions from local Turkish, Azerbaijani and Kurdish leaders. The alliance that was forged between the Assyrians and the Russian Imperial Government ten years earlier now came under scrutiny, and it looked more and more like treason. Suspicions surfaced, accusations were vented. Had the Assyrian bishop made a dreadful mistake seeking the Tsar's protection? What must have seemed like a clever manoeuvre to empower the Assyrians after centuries of persecution under their millet status, turned out only to place the whole community in greater jeopardy.

The Assyrians of Persia and Turkey found themselves vilified as traitors, both to the Shah and the Sultan. The sinister threat of violence crept through the highlands again. It didn't take long before the Hamidiye cavalry swooped like birds of prey on the Assyrians, committing a spate of pogroms in villages and hamlets that dotted the borderlands of the Hakkari and the Zagros Mountains. Their fate hung by a thread, just as it had done 70 years prior, during the Ascension Day massacres. But life had not always been that way for the Assyrians of the Near East, where once they reigned supreme.

o o o

Chapter Seven
Bethnahrin

*Between us and heaven or hell there is only life,
which is the frailest thing in the world.*

Blaise Pascal

Vast and inhospitable, the Zagros Mountains extend for 1,500 kilometres from the Anatolian plateau in Turkey and Armenia, stretched between Iraq and Iran, curving southwards to the Persian Gulf where, they bow beneath the waves under the Straits of Hormuz.

Truth be told, no one really knows who appeared first in the Zagros Mountains or from where they came. What is known is that at some point in unrecorded time, a host of nomadic clans wandered over the alps and plains and rivers throughout the Near East, and from among them arose the Assyrians.[90]

Forests of dwarf oak, maple and pines and dense groves of chestnut and almond trees covered the ranges. Juniper bushes, narcissus, rhododendrons and cyclamen grew over the forest floor. Leopards, bears, wolves and stags grazed in the woodlands, while herds of deer and ibex wandered over the plains.[91] Spring unfurled like a magic carpet across the Zagros, flush with wildflowers and clover. Rich soil yielded quinces, figs, mulberries, muscatels, pistachios and pomegranates.[92] Melting snows filled the Tigris River which hurtled through ravines, across the plains of northern Mesopotamia into the Arabian Sea. Neolithic pioneers grazed their herds in warmer months and retreated in winter to shelter in caves and forests, probably subsisting on alpine staples such as sheep curd, goat meat and roasted acorns.

Between the western slopes of the Zagros Mountains and the plains surrounding the Tigris and Euphrates rivers, is the Fertile Crescent where humans decided to settle down for the first time. According to the archaeological record, a cultural revolution commenced there on an inconceivable scale. The first cities and temples, the first deities and religious ceremonies, the first royal mint, banks and taxation systems, the first legal code and political treaties all originated in the Fertile Crescent. It is the birthplace of the alphabet and the abacus, and where the first hymns and love songs were recorded.[93] It was a land of firsts, a land of wonders.

Long before Alexander the Great conquered Asia Minor, before the Persian King Xerxes sacked Athens, and even before the Babylonian King Nebuchadnezzar dragged the Jews into exile, there was the Kingdom of the Assyrians, the hell bent city folk.

The Assyrians were among the first tribes to settle in the Fertile Crescent, or what the Greeks called Mesopotamia, 'the land between the two rivers'. By 9000 B.C. people had begun to cultivate grains like barley, millet and legumes, and to domesticate animals for food as well as altar sacrifice. By 5400 B.C. the first cities began to rise and they had dug canals and weirs along the northerly reaches of the Tigris River. Later they built temples and ziggurats and organised trades and crafts, such as papermaking and pottery.

Between 2900 and 2350 B.C. the Sumerians, another Semitic group thought to be from the southern delta, gained predominance in Mesopotamia. Under the umbrella of Sumerian civilisation, Assyrian and Babylonian societies flourished. Around 2350 B.C., Sargon, a man of untraceable origin and ancestry rose to power full stop. A Babylonian inscription about Sargon reads:

> My mother was a priestess; I did not know my father.
> My priestess mother conceived me, in secret she bore me;
> She set me in a basket of rushes and sealed my lid with bitumen;
> She cast me into the river which rose over me;
> The river bore me up and carried me to Akki.[94]

With his throne at Akkad on the western bank of the Euphrates, King Sargon, a self-sufficient, visionary leader, united the Sumerians, Babylonians and Assyrians under the new Akkadian Empire. The Akkadian population spoke Aramaic, the mother tongue of the Aramaens, who are the descendants of Aram, the son of Noah. The original Aramaic name for the region is Aram-Nahrim and their language gradually became the lingua franca of Mesopotamia until the seventh century A.D. when it was superseded by Arabic.[95] The Akkadian Empire was the first of its kind, and ever since then King Sargon has been emulated by Eastern despots, including Nabonidus, the last king of Babylon, and the Iraqi dictator former President, Saddam Hussein.

In the twilight of the Akkadian Empire the Assyrians emerged with great force and capability. These highly organised, self-confident people developed a predilection for weapons, hunting parties and fantastical beasts, such as the five-legged, winged lamassu that stood guard outside their palaces and tombs. They also had a penchant for grooming. Assyrian charioteers are depicted wearing ostentatious hairstyles, curled and plaited like rope with unforgettably wide sideburns.

Over time, the Assyrians perfected the bow and arrow and their spoke-wheeled chariots. These were indispensable assets for an epic real estate hunt that was to last for the next twelve hundred years. From the ramparts of their sacred cities at Nimrud and Nineveh and their imperial capital Ashur that overlooked the Tigris River, they coveted their neighbours' kingdoms.[96]

Like a wolf upon the fold, the Assyrian Army came down on their panic-stricken enemies—the Elamites, Medes, Egyptians, Hittites, Persians, Israelites, Edomites and the Phoenicians. Under the command of their kings—Shalmaneser, Esarhaddon and Sennacherib—battalion after battalion of mounted bowmen galloped over the hills and plains in bentwood chariots. They plundered horse studs, devoured crops and tore up villages.[97] They swallowed towns and cities along the Mediterranean coast and the Lower Nile, from Tarsus and Tushpa all the way to Thebes, leaving in their wake smouldering fields and roads lined with piked heads. Such were the brutalities of an Assyrian pogrom—with their lightning raids and mass deportations of captives—that their victims believed Assyrians to be the envoys of Satan himself.[98]

Lying at the southern foothills of the Zagros Mountains is the ancient city of Susa, capital of the mysterious kingdom of Elam, the playground of the royal court. Susa was the target of the Assyrian Crown Prince Ashurbanipal. British archaeologists uncovered gigantic tablets there in the 1850s, on which were recorded how the Assyrian warrior prince dealt with his enemies:

> Susa, the great holy city, abode of their gods, seat of their mysteries, I conquered. I entered its palaces, I opened their treasuries where

> silver and gold, goods and wealth were amassed...I destroyed the ziggurat of Susa...I reduced the temples of Elam to naught; their gods and goddesses I scattered to the winds. The tombs of their ancient and recent kings I devastated, I exposed to the sun and I carried away their bones toward the land of Ashur. I devastated the provinces of Elam and upon their lands I sowed salt.[99]

At the peak of his reign, Emperor Ashurbanipal's domain spanned from the Zagros Mountains northwards through Cappadocia to the Black Sea, westwards through Syria, Palestine and Phoenicia and southwards to the Red Sea frontiers of Egypt and Abyssinia.[100] But he was to be the last sovereign of Assyria. After 12 merciless centuries, it all came crashing down around his ears when Nineveh fell to the Babylonian King Nabopolassar in 612 B.C. Within two years, Ashur was wrecked. When the ruins of Ashurbanipal's palace were excavated, hundreds of gold-plated ivories were found lying in a layer of ash two metres thick, the headquarters of the Assyrian Empire had been incinerated.[101]

And after the siege, their splendid temples defiled and laid bare, their palaces trampled and ablaze, what then became of the Assyrians, the ordinary men, women and children of Nineveh and Ashur? It is impossible to know exactly, but more than likely they did what survivors have always done. Brick by brick they rebuilt their houses and workshops, field by field they replanted their crops and day by day they carried on. One renowned Assyriologist described it this way:

> Descendants of the Assyrian peasants would, as opportunity permitted, build new villages...remembering traditions of the former cities. After seven or eight centuries and after various vicissitudes, these people became Christians...These Christians and the Jewish

communities scattered amongst them, not only kept alive the memory of their Assyrian predecessors but also combined them with traditions from the Bible. The Bible, indeed, came to be a powerful factor in keeping alive the memory of Assyria.[102]

Aramaic speaking people were among the earliest converts to Christianity, exchanging the brute force of bow and arrow for the spiritual powers of prayer and Eucharist. Once the potentates of the most ferocious military machine of the ancient world, the name before which every satrap and emissary kneeled, the Assyrians dissipated and dispersed across the towns and cities of Judea and Syria, into the northern reaches of the Tigris, the highlands of Eastern Anatolia and the plains of northern Persia. Although it does not appear on any map, neither ancient nor modern, neither mythological nor cartographical, the Assyrians named their homeland Bethnahrin.

The crucifixion of Jesus Christ in the year 33 A.D. heralded a new epoch—an empire of hearts and minds. From its epicentre in Jerusalem the Christian gospel rippled across the mountains and valleys right to the front doorsteps of Bethnahrin. Saint Thomas (Mar Thoma) and Saint Thaddeus (Mar Addai), the Apostles of Jesus Christ, founded the Church of Antioch in 37 A.D. and to this day it remains the mother church from which all the Aramaen or Syriac Christian churches originated. From the first century A.D. onwards, Aramaen Christians set off on foot to evangelise communities throughout Persia, the Mediterranean, Asia Minor, and as far as India, owing to the evangelical mission of Saint Thomas.[103] Edessa was the host city of the first Church Council in 197 A.D.[104] The Syriac Church spread and flourished throughout the region and beyond during the first few centuries of the new millennium.

Aramaen Christians were instrumental in the formation of a new mystical tradition, which arose from the men and women who abandoned the flesh pots of the Near East for a life of prayer, fasting and contemplation of the Holy Scriptures in the desert wilderness. Abbesses, monks and hermits, namely Saint Ephrem the Syrian, established chapels, hermitages and monasteries by the hundred, over the Nile Valley and across the hills of Palestine and the mountains of Lebanon. Their numbers grew to the point where, it is said that the desert thronged like a city. As one fourth-century Palestinian visitor put it:

> One can see them in the desert waiting for Christ as loyal sons watching for their father...There is no town or village in Egypt or the Thebaid, which is not surrounded by hermitages is if by walls.[105]

Later, under the aegis of the new Christian headquarters at Byzantium, the Syrian cities of Antioch and Edessa became theological powerhouses of Eastern Christianity.[106] During the fourth century, Aramaic-speaking monks started translating Greek scholastic, philosophic, scientific, medical and literary works into Arabic, from which new intellectual inquiry flourished.[107] In 431, the Syriac Patriarch of Constantinople, Nestorius, was denounced for heresy at the Church Council of Ephesus.[108] He was banished from Byzantium by the Emperor Theodosius II, retreating to his monastery in Antioch. This schism marked the separation of the Church of the East from the Church of Rome, and sparked an exodus of Nestorians away from Byzantium.

After this schism, there remained two distinct denominations of Syro-Aramaic Christians in the Near East; Orthodox and Nestorian. Each had its own ecclesiastical hierarchy based in various cities across the region. The western provinces of Mesopotamia and Syria were predominantly Orthodox and lived under the authority of the patriarchate centred in Baghdad and Aleppo. The Nestorians living in the eastern provinces around Persia and eastern Turkey followed the authority of their own patriarch, called the Mar Shimmun, a title meaning Holy Father. Altogether they are referred to as the Church of the East, and sometimes as the Oriental Church.

Following the Muslim conquest of the Middle East, the Church of the East remained the predominant Christian denomination in Asia Minor and Central Asia. The Chinese emperors of the T'ang Dynasty (618–907 A.D.) and the Mongol Empire welcomed the Syriac missionaries, and Aramaic-speaking Chinese monks were even sent to Bethnahrin for theological and cultural exchanges during this period.[109] The legacy of the early Syro-Aramaen Christians is a mosaic of Orthodox, Nestorian and Chaldean Christian traditions that live on in modern-day Iran, Iraq, Syria, Lebanon, Egypt, Turkey and Jordan.

The history of the Church of the East and its enormous influence during the first centuries after the collapse of the Roman Empire are familiar to Western scholars, however, following the advent of Islam, the life of the Aramaen Christians in Mesopotamia and Persia becomes more obscured, especially during the medieval period. From the seventh century, Christian communities throughout the Middle East were deemed *ahl al-dhimmi*, an Arabic term meaning 'people under protection'.

Dhimmitude is a Koranic contractual relationship that was personally bestowed by the Caliph whereby all his non-Muslim subjects were given special religious protection. The Arab Abbasid Caliphate, spanning from 750 until 1258, allowed the Assyrian patriarchs of Baghdad, Aleppo and Mosul to practice Christianity. However, the price for this protection was dhimmitude, the crippling tax regime imposed on non-Muslim subjects.[110] The flourishing ancient Church of the East began to decline under dhimmitude, mainly due to the confiscation of original land and properties, as well as diminishing congregations due to forced conversion, poverty, persecution and assimilation. Perhaps the last contact between the Western and the Syro-Aramaen Christians was forged by Monk Rabban Sauma, an envoy of Mar Yavallaha III, when he visited the Vatican and the Royal courts of Europe in the late 13 century.[111]

Without warning, in 1258 an untameable force stormed over the Zagros Mountains and fell upon the people of the Near East, the Caucasus, and the Levant. Mongol Prince Hulagu, the grandson of Ghengis Khan, trashed Baghdad and took the Caliph himself prisoner. Hulagu's cavalry pillaged the fortresses, mosques and hospitals that lined the Tigris and Euphrates. Worst of all, the Grand Library of Baghdad, a treasury of ancient texts and illuminated manuscripts, was looted. Some say the river ran black with ink.[112] Once the wild horsemen of the steppes bolted away, the Abbasid Empire was no more.

Then came Tamurlane, the Shadow of God. He was ferocious and unbeaten, and the most feared of all the Khans who 'opened the locks of terror, tore men to pieces like lions and overturned mountains'.[113] With his rebel horsemen Tamurlane burst out of his imperial resort at Samarkand on the shores of the Black Sea to demolish Hulagu's dynasty.[114] Not since the tyrannical years of the Assyrian Prince Ashurbanipal 2,000 years earlier, had the people of those parts experienced such unbridled demolition and bloodlust.

From Egypt, through Syria, Georgia, the Zagros Mountains and Persia to the Eurasian Steppe, Tamurlane shattered the nerve centres of Islam, Judaism and Eastern Christianity. Some would say that they have never fully recovered.[115] In their bid to survive the hammer of the Khans, the Assyrian Christians ran for the hills. Hundreds of tiny parishes, hamlets, hermitages and monasteries were abandoned. Some clans migrated to established communities in Mosul, Aleppo, Damascus and Baghdad, some resettled into diocesan centres around Lake Urmiah, Van, Sirt, the Salmas Plains and Dyarbakir. Others moved higher into the remote enclaves of the Zagros and Hakkari mountains, carrying their sacred relics and rites with them.[116]

In 1456, the Ottoman Turks seized Constantinople, the last fortress of the Byzantine Empire. From this vantage point the Ottomans began rolling out a new system of religious administration. Millet is any non-Muslim community given the official status of a distinct religious nation within the Caliphate. Greeks, Jews, Armenians and Zoroastrians were all millet nations under dhimmitude.

Chief rabbis and archbishops kept handwritten letters from the Caliph that outlined their millet status as non-equals. After hundreds of years of cultural transformation and catastrophic events, the much-reduced mountain dwelling Assyrian Christians lived under the thumb of the Ottoman Caliphate and the Persian Shahs. Being thus situated between Turkey and Persia, the Assyrian Christian community was spread across the dividing line between the two great Muslim sects, the Shiites and the Sunnis.

In 1552, the community experienced another schism, which manifested in two distinct denominations; the Assyrian Church of the East and the Chaldean Church, which was aligned to the Roman Catholic Church. The Chaldean Church had centres in Mosul and Baghdad and other parts of the Near East where the Catholic Church was influential, such as in Syria and Lebanon. In 1796 a French Catholic priest, Fulgence de Sainte Marie, undertook a census of the Country of the Church of the East. He estimated the various dioceses of Amid, Mosul, Baghdad, Mardin and Sirt to be around 19,500 parishioners with a further 4,033 extended families.[117] Taken together these dioceses correspond to the country known as Bethnahrin, a triangular zone lying between Mosul in central Mesopotamia (Iraq), Van in eastern Anatolia (Turkey) and Urmiah in north-western Persia (Iran).

In the seventeenth century, the Assyrian Church of the East established its headquarters at Qudshanis, a mountain citadel in the heart of Bethnahrin in the Hakkari ranges, where the Zagros Mountains fold over the Persian border into Turkey. There stood in the heart of Qudshanis a large, squat, stone house—the patriarchal seat of the Mar Shimmun. His title means Holy Father in Aramaic, with reference to the apostolic succession from Simon Peter.

Mar Shimmun incorporated the religious and political identity of the whole congregation of the mountain 'Nestorian' Christians, as distinct from the Christians of the Nineveh Plains. Not only was the patriarch's home located in Kurdistan under the authority of the Ottoman Sultan, it was also controlled by the local Kurdish Emirate of Hakkari. When the Assyrian Church of the East chose Qudshanis as their new patriarchal home, it was a long way from anywhere, and deliberately so.

The imposing stone house, similar to a Swiss chalet, was made to keep the weather and intruders out. At first glance, Qudshanis could have inspired the scene of a Persian ballad; wild, haunting and rustic. But it was much more than just a house. Qudshanis symbolised what it meant to be Assyrian—their imperious heritage, tribal traditions and religion. The house stored their most treasured possessions—writings, crafts and sacred artefacts, such as sacramental vessels, liturgical garments and the Peshitta, an Aramaic Bible. Qudshanis stood for the centuries of joy and loss, the young and the old, and struggles past and present. Above all Qudshanis embodied their faith and hope.

Qudshanis was out of sight, but not out of harm's way. The Assyrians hoped the alpine homestead would be overlooked by the Shah's tax collectors and by the Sultan's troops. They wanted to be left alone by the Kurdish Emirs' hit men. So remote were the Assyrian parishes that some said their patriarch received the millet edict from the Prophet Mohammed himself.[118] Even so, in this restive nest of provincial affairs, the patriarch needed diplomatic skills of Shakespearian quality to broker the peace. And when he failed there were always reprisals. It could mean the difference between a horse trade and an empty barn, or a tea ceremony and a funeral.

And so there they were, the Assyrians of Bethnahrin, the remnant people of 7,000 years, who traced their genesis to the clans that emerged from the antediluvian fog of unrecorded time. Those tented tribes who roamed the plains and pastoral valleys of the Fertile Crescent, who settled on the banks of the Tigris and Euphrates, the rapacious empire builders who conquered the Persians and the Egyptians, the inventors of cuneiform and chariots, who became a religious caste of Christian mystics, saints and martyrs.

The Assyrians had eked out a precarious existence as a pariah nation under the yoke of the Ottoman Empire, forgotten by the outside world until the Sayfo, the Year of the Sword—when everything changed. It must have seemed to Mar Binyamin Shimmun and his people as though Tamurlane, the Shadow of God, had returned from the underworld to stalk them through the mountains once more.

o o o

Chapter Eight
The Generals' Ruse

The advance of the Turkish Army on the Armenian Front continues slowly...since the Assyrians are a tiny minority and lie in the path of the Turkish advance, they are probably doomed.
Secret cable from Intelligence Bureau,
Baghdad to British War Cabinet,
London, 12 March 1918

A British aviator flew over Lake Urmiah on 10 July 1918 in search of a favourable landing spot. He was delivering a classified letter from British army authorities to General Agha Petros, the Commander in Chief of the Assyrian Army. Circling the lake, the pilot could see soldiers and civilians swarming on the ground below, gazing skywards in wonderment as the plane floated down like a leaf from the clouds. The Assyrians had never seen or heard such an unearthly machine before and they ran for cover.

A rumour had spread through the northern Persian provinces that the British Army had reneged on their agreement with their smallest ally, withdrawing from Persia back over the border to Mosul, and abandoning the Assyrians to face the Turkish Army alone. A few of the Assyrian mountaineers suspected that the flight was a ploy of the Turkish Government and fired off a burst of bullets at the aeroplane, but missed.

As it came into view like a deus ex machina, the bold red and blue circular symbol of the British air force became clearer and the Assyrians started to cheer ecstatically and fire their rifles in the air. They dragged the airman, Lt. Pennington, from the cockpit and carried him over their heads, as though he was the lone survivor pulled from the rubble of an earthquake. The women of the town were dismayed at the pilot's bare, white legs. Believing that he had cut off his pants to make ends meet, they started making him a pair of traditional patchwork trousers.[119] In the meantime he was whisked off to meet their commander, General Agha Petros.[120]

Petros was an imposing, debonair man with a chequered past but proved to be a natural leader who lead his cavalry from the front. He was born into the Assyrian Baz tribe and educated in the European missionary schools in Urmiah, where he became fluent in Aramaic, Arabic, Turkish, English, Russian and French. In previous years, he had been the Turkish Government's representative in the Urmiah district.

When war was declared in 1914 and the province was occupied by the Russian Army, being an educated Christian, the Russians appointed Agha Petros as the commander of the Assyrian and Armenian forces in the service of the Tsar.[121] In the three years since the war had begun, Petros had watched the city being transformed into a Christian ghetto—garrisoned by the Russians, engulfed by refugees and encircled by the Turkish Army. At that point, General Petros and the Assyrian Army were guarding the 130,000 Assyrian and Armenian civilians trapped inside Urmiah and the city was on the verge of collapse.

General Petros was on the cusp of making a drastic decision: whether to shunt his entire force of mountaineers westwards 400 kilometres from Urmiah into Mesopotamia, or whether to dig in and wait for British reinforcements. He believed it was possible to connect with the British Army in Mosul but he risked his mounted troops being minced by the superior Turkish Army. That is when the sound of the British aeroplane could be heard buzzing over Lake Urmiah. Lieutenant Pennington handed Agha Petros the letter from the British commander of the Persian Campaign, Major General Dunsterville.

In the letter Dunsterville proposed that the Assyrians should collaborate with his forces to create an elaborate ruse. If General Petros remained in northern Persia to fend off the Turkish Army around Urmiah, this would create the illusion that British units were taking the overland route to the Caspian Sea, rather than the sea route via the coastal roads.[122] In return the British authorities in Baghdad guaranteed they would supply the Assyrian Army with the necessary arms, ammunition and coin to stay in Urmiah. The ruse was intended to alleviate the pressure on Dunterville's force by drawing the Turkish forces back into the Persian mountains, well away from the Caspian coast, sparing the British forces precious time and resources.

In effect Dunsterville's strategy would kill two birds with one stone. Firstly, it might avert the pending annihilation of the Assyrians by the Turkish Army, and, secondly, it opened a tiny window through which the British units deployed in northern Persia could scramble towards Baku and capture the oilfields. But before the plan could proceed, British authorities at Baghdad General Headquarters (GHQ) needed to know General Petros' capabilities and requirements; Baghdad GHQ wanted assurances that Petros was willing to back the scheme without reservation.[123]

Assyrians were alert to false promises made by foreigners in the name of cooperation. They could remember such promises being made to their patriarchs Abraham and Ruwil, and then broken by the Emirs and the Sultans and the Archbishop of Canterbury. Would the English let them down again? Was the general as good as his word, or would they be usurped? Other inducements were fresh in their minds, such as those offered in the early days of the Great War by the Russians, Turks and Germans at Qudshanis.

One year earlier, in 1917, General Petros had escorted Mar Binyamin Shimmun to a meeting with the Tsar's Consul Nikitin at the Russian embassy in Urmiah, where military negotiations took place. Nikitin promised Mar Binyamin Shimmun that in return for Assyrian service to the Imperial Russian Army, they would be granted community lands in Russia after the war. As with similar guarantees, it turned out to be a perfidious deal and each time the Assyrians had come off much worse. From this point, Mar Shimmun advised Agha Petros to refrain from military engagement with Persian and Turkish forces and to maintain peace.

In February 1918, Mar Binyamin received a written invitation to meet with the Ottoman governor of Khoi at which both parties agreed to the terms of a peace arrangement for the whole region. One month later, the Mar Shimmun received another letter from a Kurdish leader, Ismail Agha Simko of the Shikak Kurds, who wanted to arrange a truce with the Assyrian chiefs. The meeting took place on 3 March at Dilman, north of Urmiah. Mar Binyamin was accompanied by a mounted retinue of around 150 people, including his brothers Daoud and Isaiah, clan chiefs, and Russian military representatives comprised of Colonel Kondratyev and his officers. Daoud described the meeting:

When Mar Shimmun stepped out of his carriage, Simko himself went out to meet His Holiness, bowed twice after the custom, took his guest to the house. The meeting took more time than usual...To be on the safe side I entered the house myself...I saw that the meeting room was overcrowded. Mar Binyamin was sitting in the centre, on his right—Colonel Kondratyev, David Shimmun, Shmuel Khan and four Russian officers, and on his left—Simko and his people. A Persian servant entered the room and started to serve tea.[124]

When the meeting was over, Agha Simko Shikak farewelled the patriarch and the Assyrian Russian delegation began to saddle up. Gunshots rang out from the rooftop of nearby houses and they ran for cover. Mar Binyamin fell backwards off his horse, hitting his head on the ground, covered in blood. Several Russians officers were killed. The Assyrians went to Urmiah for reinforcements and returned later that night to retrieve the body of the beloved patriarch. Agha Simko was later captured and shot by Persian police.

In the absence of the Mar Shimmun, General Petros and the chieftains now considered the implications of another foreign deal. For Petros the British tactic posed a huge dilemma; the safety of his troops over and against the wellbeing of the Assyrian civilians trapped at Urmiah. What's more, when the war was over and the British left, the Assyrians still had to live among their adversaries. General Petros sent the pilot back to the British base with his reply. In exchange for men and matériel, the Assyrian Army would remain at Urmiah to hold back the Turkish Army. Supplies, currency, vehicles and ammunition were critical for the Assyrians and there was no way that the disparate British units could wrestle the Turks out of Baku without additional resources. It was a decision that would impact the final outcome of the British mission in Persia.

From that point onwards, the Assyrians became Britain's only native ally in the eastern theatre of the Great War. Once more the imperial powerhouse was forced to rely on its smallest ally. The British commander made an urgent flight back to Baghdad G.H.Q. to organise the materiel for General Petros.

At Baghdad G.H.Q. the next day, General Dunsterville worked himself into a lather waiting for a wire from London; the War Office may as well have been on the far side of the moon. The wire came back; the deal was out of the question. It was irresponsible. How could the stratagem succeed without a huge loss of life and hardware? The answer was final and no negotiation would be entered into. Thinking on his feet, the general requested that at the very least he should be granted permission to protect the Assyrians from Turkish attacks in northern Persia and Azerbaijan. The Baghdad office finally relented.

The general dashed back to his field base at Hamedan, in central western Persia, to arrange the meeting point with the Assyrian forces where the promised arms and coin were to be delivered. The handover date was set for 23 July at Sain Qaleh. Although spread far and wide in the field, British mission units were on notice of immanent action. At Bijar, on 17 July, it was Captain Stanley Savige who received orders to implement the generals' ruse:

1. You will be in charge of the party detailed hereunder proceeding with Major Moore.
2. Instructions as to time of departure, transport, etc will be notified later.
3. You will draw from the Q.M. sufficient ammunition to make up to 200 rounds per N.C.O. and O/R.[125]

Further instructions would be issued only when Captain Savige and the 'Bijar' party were well down the road. There were horses for each man and fodder for the pack animals, but no wireless devices, and no details. The Turkish Army was on the move somewhere in the mountains to the north. If this was a foil, only a sideshow to the main event, then what was the actual nature of the secret British military mission to Persia? And why was Captain Savige, an Australian officer, involved?

Part Two
MISSION

○ ○ ○

Chapter Nine
A Great Stunt

> We shall draw from the heart of suffering itself
> the means of inspiration and survival.
> Sir Winston Churchill

At daybreak on 12 January 1918, dressed in the trademark greatcoat and slouch hat, Captain Stanley Savige walked along the frosty, brick lanes of Westminster to the Tower of London. He had been summoned from the Western Front by the British Imperial High Command to take part in a covert military operation in an undisclosed theatre of the Great War. After three years of hard battle, the serenity and orderliness of the city must have felt strange at first—cobbled streets instead of rancid trenches, horses carting fresh milk not cannons, and not a single dead soldier in sight.

Christmas had come and gone only a few short weeks beforehand; it was Captain Savige's third since leaving Australia. He had shifted into the Ploegsteert Sector of Flanders with the 6th Brigade on 15 December where he had remained on duty. On Christmas Eve, while the captain and his brigade celebrated with roast pork and plum pudding, General Birdwood, their commanding officer, opened a classified letter from the British War Office. It outlined orders for the organisation of a secret mission. Birdwood commenced immediately, as did the British commanders in Salonica, Palestine and Mesopotamia. With that, the Dunsterforce Mission was underway.[126]

At the Chateau Flêtre, where Birdwood had established the Australian Corps Field Headquarters (HQ), he began the selection process for Dunsterforce. Only those officers who demonstrated 'initiative, resource and courage and power of dealing with and managing men' would be chosen.[127] Officers of the 6th Brigade were notified of the opportunity, and Captain Savige nominated himself for what he called a 'mysterious show'. He was less than enthusiastic about spending another excruciating winter in the trenches and did not want to miss out. For Savige the prospect of a daring and prestigious adventure was also an unprecedented opportunity to serve Australia and to advance his military career.

Despite the fact that a sizeable portion of the finest Commonwealth officers was already dead or missing in action, each commander prepared a register of his best men. It is possible to piece together a sketch of some of the other officers who were nominated for the mission based on General John Monash's original list of men from the 3rd Australian Division with his own personal recommendation:

> Captain R.J. Stewart, MC, 34th Battalion...Constitutionally robust, brave and resourceful and has an excellent command of men;
>
> Lieutenant F.W. Stackleberg, 33rd Battalion...has shown great initiative. When with his company in the line he has displayed both coolness and courage;

Captain E.W. Latchford, MC, 38th Battalion...a resourceful and daring leader;

Captain C.L. McVilly, MC, 40th Battalion...has a strong personality and distinguished himself in action. Is young and athletic;

Second Lieutenant W.A. Fraser, DSO, 41st Battalion...served for five years in the Australian Navy and for two years with the Royal West Kents..a gallant man is shown by the fact that he was awarded the DSO;

Lieutenant C.D. Lintott, MC, 44th Battalion...He personally captured three prisoners...resourceful and courageous above the average.[128]

The renowned Australian war correspondent and historian C.E.W. Bean described these Anzacs as 'the cream of the cream'.[129] Captain McVilly had been decorated for outstanding sporting prowess before the war. Born and bred in Hobart, the six-foot 'iron man' had held the Australian Sculling Champion title for three consecutive years prior to enlisting. In 1912, he robbed the English of the Diamond Sculls title for the first time on record and, in 1913, he won the Helms World Trophy as Australian athlete of the year. Captains Lay and Latchford had performed gallant feats both at Gallipoli and the Somme.[130]

On 2 January 1918, Stanley wrote, 'Have been asked by Gen. Smyth our commander if I would undertake a desperate venture which would probably cost me my life but had a sporting chance. Nature of work and place not known. Accepted'.[131] Within a week, he was in the grand drawing room of the Chateau Flêtre with the other candidates waiting for a senior officer to address them.

All stood to attention and saluted Colonel Byron, the general's headhunter. Colonel Byron looked around the room and made a proposition:

> Gentlemen, are you prepared to undertake a desperate venture which will probably cost you your lives, but if successful, will mean everything at this stage of the war to the British Empire?[132]

Stanley explained that 'after so many years of war, on Gallipoli and in France, especially through the fighting of the Somme and Flanders, nothing could possibly be worse than that of the past, so nineteen of us accepted the proposition'.[133] But he still knew next to nothing about the mission to which he signed up.

Colonel Byron was appointed by the War Office to select and manage the new, elite unit and was one of the few people who knew anything about the mission. As a boy, Stanley had read about men just like Byron in books—men born for war. He was an officer's officer, an Irishman with an intriguing and impressive past, who had commanded the Queensland Artillery during the Boer War and led an attack against the Germans in East Africa.[134] Stanley learned for the first time the actual purpose of the mission as the colonel read aloud from the War Office letter:

> You will realise what a big question is involved—nothing more or less than the defence of India and the security of our whole position in the East. If we can only stem the rot in the Caucasus and on the Persian frontier and interpose a barrier against the vast German-Turkish propaganda of their Pan-Turanian scheme, which threatens to inflame the whole of Central Asia including Afghanistan, our minds will be at rest as regards Mesopotamia and India.[135]

The War Cabinet finalised the selection of a total force of 370 men from across the entire British army, with 120 officers and 250 regimental sergeants. Captain Savige was one of 20 Australians selected. There were also 12 New Zealanders, 20 Canadians and 12 South Africans whose names appeared on the roll. The remainder were British. An additional 20 Non-Commissioned Officers (N.C.Os) of 'relatively similar qualities' were also selected.[136] Dunsterforce, named after their commanding officer, Major General Dunsterville comprised of 390 men in total, each distinguished in character and in combat.

At the beginning of 1918, after three years of unmitigated devastation there was still no outright victor of the Great War. In the east, the Balkan states were in disarray. The Ottoman Empire was crumbling. Russia was imploding under the Bolshevik Revolution and Lenin's tenuous armistice with Germany threatened to break at any moment. Lenin had withdrawn Russian armies from the Eastern and Caucasian fronts, generating a fearful vacuum that was filled by Enver Pasha who redirected his 60,000-head Army of Islam into Persia. All the while, the British High Command were in a paroxysm at the idea of Turkish forces leading a jihad through Afghanistan to India.[137]

And everywhere there was tumult and anguish. Millions of displaced, homeless people searched for a safe haven, and countless thousands of refugees poured into ports on the Mediterranean, the Adriatic and the Caspian Seas. France and Belgium were shattered. Germany and Austria were counting the imponderable numbers of dead, wounded and missing.

With victory over the Germans in serious doubt, Britain was in no position to withdraw a substantial group of competent officers from the front lines at the height of the Great War. It begs the question, what kind of urgent conditions had impelled the High Command to marshal its finest officers into this covert venture in the first place? It may have belied a shrewd strategic manoeuvre by the British Government. On the other hand it could have been a desperate backup plan for the worst-case scenario.

Dunsterforce's mission was to secure British colonial territories and assets in Central Asia and the Middle East, and Captain Savige would be at the vanguard. Being selected for the mission meant that the Imperial High Command and the War Cabinet regarded him as one of their finest warriors, exactly the sort of man they could rely on to fulfil the mission. It was no surprise to the men of the 6th Brigade that Captain Savige was selected. Inside the brigade barracks at Broodseinde, officers and men gathered to congratulate him and to wish him sterling fortune for the mysterious new venture. General Smythe had organised a staff car and driver to collect him early the next morning. Before the first streak of dawn, Captain Savige stepped into the motorcar waiting outside and disappeared off the map of Flanders.

The four-hour journey across the bleak countryside to the French port of Boulogne would have cured his bones like cement. Mile after mile the waves of barbed wire and rotting trenches and the whole blood-tub of war faded out of sight. Captain Savige had dreaded the farewells at the barracks the night before and although he was sure that it was the right decision to join the mission, he must have felt apprehensive about the unknowns. Would they travel over land and sea to fight a foreign enemy again? He may have doubted what his family would make of it—was it reckless, was he selfish? These were things that he could dwell on during the Channel crossing to England because he had sworn himself for service to the King and his appointment at the Tower of London was now inescapable.

Alighting at Waterloo Station, Captain Savige headed directly to the Australian Imperial Force (AIF) Headquarters on Horseferry Road, Westminster to report his arrival to army authorities. It was an antipodean outpost in the centre of London; a home away from home for thousands of diggers on leave from the front. There he joined two other officers from the 2nd Division, Lieutenant Turner of the 27th Battalion and Lieutenant Hitchcock of the 6th Machine Gun Company.[138] They would have to wait until the next day for further instructions about the mission.

On the morning of 12 January, Captain Stanley Savige entered the Tower of London. There was a wide, hollow quadrangle where a company of officers had assembled, straight and tall like a poplar forest, facing the internal barracks. The company stood in rows according to dominion, imperials at the front, colonials at the back. Captain Savige moved into the back line. A party of Russian officers marched across the parade ground in front of the main assembly.[139] The thought flashed into Stanley's mind that he may be on a rescue mission to Moscow to save the Tzar from the Bolsheviks, but a sharp call to attention killed the notion. The Chief of the British Imperial General Staff, General William Robertson appeared on the balcony and addressed the men of Dunsterforce:

> Gentlemen, I am indeed pleased to see you, for I recognise that before me I see gathered from the Imperial Army and the troops of the various Dominions, the cream of the British Army, and in whatever you undertake, I wish you good luck and God speed.[140]

The Imperial High Commanders explained the main objective of the mission: to do whatever was necessary to protect British interests in the Middle East by thwarting German–Turkish expansionist schemes that were undermining British security throughout the entire region. The next person to address them was Andrew Fisher, former prime minister of Australia, who had been appointed as the Australian High Commissioner in London. He cast a benevolent eye over the men below and yelled, 'Now boys, you're going on a great stunt—live clean!'[141]

After the formalities of the Tower muster, the men underwent stringent medical examinations. Stanley's results showed that he was virtually unblemished by two and half years of front-line service. He had no bullet wounds, no shell shock or nervous disorder, no broken bones or hearing loss, not even a close shave with shrapnel. Although he wondered how this was possible he also felt a sense of accomplishment and confidence.[142] It seemed that the worse the conditions and the steeper the challenge, the better he became at soldiering.

Each man was given a list of items to purchase with his own money and headed to the nearby army stores. Two kits were necessary, one tropical and one arctic, as well as medical supplies. Their gear would need last for two years. The inventory read: 'Leather or fur jerkin or a fur coat; fur gloves; fur cap with ear flaps; field boots large enough to take extra socks.'[143] Rumour had it that the plan of operations was 'somewhere east of Suez', which left little to be desired 'in the way of adventure' and they remained in the dark regarding all details.

Dismissed from the Tower with a week's leave, Captain Savige went out with the others that night to catch a show in the West End while some men left the city to visit relatives and friends.[144] Others, like Captain Stewart who stayed in a dreary bedsit, found the solitude almost unbearable: 'And never for the rest of my life was I to feel so lonely as I did during that week in the heart of big busy London.

I used to go into shops and buy something I didn't really want, just to be able to talk to someone'.[145]

Nights were interrupted by German zeppelins as they hatched their deadly packages, destroying neighbourhoods below. Each morning the London papers published a list of the dead and wounded, and in the evening the city squealed with air-raid sirens. One night, as they prepared to depart for the mission, the first Luftwaffe bomb of the New Year burst over Canary Wharf.[146] Leaving Australia for the Great War almost three years earlier, Captain Savige only dreamed of such an adventure, but now he would be part of a perilous, secret mission from which he might never return.[147]

Chapter 10
A Pioneer Boy Enlists

The glory and the freshness of a dream.
William Wordsworth

The flagship HMAT *Ulysses* embarked from Port Melbourne laden with the 1st Division of the Australian Imperial Expeditionary Force in October 1914 headed for Egypt, but Stanley Savige was not on board. Murmurs of war had floated around Melbourne long before the first troops departed. The royal cousins of Europe, England and Russia had taunted each other for years and the broadsheets covered the darkening atmosphere in Europe. There were reports of the German Kaiser standing on the deck of freshly minted battle cruisers at the Hamburg shipyards, and aeroplane pilots buzzing the crowds at the Paris World Fair and Zeppelins flying like armoured bumblebees over the open countryside. But the burgeoning conflict was a world away from Melbourne and besides all that, Stanley was in love.

On New Year's Day 1914, Stanley proposed to Miss Lillian Stockton. It may have been in the winter of 1911, just before his twenty-first birthday, when Stanley first noticed her at the South Yarra Baptist

Church, where they both worshipped. He most likely saw her every Sunday, sitting with her parents in the wooden pews. Once or twice a week, when he went to choir practice after work he may have had the chance to talk to her and her friends.

Lillian Stockton was a successful milliner, which was a clever career choice in a day and age when hats were mandatory attire for women and girls and there was no shortage of business among the well-heeled and the Saturday race-set with whom she could show off her fancy creations. Lillian was demure, devout, talented and popular and, not surprisingly, appealing to a young man like Stanley.

Stanley was raised in a church-going family. He had a steady job at the haberdashery, and his own bank account. Despite his meagre clerk's wages, he had managed to knock together a deposit for a block of land. Lillian may have made discreet enquiries of her own about Stanley, the Sunday School teacher. In any case, by the summer of 1913, she became a frequent guest of the Savige family, showing up at their inner-city, working-class home in Prahan for tea parties, social outings and family celebrations. Things were off to a good start when, there was some hint of a falling out, a lovers' tiff, but Stanley must have smoothed it over when he confessed his ambitions in a letter 'to be a man with a character following the great ideal of Jesus Christ...that's my ideal Lil'.[148]

During their extended courtship, Stanley and Lillian most likely enjoyed things that other young couples liked to do in Melbourne at that time—evening dances at the town halls and picture shows, where they could sit side by side on the bucket seats. On weekends there was bathing and picnics at St Kilda beach, cricket and the thrill of Luna Park. On Sundays, perhaps Stanley got up early so that they could walk to church, arm in arm.

Six months into Stanley and Lillian's engagement, the freshness of their hopes and dreams curdled. On 4 August 1914, the Prime Minister announced that Australia was at war, triggered by the assassination of the Austro–Hungarian Archduke and his wife a few days earlier. One by one, the Kaiser, the Kings, the Sultan and the Tsar, caved into a pit of enmity taking Europe, Russia and the Middle East with them. Within weeks of the first exchange of fire, thousands of soldiers lay dead in the paddocks and fields that only weeks earlier they had been ploughing and sowing around the ruined villages of Belgium, France and Austria. Some speculated that it would be over by Christmas, but the conflict steadily worsened.

Unlike many who rejoiced at the declaration of war, Stanley's mother, Ann, was 'bitterly opposed' to it. She believed that the war was driven by imperial power and greed, and was concerned about the pending exploitation of workers and the poor. She made no bones about it, taking to the soapboxes around the city, declaring her left-wing, pacifist views in front of crowds that gathered at parks and street corners for debate.

Ann was also anxious about her sons enlisting for military service. In particular, Stanley, who was due to be wed, fearing that he would be targeted by recruiters. Ann's dream for her son was that someday he would run for a seat in the Victorian parliament, or that he would enter church ministry. The war meant that all the hardships and sacrifices she had made for her family for the sake of that dream might come to nought. That was when her heart trouble started.

Ann Savige was born and raised on the Bendigo goldfields. She was a tough woman—enterprising, determined and warm-hearted. In 1888, she moved with her sister to Morwell, a small farming settlement in Eastern Victoria, where they opened a haberdashery. Next door was Samuel Savige's butcher shop. Ann and Samuel were soon married, and on 26 June 1890 Stanley George was born, offspring of the pioneer generation.

It wasn't the easiest time to be born in Australia. Economic depression and drought were entrenched, pushing men and women out of work in the shearing sheds, hotels, factories and farms across the country. Things began to go backwards for the Saviges. When Stanley was three years old, they sold their business and moved to a tiny farming town, Korumburra, to ride out the downturn as best they could. They lived in a shingled, earthen-floored shack with two bedrooms, an outdoor bathroom, and a kitchen with an open fireplace for cooking and laundering. It was ramshackle but Ann wasn't one to complain and Samuel was no stranger to hardship.

Samuel's father, John, was born at Towcester, Northamptonshire in 1832 into a family of merchants, school teachers and farmers. The family name was altered from Savage to Savige in order to avoid confusion at the Towcester post office—presumably villagers of the same surname had been collecting the wrong mail for decades.[149] When John Savige got wind of the mad flurry of wealth and opportunity on the Victorian goldfields, he became the first in his family to depart permanently from England.

According to a genealogical study of the Saviges undertaken in 1966, the family tree is laden with knights by the name of John. From his earliest recorded ancestor, Sir John Savage, a knight to King Edward III who became heir to the Viscounty of Savage in 1376, there were 17 generations of Savages with the first name John. For 300 years, the family resided in the counties of Derby, Cheshire, Worcestershire and Chester.[150] Most of the women of this lineage brought lavish trousseaus of capital, title, land and children.

The Savage family served the English monarchs for hundreds of years. One was the Groom of the Royal Bedchamber of James,

Duke of York, one was the Sheriff of Worcestershire in 1498, another became the Archbishop of York in 1501, and another placed the crown on the head of Henry, Earl of Richmond, at his coronation as King Henry VII. Then in the early 1600s there arose an heir called Thomas, severing the familial attachment to the name John.

Sir Thomas Savage, Knight became the first Viscount Savage in 1626 by marriage to Countess Elizabeth Rivers, who belonged to the baronial house of D'Arcy.[151] Among the countess' relatives was the knight Sir Thomas D'arcy, who was constituted by Henry VIII as the 'Master of the King's artillery' at the Tower of London.[152] The tutor to the Viscount Savage's 13 children described his impressions of their household in a letter to a friend:

> For I never saw yet such a dainty race of children in all my life... for a cheerful, rising ground, for groves and browsing ground for the deer...from the gallery one may see much of the game when they are a-hunting. Now for the gardening and costly choice flowers, for ponds, for stately large walks green and gravelly, for orchards and choice fruits of all sorts, there are few like it in England.[153]

As Roman Catholics, Viscount Thomas and Elizabeth were persecuted during the English Revolution by the Cromwellian mobs who sacked their estates at St Oswyth and Long Melford. In the early twentieth century, a survey of church heraldry uncovered a curious hatchment, a small coat of arms hanging in the family church of Long Melford. When Viscount Savage died at Melford Hall on Tower Hill, London in 1635, the hatchment was hung on the portico. The prodigious, loyal Savage family became extinct at the turn of the seventeenth century, when Sir John Savage, a Roman Catholic priest, died intestate in 1628. According to the *History of Dormant, Abeyant,*

Forfeited and Extinct Peerages of the British Empire, the Savage coat of arms was cast in silver and depicts six lions rampant. Such was the ancestry into which Stanley George Savige was born.

By the time Stanley started school at Korumburra he had five siblings, Edna, Harry, Jack, Hilda and Bill.[154] He didn't excel at anything, neither academically nor on the sports field, rather he was a natural orienteer, alert to the life of the bush. Once the school day ended, Stanley went roving through the scrub with his brothers and sisters, swimming in billabongs, rambling through the dense tracks and gullies around Korumburra.[155] Once he brought home a koala that had scratched his face to bits and a tiger snake in a jam tin.

At nine years old Stanley got his first taste of war, when the residents of Korumburra and Morwell celebrated the inauguration of the District Patriotic Fund to aid the Boer War effort with Great Britain. Korumburra was so riveted by the conflict that a Junior Cadet Detachment was assembled and a contingent of mounted 'Rangers' was put on standby.[156] The first Australian soldiers, including seven of the local Morwell Rangers, departed for Cape Colony within a month of the Boer War declaration.

Letters from local soldiers were frequently published in the local paper describing their victories and setbacks in South Africa, as well as candid criticism of the British officers. Stanley may have overheard adults discussing the letters in the main street. Perhaps his teacher pinned newspaper articles on the classroom walls or the vicar mentioned them in a Sunday sermon. When news arrived of the relief of Mafeking in May 1900, the town erupted with joy:

> Someone rang the church bells, others fired off guns and fireworks, flags were hoisted, bunting displayed, cheers and songs rent the air; whilst everyone felt like standing on their heads… the President of the Shire got on top of a large box and gave a

stirring address. He eulogised Colonel Baden-Powell and his gallant six hundred men, referring at length to the hardships they had endured...and to the manner in which they had repulsed every attack made on them by the Boers...In the evening a public meeting was held...when there was a large attendance.[157]

In his child's mind, Stanley's earliest impression of war was, on the one hand, a miscellany of faraway battles against implacable enemies with strange names, and, on the other, patriotic celebrations where main streets and front verandas resembled florist shops blooming with red, white and blue paper garlands to welcome home local men, lionised on cenotaphs, never to be forgotten. Of the 16,175 Australian soldiers who served in the Boer War, 19 men from Morwell district were killed. Perhaps they were from Korumburra, perhaps the Savige family knew them, but whatever the case, Stanley was so gripped by what he read and witnessed that he kept newspaper clippings and copies of the soldiers' letters stashed away in a suitcase for the rest of his life.

The Victorian Inspector of Schools released student No. 131111 from the confines of the public education system when he was 12 years old. His first job was in a forgery as a blacksmith's striker, then at the local butter factory, after that at the *Korumburra Times*, but he tossed that in for work in a haberdashery. He landed a role in the town's Junior Cadets by fabricating his age and falsely declaring that he could play the bugle, and with that Stanley commenced his military career.[158] Looking back years later, he said, 'the best education I ever had was swinging a pick as one of a gang of navvies when I was a young fellow.'[159] In his free time he enjoyed cycling, pony club meets, debating and bush dancing.

Beyond school and work, Stanley harboured a desire for self-development. He badgered his mother to allow him to attend the Melbourne Continuation School but the family could not afford to lose his measly pay packet, so he spent his pocket money on books. At 17, Stanley decided to be baptised at the Korumburra Baptist Church. One boss described him as 'always diligent, punctual and thoroughly honest and industrious' but there was nothing particularly outstanding about Stanley. There were no glowing reports from his teachers or the principal, no tertiary qualifications, no promotions or pay rises. He was simply an affable, likable young man.

Ann worried that Stanley had no career prospects. She didn't want him undertaking the kind of work that other young men of the district had to do—navigating the life-threatening hazards of the mine, the seasonal ups and downs of farming, the dead-end factory jobs. Perhaps Ann feared that none of her children would reach their full potential if they stayed in Korumburra. Poverty is many things, and tedium is one of them. Ann fretted for something better, not only for Stanley, but for the whole family.

In October 1907, the Saviges sold their house for ten pounds. Ann piled the kids and the household furniture onto the train and went to live in the city, while Samuel stayed behind to work. In those days, the train trip to Melbourne would have taken all day. Children could bounce over the sprung leather seats, waving to strangers on the platform, as clouds of sooty smoke filled the carriage and blew through their hair. The bush grew so close to the tracks in some parts that they must have felt as though they were in a forest tunnel. Around the final bend, they would have caught their first glimpse of St Paul's Cathedral spire, and then the golden dome of Flinders Street Station.

They shifted into a little house in Prahan, a bustling, working class pocket of Melbourne, close to everything they needed—schools, markets, stores, church, parks and the river. It was the hub of the jam and rag trade and Stanley soon found work as a draper in a prestigious department store earning 12 shillings/6 pence a week. It was enough to cover the household rent and he worked there for the next five years. On Sundays he took his brothers and sisters to the South Yarra Baptist Church.

At 20 years of age, Stanley threw himself into the scouting movement, setting up the First South Yarra Scout troop, taking the boys on training exercises, weekend camping trips, mentoring, reporting and planning activities. He revelled in the experience of the bush, 'wallaby shooting in old togs and wallowing in the mud...boating, fishing and swimming'.[160] While the bush would always be a part of him, the unfettered freedom and solitude of it, Stanley had become full of grown-up, city business.

There were his job and family obligations, church services, Bible classes, scout meetings and camps, training with the Prahran Senior Army Cadets where he learned signalling, mapping, topography and scouting. On top of that he had enrolled in a three-year course to qualify as a Sunday school teacher, studying at night. At Stanley's twenty-first birthday party his best mate Percy said, 'You have qualities and a magnetic influence which will be of great benefit to all with whom you come in contact.'[161] Ann's scheme was starting to pay off. Stanley's strong faith and character, his leadership qualities and rapport with young people all pointed in one direction; he would make a fine church minister or missionary.

It was around this time that he met Lillian, but they took their time getting to know each other. Anyone could see that Stanley was a kind, reliable person; he was no show-off or charmer. He was fastidious, but not obsessive; well-mannered and always on time. His sense of fun and adventure made up for what he may have lacked in spontaneity. These were the qualities that Lillian probably wished for in a husband. Outweighing any chemistry that existed between them, it was their Christian faith that brought them together. Following their engagement on New Year's Day 1914, friends and family threw a tea party to celebrate. But a tempest brewed abroad.

The Austrian Archduke and Duchess were assassinated in Sarajevo in July. Austria declared war on Serbia, England declared war on Germany. France and Russia folded their cards and the entire commonwealth was put on standby. Prime Minister Cook pledged that Australia would defend England against all comers but it took a while for the news to sink in. Nobody knew for certain how the fledgling nation would mobilise for a war in Europe, especially as it had not long dropped its colonial shorts and changed into a pair of ill-fitting, sovereign trousers.

The brand new Australian naval ships were the first to see action in the islands off New Guinea, and by the end of September 10,000 men were ready to sail. The navy looked for seamanship, but despite the countless hours Stanley had spent fishing creeks in wooden canoes he would never pass for a sailor. Lillian could breathe a sigh of relief. His mother would not tolerate a bar of the war. In Ann's opinion it was obscene and pointless, waged by the rich and powerful for more riches and power.

Stanley had let on nothing about the idea wafting, like a daydream, in his conscience. At the time, he was engrossed in a book called *The Fire on the Snow*, a gripping account of Scott's expedition to the South Pole, one of the bestsellers of the day. It may have been what brought Stanley's daydream to the surface. Perhaps it was living in the shadow of war, or the rising of a long-held boyhood reverie about those Boer War heroes that he had locked away in that suitcase. Perhaps it was longing for a heroic challenge that his job at the draper shop could never offer. Whatever it was, Stanley felt a strong affinity with the Antarctic hero. Given his Baptist sensibilities, Stanley began to interpret his rapport with Scott as a spiritual sign to take courage. He believed that his personal decisions would be guided by God, and that he would make a real difference in the world oneday.

Stanley's way of wrestling with his conscience was to slip away into the bush alone. It was a sort of self-imposed solitary confinement in a familiar location where he could pray for guidance and listen without distractions. He emerged from the bush a few weeks later and enlisted on Saturday 6 March 1915.

When Stanley told Ann what he had done, that he had signed up for the war and would be heading off sooner rather than later, she broke down, wailing and sobbing for days. His father, Sam, was shaving in front of the mirror when Stanley told him the news. His only response was 'Lad, I always thought you were a bit of an arse, but not such a damned fool as to take that game on!' and he carried on shaving.[162] Stanley later wrote of that day how hard it was to forget 'the mental picture of a line of men waiting to be examined...and the feeling 'I hope I pass, I hope I fail'', but that wasn't the worst bit.

How would he tell Lillian that he had joined up and that he would be leaving in a few weeks time? Should he explain to her that if he plodded on with his ordinary civilian life he would always have regrets? He knew he risked losing Lillian before he even tried on his uniform, and whichever angle Lillian looked at it she would be losing out. If he married her before he left she might be widowed and childless in her early twenties, but if he called it off altogether they would both be heartbroken and she might meet someone else.

It's not known how Lillian reacted to Stanley's news but perhaps she suspected it was coming. Lillian may have appreciated better than his own mother that Stanley's decision to enlist made sense; important principles were involved. One must serve God, king and country. Good people should always make a stand for what is right and fair, and bullies must be taught a lesson. It was a matter of faith and trust, nothing less. Fate never came into it. Stanley and Lillian didn't believe in fate; they trusted in God's will and purpose. Although she had to accept that their wedding day would be postponed indefinitely—Lord forbid permanently—she could also trust that their relationship was based on a binding promise and vow of intention. And it would turn out to be bigger and more important than either of them could possibly imagine. Stanley and Lillian spent eighteen precious days together before he left. Such is the lot of wartime lovers.

○ ○ ○

Chapter Eleven
Preparations in Egypt

*If there is a heaven, which I believe with all my heart,
we shall meet there.*
Letter to Lillian from Stanley Savige

Being sworn in at the Victoria Army Barracks in March 1915 brought Stanley Savige's latent boyhood dream of becoming a warrior one step closer to fulfilment. That day, he became a new soldier in a new army in one of the world's newest nations. Along with 'about 300 men whose dress and bearing denoted that they were drawn from ever class in the community' he departed from Flinders Street Station headed for the training camp at Broadmeadows on the outskirts of the city.[163]

Three days later, standing in his blue dungarees on the dusty parade ground, an officer burst out of his hut with a tin of white paint and slapped two stripes on Savige's shoulders. He was now acting corporal. The brief painting ritual may have fallen short of the illustrious occasion Stanley had in mind for a promotion in the field, but it was a start. The corporal's stripes meant that he, the 'bespectacled Sunday school teacher', had been noticed. This was the moment when something seems to have set inside him. His vocation became crystal clear. It was, therefore, almost too good to be true when he was given the tap to try out for the Officers' Training School.

Savige passed each test in drills, tactics, orienteering, basic fitness and essay writing but was not selected; and it stung, not least because he had been rejected after putting himself on show. This failure apparently knocked around in his head for weeks because he recalled later that:

> On the second last day we were lined up when the Adjutant called out, 'Private so and so, one pace forward'. Two men stepped out. The Adjutant looked puzzled and then said, 'I want so and so, the son of a certain mining manager.' The right one was selected and marched into the officers' school.[164]

Stewing over the incident as he did, about how unfair it was and how demoralised he felt, how livid his mother would have been, he probably realised that skills and aptitude weren't going to be enough to get ahead.[165] He was overlooked on the basis of his lowly background or a lack of family connection; something he could never change. He wrote to Lillian that the authorities would soon find out that he was 'no lamb'.[166]

In that stinking dust pit of a training camp, sleeping under the stars at the bottom end of the British Empire, it seemed to Savige that the only way he would ever attain a commissioned rank was to somehow compensate for what he never had in civilian life. The incident coloured his perspective about army life and authority, and from that point onward he seemed to become all the more determined to excel in the field.

On 15 April 1915, Corporal Stanley Savige was officially transferred into the 24th Battalion of the 6th Brigade, 2nd Division of the Australian

Infantry Force (AIF). With only two days left before their departure they had no clue that the battalion was in a shambles.[167] The commanding officer (C.O.) was on active service in the German New Guinea campaign. The adjutant was held up at the Sydney barracks. Some troops had not yet been issued their boots or uniforms.[168] Regardless, the 24th Battalion would depart for active service, ready or not.[169]

The official history of the 24th Battalion, entitled *The Red and White Diamond*, is one of the chief sources for the first phase of Savige's army career. Named after the coloured shoulder patch worn by each member of the 24th Battalion, it is their war story. Written by serving members including Stanley himself, after the war, it contains narrative descriptions and highlights from all their minor and major engagements, their perceptions of the enemy and their own commanding officers, as well as idiosyncrasies of particular individuals and places. It also contains the Honour Roll; those who were awarded for distinguished conduct, those who served and those killed in action. Stanley is mentioned throughout the pages of *The Red and White Diamond*.

The second source is the 24th Battalion war diary, which is the military record of the battalion's activities in the field, held at the Australian War Memorial. It is their record of operations. Filling in the diary was an essential daily task of the unit, usually kept up-to-date by an officer. It is a detailed account of weather, rations, terrain, training regimes, manoeuvres, points of arrival and departure, casualties and deaths. On quiet days, the record is sometimes at hourly intervals but on the worst of days, it is blank, except perhaps for a scrawled word or two in pencil. Together *The Red and White Diamond* and the Battalion war diary comprise a fascinating and moving insight into the Great War as experienced by the staff and soldiers of the 24th Battalion. *The Red and White Diamond* began with their enrolment in April 1915 and ends with their devastating final battle at Montbrehain in October 1918.

The 24th Battalion's embarkation roll shows that the recruits came from various stages and walks of life. There was 'a 33 year old, married orchardist from Harcourt; a 19 year old boundary rider from Dhurringile; a bricklayer from Shepparton; a 24 year old, married chemist from Collingwood; a 37 year old married saw miller from Portland and a hospital orderly from Ararat'.[170] And there was Corporal Stanley George Savige, 24 years old, measuring five feet seven inches tall with black hair and brown eyes. His best mates, Ted Shepherd and Bert Stevenson, enrolled alongside him. On 8 May, Stanley stood on the deck of HMAT *Euripides* as it pulled away from the quay at Port Melbourne bound for Egypt.

Some of those who made the same voyage months earlier with the AIF when the war began commented in their diaries about the tranquillity of Port Phillip Bay. That was until they reached the rip at Point Lonsdale, where massive currents pummel through a narrow neck out into Bass Strait, making it 'a bit bouncy'. Many men who had grown up in the bush and travelled from outback stations, farms and country towns, saw the sea for their first time in their lives. They were not used to the open ocean, the navy food, or sleeping in hammocks, rocking back and forth all night in the stuffy cabins.

Savige wasn't as sick as some of the others who could be heard during the night cursing the weather, the rear admiral and the royal family. Some poor fellows, beside themselves with seasickness, would recite incoherent rhymes or declare that they no longer cared whether the ship floated or sank. The next morning it was easy to pick those men who struggled being on the waves for the first time. They were the ones stumbling around the decks, doubled over the railings with faces as green as split peas, throwing up for Australia.

Shipboard life was a constant challenge for the officers to maintain some semblance of military routine, which usually involved daily drills, machine gunning, inoculations, kit inspections and parades. There was even a mock court martial. Spare time was often spent playing chess, card games and cricket, lazing around on deck, sunbaking and writing letters. But the favourite entertainment was the tug-of-war competitions between the 23rd and 24th Battalions.

Each side gathered in the centre of the deck while men hung from the railings to get a better view. Stanley and the other men in C Company took hold of the rope, and when the sergeant blew the whistle, the game was on. On one occasion, both sides heaved and huffed and those on the sidelines yelled and shouted but neither side budged an inch. They heaved some more and still could not shift the rope. The 24th team discovered that the anchorman on the 23rd team had tied the rope to the ship's ventilators. To be fair, the match was replayed and 'the giants in 'C' company displayed so much strength that had they been ashore with the rope they might have pulled the ship uphill'.[171]

Having departed Melbourne in the late autumn, the HMAT *Euripides* now steamed over the equator into the northern, early summer. The humidity became stultifying. Stanley was stationed below deck for three weeks without a break, and began fading away, until the company commander finally relieved him of his duties. It was more than just uncomfortable; the ship's chaplain conducted eight sea burials during their voyage.[172] In July 1915, after six weeks at sea with one stop in Colombo, the first sight of the mountains beyond Suez came into view.

Corporal Stanley Savige marched down the gangplank at Helmiah with the rest of his sea-weary battalion, assuming that they would be allowed to stay put and rest for a while. But that afternoon they loaded up again for a further five-hour train trip and a three-mile march across hot dunes under the weight of full gear. Their destination was Heliopolis, the Egyptian desert training camp.

The Australian and New Zealand infantry had been training near the sprawling settlement five miles out of Cairo since December 1914. From a distance, it could have been mistaken for a gigantic Bedouin camp flapping in the wind, with horses and camels tethered outside tents from which nomads came and went, except that they wore slouch hats and khaki-coloured uniforms and went outside at the wrong time of day. Official records describe how the camp at Heliopolis

> gradually became decorated with whitewashed stone edges to the roads or with neat borders of green oats sown round the tents as time went on, spacious mess-rooms were built for the men. Shops of all sorts crowded along certain roads where they were allowed-shops of tobacconists, hairdressers, dyers and cleaners, newsvendors, tailors, photographers, sellers of antiques.'[173]

Major General Birdwood had arrived in Cairo near the end of December 1914 to organise the disparate commonwealth forces. On Christmas Eve, having made his plans, Birdwood proposed the constitution of the Australian and New Zealand Army Corps, ANZAC.[174] The 24th Battalion joined the other ANZAC units to prepare for deployment.

Six weeks at sea had eroded the men's general fitness and therefore they commenced a rigorous training schedule—a five o'clock morning reveille, six o'clock fall-in, followed by drills until breakfast at nine o'clock, lectures until midday, then lunch and a rest until four o'clock, followed by more training and pack marches until evening. All-night manoeuvres were also undertaken: 'A ten mile march on top of the day's training... Then after a sleep in the sand, they would attack at dawn and advance over five miles of sand ridges to march home over another five miles of burning sand in the mid-morning sun.'[175]

In an effort to cope with the heat and dust storms, Corporal Savige adopted a few new vices which he was never quite able to shake—tobacco, liquor and profanity. With his love of history and his penchant for adventure, he snooped around the Sphinx, the archaeological museum and the zoological gardens with his mates Ted and Bert. He also volunteered in nearby military hospitals, such as the one converted from an old hotel, visiting wounded soldiers and others who had contracted embarrassing recreational ailments.[176] As often as training permitted, he took time to pour out his feelings in letters to Lillian: 'If there is a Heaven, which I believe with all my heart, we shall meet there. I think my faith is simpler and my trust in God greater than ever before.'[177]

During those months of arduous training in the shadows of the pyramids, Corporal Savige started to stand out in small ways. He became the battalion shooting champion, aced the Imperial Army Certificate for Sergeants and gained a reputation for mapping and field-sketching skills. At the end of August 1915, the 24th Battalion was ready to ship out to Gallipoli—that 'mad country'.[178]

Chapter Twelve
Chewing Sand at Suvla Bay

They went to look at War; the red animal, the blood-swollen god.
Stephen Crane

The 6th Brigade travelled overnight in open-freight carriages through the desert to Alexandria. By daybreak, the 24th Battalion was loading onto the *Nile*, an old packet steamer, headed for the Dardanelles. There were 32 officers and 233 soldiers and crew on board. The other battalions sailed on the troopship *Southland*, which carried 30 2nd Division officers and 991 men. Just off the coast of Alexandria, Colonel Watson was ordered to take all necessary precautions against German submarine attack during the night; ammunitions were issued.[179] The *Nile* weighed anchor in the harbour at Lemnos Island the next morning to wait for the *Southland* to catch up, but by ten o'clock there was still no sight of it. Anxious staff began to speculate about the cause of the delay. They had a deadline to meet but they were under orders to stay in the harbour.

Half an hour later the officers were informed that the *Southland* had been torpedoed by a German submarine. Eight boats surged to the aid of the stricken vessel; officers paced the bridge. Finally the news came through; all hands had gone down with the *Southland*, as it sank *'port under easy'* into the Aegean Sea. Rescue boats managed to salvage 1,324 men from the water. Thirty-four souls drowned during the attack. They were buried on Lemnos Island on 3 September.[180] Marking their arrival in the Dardanelles with a funeral was not a good omen. A message of condolence from the General Staff of Army Corps Headquarters was read out to the 6th Brigade:

> In welcoming the 2nd Australian Division to join the Australian and New Zealand Army Corps, the General Officer Commanding, on behalf of all their comrades now serving on the Peninsula, wishes to convey to them our general feeling of admiration for the gallant behaviour of all ranks on board the transport Southland when that vessel was torpedoed on the 2nd... with men like those on the Southland we are full assured that our new comrades are going to prove themselves equal in all ways to the old hands who have fought so well.[181]

On Sunday 5 September, the 24th Battalion changed ships from the *Nile* to the S.S. *Abassiah* for the last leg of the trip. In the grey darkness, the officers did their rounds through the sleeping quarters to rouse the men. Most of them were probably already awake, helping each other gear-up with packs and rifles. Stanley was on deck with his company waiting for last minute instructions. Behind them the green lights of hospital ships flickered over the bay. Armour-plated landing craft ferried the men over the waves with the dim outline of dunes and cliffs in the distance. Bullets darted into the water and every now and then flares lit up the clouds like gigantic lampshades.[182] In his hands, Stanley held a tiny, leather Bible. He opened it at random and let his eyes settle on Psalm 91. There was time to read one verse: 'A thousand shall fall at thy side and ten thousand at thy right hand, but it shall not come nigh thee.'[183]

As they pulled into the shoals the men could see a cemetery with crooked crosses sticking out of the sand at all angles.[184] Stanley clambered from the boat, waded out of the water at Anzac Cove and ran up the dunes with the rest of his company until they reached Rest Gully, where they dropped to the ground with their ammunitions and stores. From there they had a clear view of the whole area, which resembled 'a vast mining camp'. The pungent stench of death and latrines and unwashed men shrouded the cove like a rotting blanket. And no one warned them about the other enemy, which could never be defeated—millions of blowflies. At least the worst of the summer was over.

Stanley's company got the order to crawl along the maze of gravelly trenches parallel with the coastline up to Monash Gully and stay low until they got to Quinn's Post. This spot, described by C.E.W. Bean as precarious, uninhabitable and the most critical position at Gallipoli, was where the 24th came into contact with Turkish troops for the first time. Their trenches were so close that they could smell each others' tobacco. Shortly afterwards, the 24th moved to Wire Gully where they occupied Courtney's and Steele's Posts, overlooking Anzac Cove.[185] Surrounded by menacing terrain, the newcomers of the 24th Battalion were was amazed at the feats accomplished by the 1st Division who had landed there on 25 April and scaled the ridges under heavy fire.[186] Seeing those soldiers all sunburnt and louse-ridden, wasted by dysentery and incessant shelling, it was difficult to comprehend how they maintained their good humour.[187] Colonel John Monash wrote that they had nothing but what we stood up in for the first 5 days, then gradually came water and food and boxes to sit on and boxes to burn to boil our camp kettles, then blankets and waterproof sheets...We have been fighting now continuously for 22 days, all day and all night...the longest period during which there was absolutely no sound of gun or rifle fire was 10 seconds...(the men) are as docile and patient and obedient and manageable as children, yet they are full of the finest spirit of self-devotion... I am convinced that there are no troops in the world to equal the Australians in cool daring, courage and endurance.[188]

By the time Stanley arrived in September, the Gallipoli campaign had been underway for almost five months. The 24th Battalion missed the massive August Offensive by a few weeks, arriving at the tail end of the allied push to snatch the peninsula from the Turkish Army. In the lead up to the offensive, Constantinople was rife with rumours about the not-so-secret British plans to bring ashore 100,000 commonwealth reinforcements that would take the strategic posts above Suvla Bay and Anzac Cove.

Winston Churchill, the First Sea Lord of the British Admiralty, inadvertently flagged the plans in a speech he had delivered in June, boasting about an allied victory. Such clues would never be overlooked by the meticulous Germans. General von Sanders, Commander of the Turkish forces, deciphered Churchill's speech as an imminent, redoubled effort at the Dardanelles. Given von Sanders' battle instincts and Mustafa Kemal's strategic brilliance, there were no surprises when, on 7 August, the Anzacs stormed the heights of Gallipoli. The New Zealanders made a rush for Chanuk Bair and the Australians smashed the Turkish line around Lone Pine.[189]

It was a strange place for their first engagement and the Anzacs would be forgiven for wondering why the British Admiralty were involved with land warfare at all. The Australian troops assumed that would be deployed to the Western Front against the Germans but instead, they were fighting Turks on a an Aegean beach. The Anzacs were tangled up in an elaborate scheme instigated by the British Royal Navy.[190]

At the centre of this fiasco was Tsar Nicholas Romanov. Russia joined the Great War from the moment it was declared, but it was already in trouble by the end of winter 1915. Russian troops were engaged with two formidable enemies on two separate fronts; the Germans on the Eastern front and the Turks on the Caucuses Front. Russia was outpaced by the Central Powers. Their manufacturing output of 15,000 artillery shells per day was only one-ninth of the German–Austro–Hungarian production rate. The Tsar was also sensitive to the flagging morale of his imperial troops and could not afford to lose further ground the Turks. He implored his English cousin, King George, to invent a manoeuvre that would relieve pressure on the Russian Army by diverting Ottoman forces away from the Caucuses.

The Tsar's request aligned well with the strategic concerns of the British War Cabinet which, by that stage of the war, had reached a stalemate with the Central Powers over the Western Front. Churchill enquired of Prime Minister Asquith whether 'there were not other alternatives than sending our armies to chew barbed wire in Flanders?' What the cabinet required was an ingenious strategy to outwit the Germans; it needed a diversion, a smokescreen.

Churchill proposed to deploy naval forces to destroy the Turkish forts, batteries and sea mines that had been stockpiled around the Gallipoli Peninsula. But Third Sea Lord Tudor opposed the idea saying, 'You won't do it with ships alone.'[191] Lord Kitchener, Secretary of War, subsequently advised the Tsar that the British had a twofold strategy. British warships would attack the Turkish garrison at the Dardanelles, and commonwealth forces would be marshalled from Egypt for a land assault. The Anzacs could chew the sand at Suvla Bay instead.

On 15 March, Lord Kitchener approved 'a deliberate and progressive military operation carried out in force in order to make good the passage of the navy'.[192] A massive amphibious operation was mobilised; 75,000 allied personnel, incorporating two divisions of ANZAC from Egypt, began arriving on Lemnos Island.[193] The Turkish Minister for War, Enver Pasha, instructed German General von Sanders 'to drive the invaders into the sea'.[194] Four days after the allied landing, von Sanders began to transform the dunes into a barbed-wire fortress, a death-trap.[195] But the Anzacs were underestimated; they clawed their way up the cliffs and burrowed in until the whole cove looked more like a termite's nest than a battlefield.

Six months after the botched naval scheme and one month after the failed August Offensive, Savige's battalion were on the move to their new position near a solitary pine tree. They reached Lone Pine via tracks and tunnels, and managed to put up a garrison by late afternoon. Knowing what it had cost to wrestle Lone Pine from the Turks, the 24th Battalion would give everything they had to hold it, so they started sniping before they put their gear down. The enemy returned fire on them throughout the night. Never has a tree been fought over like that one was. Stanley seems to have avoided any serious illness or injury up to that point and he wrote to Lillian reassuring her about their conditions at Gallipoli:

> I suppose you wonder what it feels like to be under fire...the trench work hasn't affected me in the least. I felt no different

coming under fire than going down to South Yarra. The crowd were all jolly and dead anxious to have a go. The feeling is quite different to what I expected. I thought one would feel quite jumpy. When they shell you it makes you feel a bit queer and the bombs are crook. Don't worry unnecessarily, I feel sure of coming out.[196]

Over the next four months, the 23rd and 24th Battalions undertook gruelling 48-hour shifts, one relieving the other, two days on, two days off without a break. When they weren't guarding the garrison, they were standing sentry or doing fatigue duties, hauling stores of water and ammunition uphill, sandbagging, repairing parapets and trenches, sniping and scouting.[197] In any other circumstance, the routine would be called torture. In retrospect, Major General Sir John Gellibrand described the men of the 24th Battalion in the Red and White Diamond:

> they liked to do things nobly for their own satisfaction. They were giving their lives, there was no help for that; and they made it a point of self-respect to give them handsomely...Light-hearted the 24th certainly were but underlying their gaiety of mind was a stern determination to see the matter out. Their business creed was to get the most out of life, and to demand the highest price from the enemy for their casualties.[198]

Stanley was at Lone Pine with the 24th until the end of the Gallipoli campaign. During those awful autumn months, the dead often outnumbered the living. The battalion war diary recorded a slow and steady attrition of men, mostly from Turkish shells, grenades and snipers, but often from sickness, fatigue or nervous breakdown. The diary notes that on 16 September the men received their first mailbag from Australia. Two days later, almost as an aside, the diary cites the death of company Sergeant Major Tippett. Not inclined to self congratulation, Savige omitted to tell Lillian that he replaced Tippett as Sergeant Major of C Company. It was his first promotion in the field and he was soon in charge of the Lone Pine snipers' post, in recognition of his excellent marksmanship.

From October onwards, Sergeant Major Savige was given regular intelligence duties as well, due to his mapping skills. One of his tasks was to detail the company for water fatigue duty each night. Provisions were loaded or pumped off barges onto the beach and carted by 16 mules along the headlands to the fatigue parties, who would relay the supplies into the trenches.[199] It was back-breaking work and Stanley's company cursed him for it. One of his men wrote:

> I often marvel on a rough day, when the loaded carts, nearly up to their axles in mud or sand, are beached on that wild seashore, on the watery edge of which they are kept during the day; and wonder still more when, after standing there for a few hours, the mules draw them out when the convoy leaves at night. For the mules do not like the sea…Therefore all praise to the Indian Mule Corps.[200]

Fresh ingredients and potable water were in short supply on the peninsula but the 6th Brigade chaplain had a bright idea. He went foraging on a nearby island and returned with 'a rooster under his arm and another on the end of a string'; both birds were tethered outside the colonel's tent. Each morning, when the roosters started yodelling, Private Kelly, known as 'the Kookaburra of Gallipoli', would answer them from the facing hillside at the top of his lungs for everyone's amusement. Rumour had it that the officers had cut off the roosters' combs to encourage them to start laying eggs but before they had the chance, the Lone Pine 'poultry farm' came to a grisly end at the hands of the brigade cook.[201] When the short-lived promise of scrambled eggs dissolved, the battalion resumed their standard rations of dry biscuits, jam, tea, desiccated vegetables, rice, bread and bully beef.[202]

At Lone Pine, the 24th Battalion fired up five machine guns and an 18-pound field gun—two hours on, four hours off, week after week. Neither side gave ground, neither side moved forward. The monotonous routine, the permanent state of vigilance and shelling night and day, left the battalion feeling agitated and demoralised.[203] By the end of October, the 24th Battalion registered 14 men killed in action, seven wounded and 149 evacuated to hospital.[204]

Savige received his next battlefield commission on 9 November to second lieutenant, but he took no joy in the promotion because it came as result of losing his mates in the 24th Battalion. Then the cold crept in. With the lice, dysentery, jaundice, malnutrition and exposure to the elements, it took its toll on the men. Lord Kitchener inspected Gallipoli in mid-November, realising that the Germans would crush any attempt to hang on there.[205] The 24th Battalion waited for orders to advance or retreat, but they were never issued. Like a bolt from the blue, a note from the Turks landed in the nearby trenches: 'We can't advance; you can't advance. What are you going to do?' The campaign reached an impasse.

Winter nonetheless, marched onwards like a crusader. Armour is no match for it and weapons cannot hold it back. It assailed the men at Gallipoli without mercy. Icy gales swept over the Aegean, bringing frosts and wild storms to the peninsula. Rough seas damaged the piers and 'their wreckage strewed the beach'. Food and ammunition boxes were held up in the tunnels.[206] Their equipment and provisions were buried under the snow. One blizzard cut off their water supply temporarily by wrecking the condenser and freezing the standpipes.

Many Anzacs saw snow for their first time. Some of the photographic images captured during the winter phase of the campaign resemble Mawson's Antarctic expedition, except that the Anzacs were hopelessly unprepared for blizzard conditions. There was no timber or iron to use as shield against the intense cold, and it was too dangerous to go foraging. It caused them 'acute physical pain' to the point where their 'cup of unhappiness was filled to overflowing'.[207] Everything froze—food, mud, water, feet. At Suvla Bay alone 12,000 soldiers were treated for frostbite, a further 100 or so died of exposure, and dozens more drowned when their trenches were flooded by melting snow.[208] Just when Savige could not imagine anything more miserable he learned that new plans were afoot.

A secret conference took place on Mudros Island. The British Prime Minister instructed the High Command to prepare 'in the utmost secrecy a complete plan for evacuation' of Gallipoli.[209] When so much had been invested there, few believed that the campaign would be abandoned. Meanwhile, plans for the stealthy evacuation of the peninsula were implemented. On 22 November, orders were issued; landing of food and stores was prohibited, equipment and machinery was to be dismantled. A ceasefire was in place for four consecutive nights 'to teach the enemy that silence did not mean withdrawal'.[210]

Savige hoped the tactic of silence and the inexplicable lull in the crossfire would coax the enemy to attack.[211] Soon the 24th got reports that Turks were marching through the trenches with their bayonets fixed.[212] Another note landed in a trench at Quinn's Post: 'My dear Australian, how do you do? We hope that you are in good health.

Always the best. Reply if you please.'[213] What the 24th didn't know was that Howitzer tanks, the terrible new hardware of modern warfare, had arrived from Austria and were in position for the winter offensive.

The bombardment commenced on 29 November. It plunged the Lone Pine Sector into bedlam and the 24th Battalion was pulverised.[214] Dozens of Savige's mates suffocated under huge mounds of dirt and mud heaved up by the Howitzers. The 24th sustained its worst losses that day. Savige's best mate, Ted Shepherd, was killed and another mate, Harry Fletcher, was severely wounded. Savige doubted he would ever see Fletcher again. The pounding they received that day moved General Birdwood to pen a letter of condolence.[215] Another battalion had to help the 24th to 'clean up the lines', repair their parapets and give the survivors a spell.[216] Shell-shocked and battered, the 24th regrouped and stood to arms in the trenches, in the bitter cold, waiting for a second Howitzer attack.

Savige never understood why the Turks held off because knew they would have encountered little resistance from the Anzacs who had been shattered by the first attack.[217] In any case, the dreaded second tank battery never happened. A week on from the fatal fusillade, Savige and the others were still digging out men who had been buried alive when their trenches collapsed. Caught between the sea and an overpowering enemy, 'sometimes the men wondered whether they had been forgotten—whether the armies on other fronts had finished their jobs and gone home'.

On 8 December, General Birdwood received a telegram from the Dardanelles Committee to evacuate Gallipoli.[218] He was responsible for withdrawing 80,000 soldiers from two battlefields with 200 machine guns, 2,000 vehicles, over 5,000 horses and mules and matériel. Wether madness or sheer audacity, the retreat would be conducted under the cover of darkness, without loss of life, without arousing suspicions, so that by morning the Turks would not notice anything different from the day before.[219]

Gallipoli changed. There were silent spells. Ships weighed anchor in the bay. There was intermittent sniping and bonfires and noisy night-time marching. The Turks couldn't make sense of their erratic program.[220] By mid-December, 15,000 soldiers had been taken off and 20,000 remained to be withdrawn.

On 17 December, Colonel Watson called the 6th Brigade officers into his tent to give them their orders. Stanley described the ambience among the staff:

> His usual bright and debonair attitude was missing. We silently took our places around him and in a voice shaking with emotion—so rare in him—he told us that Gallipoli was to be evacuated...We left that conference with our feelings too deep for speech.[221]

It was to be a finely tuned, staggered retreat off the Peninsula but there were mixed emotions among the men of Stanley's battalion: about the news:

> We were stunned and broken in spirit if not broken-hearted... it was hard to give up the ground in any case, but it would have been easier to say farewell if the sacrifices of the dead had found the reward of success as well as the glory of noble effort. That the job had to be left uncompleted was no fault of the troops, yet it pained them to give up the task.[222]

The evacuation of Gallipoli was set for 20 December. On the last night of the evacuation, there would be three parties—A, B and C posted at each sector along the beachhead between Anzac Cove and Suvla Bay. The officers would withdraw their men down to the beach, where barges would ferry them to nearby islands. C parties would act as rearguards. They could expect significant casualties during the complex operation, particularly for the C parties, which could in fact be left behind on peninsula if things went awry.

Despite the risks, men jumped at the chance to be the last Anzac to leave Gallipoli. Savige wrote that 'three volunteers from the battalion were called from among the officers to remain in charge of the last party—C3—and it was clearly indicated that there could be no chance of its getting away. The party was to be the rearguard to cover the final retirement, no matter what happened'.[223] Savige was chosen with two other officers for the C3 Party responsible for the withdrawal of the Lone Pine Sector.[224]

The 24th Battalion officers organised a strict timetable allowing troops to converge at designated times and locations on the beach. C1 would depart at 0215 hours, C2 would depart at 0245 hours, C3 would hold their position for 15 minutes, then retreat at 0300 hours. In preparation, C3 Party started to experiment with different ways to ensure the safest, fastest evacuation possible. Any casualties would be left behind. On his last day at Lone Pine, Savige wrote:

> About midday, a Turkish plane appeared and dropping to about 1000 feet above the trenches, moved backwards and forwards along their length. Did the airman know anything of our plans? It looked as if he did. If so, our chances were not too bright. As the plane swept along the lines, every man was ordered to fire his rifle as rapidly as possible, not at the plane, but simply to impress the Turkish Infantry into believing our line to be strongly held.[225]

A Party moved out at 11 pm, a few hours ahead of B Party. To create enough cover for the men to reach the beach, Savige stuffed his pockets with grenades and went darting from post to post, firing at the enemy, flinging bombs around like confetti. After midnight the Turks began raining shells upon the 24th Battalion at Lone Pine. Watching from the headlands, the C Party officers could see the men with Colonel Watson piling onto the *Heroic*, surging towards the islands. The last barge idled at the ready near the jetty.

The C3 Party—Savige with two other officers and 34 men—was left to defend Lone Pine. At any second, the Turks would start shelling the trenches and beaches. Stanley recalled that night:

> The strange, eerie remoteness of the situation was experienced as we each collected our packs in the deserted corners usually so full of men. The strangeness was intensified by the blanketed trenches and padded boots. I remember the little shiver that ran down my spine at that moment.[226]

Savige now had less than half an hour to get the party to the barge. Smoking was forbidden; there was absolute silence. He stood at the entrance to the trench and on the signal he shoved the men forward, one at a time. Of those final minutes on Lone Pine, Savige said that 'time had been lost and to make matters worse the strips of blanket around the boots began to unwind and impede progress…The men of the last party had not slept since the night of the 17th. It was now the morning of the 20th'. The C3 men were under enemy fire all the way to the end of the pier:

> Now that we were clear of the trenches the nervous strain had its reaction. We were all loaded with packs and rifles. Some men began to drop out of line. All the Turks in the world did not interest

them. Persuasion was useless…We literally booted some of them along to and onto the last boat but thank God, we got them all aboard…We had achieved what was thought to be impossible.[227]

The men struggled onto the barge, some dropping asleep as soon as they boarded. As the sea churned behind them, a massive explosion took out the Turkish tunnels at the Nek and the sky flashed red, spewing clouds of dust above the headlands. Gallipoli fell quiet as the dawn-treaders ebbed away on the waves.

A wild storm hit as the Anzacs punted into Mudros Island harbour. It was surrounded by vessels of every description—barges, hospital ships, life rafts, rescue boats and men-of-war—and swamped with tens of thousands of soldiers, mules and army stores. Men sheltered together under canvases from the sea squalls that blustered up the dunes, resembling something like a seal colony. It was a long wait for Stanley and the C3 Party; they were left sitting on the barge in the icy wind until late that evening because the 24th Battalion could not be located in the chaos.[228] By then, Savige realised that he had not eaten, slept nor washed for four days. They started searching in the dark for their battalion; at midnight they stumbled across them asleep in the rain. Savige said that:

> Colonel Watson, on being awakened, would not believe we were there and had got away. They had given us up for lost. Without food, for there was none to be expected, and too tired to run up tents, we crawled under the tents they gave us as they lay on the ground.[229]

The Anzacs spent Christmas 1915 on Mudros Island but the atmosphere was far from festive. Instead of celebrating the end of the Gallipoli Campaign and a successful evacuation, they commiserated over the demoralising retreat. No roast dinner or brandy pudding; not even so much as a thank you. They recuperated on the island for almost a month, slowly coming to terms with the disaster they had survived.[230]

Savige pondered his experience in Egypt and Gallipoli—the filth, the flies, the hot sand and biting winds, hammering artillery, the shredding of limbs and the fiefdom of shallow graves. Armies have marched back and forth across the Dardanelles for millennia. In 480 B.C., the Persian King Xerxes crossed the Hellespont with his troops on the war path to Athens, and Alexander the Great forded the straits on his way to India, but neither Xerxes nor Alexander fought there for as long as the Anzacs. And neither did they bury as many men. How could he ever convey these things to Lillian? And then there was the emptiness of a glorious defeat.

Gallipoli taught Stanley that survival is not a virtue of the living, rather it is a debt owed to the dead. It is difficult to comprehend how Savige came off unscathed: 'A thousand shall fall at thy side and ten thousand at thy right hand, but it shall not come nigh thee.'[231] The verse from Psalm 91 that he had read when coming ashore at Anzac Cove held fast.

○ ○ ○

Chapter Thirteen
Gellibrand's Apprentice

And soonest our best men with thee do go,
Rest of their bones and soul's delivery.
John Donne, 'Death, Be Not Proud'

The dunes of Tel-el-Kebir were damp with winter showers when Sergeant Major Stanley Savige arrived there from Mudros Island with the 24th Battalion on 2 February 1916. Life at the Sinai desert army camp was demanding, but it was not all hard work. Stanley spent a whole day shopping in Cairo's bazaars for special gifts for Lillian, buying a porcelain jardinière, a wooden lamp stand, an embroidered dressing gown and a genuine leopard skin, along with some academic books to keep himself sharp.[232]

During the training program, Stanley struck up a friendship with 'a gentle giant', George Harriot, a transport officer who passed on some good news about Harry Fletcher. Having recovered from his injuries, Fletcher would rejoin the unit at Tel-el-Kebir. From then on Harriot, Fletcher and Savige spent their leave passes together. And more good news; the 24th Battalion's mailbag finally arrived. Stanley received 58 letters in all; seven were from Lillian and others from his favourite cousin Grace he read them 'over and over' again.

In March, the 6th Brigade shipped out of Alexandria for the five-day sea crossing to the French port of Marseille, escorted by a torpedo destroyer. The 24th Battalion marched from the docks through the streets of Marseille to the railway station. Along the route, the Marseillaise came out to greet them with chocolates and flowers. Children waved and shopkeepers watched from their doorsteps. Stanley didn't understand a word of French, but he could see that the Anzacs were welcome in the land of milk and pastry. From Marseille, the brigade travelled directly to Nord-Pays-de-Calais without stopping in Paris. They alighted at Aire-sur-la-Lys and marched through the cobbled streets of northern villages—Merville, Estaires, La Gorgue and Sailly-sur-Lys—until sundown. On 8 April, at Haverskerque, Savige wrote to Lillian:

> If a Frenchman would not fight for France, he would fight for nothing. It's a glorious country...I've been billeted in several farmhouses and they can't do enough for you...The farmhouses are very quaint...All the places are two-storey and half the top is filled with hay...There is always a cellar...They drink a lot of wine and home-brewed beer...They live chiefly on bread dipped in milk...The women all wear hob-nailed boots and short skirts. The women are at present doing all the ploughing, as the men are away.[233]

For the Anzacs, the low-lying region meant that they spent more time sandbagging than trench digging. When the war commenced 18 months earlier, troops had converted houses and barns into sandbag fortresses, which were now sodden and lousy and full of mildew. In one billet, a colony of rats had taken up residence with the 24th. They were 'numerous enough and big enough to defend the position without the aid of men'.[234]

After a month in transit, Stanley arrived at Armentieres, the Australian sector of Flanders, where the trenches almost abutted the back steps of houses. There had been unspoken agreement with the Germans to preserve the medieval city of Lille, but the hiatus was over.[235] The British High Command was set to launch the allied Spring Offensive and the arrival of the Anzacs, 'especially the artillery, was the signal for more activity'.[236] It wouldn't be long until the citizens of Armentieres would be complaining that the Australians had robbed them of 'quiet days and restful nights'.[237] That first evening in Armentieres, Savige watched the battalion's band pack away their instruments.

On 12 April, Stanley was appointed as the Battalion Intelligence Officer, a dual role that incorporated Platoon Commander. He was in command of 30 men—snipers, observers, bombers and scouts.[238] The Australian Government insisted that the Anzac Corps staff should not be separated from their men; it was a matter of morale. From now on,

> under the defence scheme laid down by the III Corps for the Armentieres sector, each frontline battalion had all four companies in the front trench; but each company retained one of its platoons in close support. The supporting platoon formed the reserve of the company commander, upon which he could call if attacked; each frontline battalion commander could similarly call upon a company of the battalion supporting him.[239]

During the day, Savige's platoon started locating and disabling enemy snipers, machine guns and observation posts, and reporting on the progress of the enemy's forward and support trenches. But late at night, the knives came out. On nightly patrols, Savige's platoon crawled through the barbed wire onto No-Man's Land, where they encountered German units also patrolling the void. Brutal hand-to-hand brawls broke out. Often Savige's platoon would pounce on the unsuspecting German soldiers in their trenches, smashing their heads with truncheons, carving them up with blades and shanks like sides of beef.[240] It was dangerous, gory, exhausting work and while it is not something soldiers usually speak of after war, it seems Stanley was very good at it.

About 25 kilometres north of Armentieres, the Germans were about to introduce a new weapon to the world—mustard gas. The 24th was aghast:

> What atrocity of the war was more dreaded than the use of poison gases? This horror had already been used by the Boche when we arrived on the Western front, and at that time not having the effective defensive equipment, we almost trembled at the thought of the deadly fumes, for we had heard all about the torture they inflicted, of the cemeteries in the Ypres sector full of their victims.[241]

One night at Fleurbaix, only few hundred yards from the German front line, where Savige lay asleep in a barn, the gas siren blasted. The whole village flew into panic. Guards ran around like meat ants and soldiers scrambled for their masks in the pitch dark. Farmers ran outside with their wives and children into the square, and then fled in the confusion. The men were ordered to 'stand to', mask or no mask. Troops fell into line where they were, in the barns and on the roadside, in readiness for the inevitable German artillery fire and infantry assault that followed gas attacks. On that occasion, it was a false alarm and everyone returned to the village.[242]

On 1 May, Savige was made lieutenant. Summer was on its way, the season when infantry commanders traditionally get their game faces on. The summer of 1916 signalled the British Offensive on the Somme Valley, planned for 1 July. Stanley moved with the 24th Battalion into the front lines near Albert. As soon as they were in position, artillery shelling got heavier, mortar and gas attacks became more regular, night raids and aerial bombing of enemy stores and facilities more frequent.[243]

Amid the preparations for the big push on the Somme, Savige was summoned to the 6th Brigade HQ for an interview with Brigadier John Gellibrand. Savige went back to tell his mates that he been made the 6th Brigade Intelligence Officer (BIO).[244] It was his twenty sixth birthday. Not long afterwards on 29 June, 300 men including Lieutenant Stanley Savige, stole across the trenches to the German lines where they launched themselves on top of the witless enemy. It was a successful patrol, resulting in one dead, two casualties, five prisoners and numerous documents and maps that Savige seized for the Brigade staff.[245]

Once the Battle of the Somme commenced, the brigade was on the move amid bursting shells and a haze of artillery smoke, through the ruined towns and villages of Flanders, Baillieul, Strezeele and Ebblinghem Hozebrouck.[246] In one badly damaged village, children appeared from behind the rubble and ran to the men with their hands full of cakes and bonbons. The battalion diary records that 'when we start we know not when we are going to stop. These long tramps are a delightful pastime! They are the nightmare of a soldier's life.'[247] Exhausted and unable to go any further, they stumbled and fell out of line.

At daybreak, the officers could see that the brigade was scattered across the road and nearby paddocks, like driftwood after a storm. The march ended at Wardrecques where they collapsed into sheds and stables. Amiens, the beautiful canal town, was not far away, and they would train there in the morning.

Early on 26 July, the 6th Brigade marched through pastures dotted with cornflowers and poppies to the brickfields of Albert. When the offensive started three weeks earlier, the 1st Australian Division had been in the thick of fighting was replaced by the 2nd Division. Later that afternoon, Lieutenant Stanley Savige dressed for battle. The men strapped their boots, oiled their rifles and handed personal belongings to the padre for safekeeping.

The 6th Brigade filed down to Sausage Valley from the Contalmaison Road, the arterial for all traffic to and from the battlefield. It was gouged by bombs and littered with debris—gun carriages, shell casings, bloated horses and wooden crosses. By the time Savige arrived it was pitch dark and field guides were required to lead the men into position. To their right was the 5th Brigade, supported by the South Wales Borderers, and to their left were the Warwickshires, who now held the Pozieres front line.[248]

For the next 36 hours the Germans smashed the battlefield with tanks, minenwerfer mortars and heavy field artillery. The field ambulance was called in from the moment the first shells detonated; the stretcher bearers' arms were so strained they could barely grip the handles. Amid the deafening shells, the squealing of horses could be heard. One man was killed every minute.[249] The 24th Battalion was pummeled during those diabolical days and nights at Pozieres. Their war diary becomes patchy and mechanical; entries are scribbled each day in a different hand. Such was the bedlam that only the names of officers killed in action were recorded. Many dates in the last few days of July and early August record only a single phrase:

> Heavy causalities owing to barrage. Boche noted carrying cylinders. Move to Mouquet Farm. German shelling very heavy the whole day. Expect heavy fusillade of Potato Masher bombs...43 killed, 156 wounded...4:48am exhausted all their bombs, could not hold on...5am relief completed...resting Sausage Valley.

Savige made it out alive and back to Sausage Valley, but there was nothing left of Pozieres. The beautiful town vanished beneath heaps of smoking wood and rubble, as scene from an earthquake. The 6th Brigade sat to one side of the Contalmaison Road, shell shocked and damaged watching others limping back from the battlefield, all glassy-eyed, bandaged and mute.[250]

At the beginning of August, Savige's skills as the Brigade Intelligence Officer were put to the test during preparations for the second attack on Pozieres Ridge. Brigade staff officers were concerned about the state of the jumping off trenches and that the enemy wire had not been sufficiently damaged. It was Savige's job to fix things, and the attack on the ridge proceeded as planned. Brigadier Gellibrand went into the line with his men and stayed out with them during 'that night of terrible suspense and agony'.[251] Gellibrand wrote of Stanley later that he:

> expected a lot of the new Brigade Intelligence Officer...and we got it. The job is pretty strenuous at the best of times, but at Pozieres there was enough to warrant three men at the work. I remember one of his jobs was to clear up a doubtful position on the flank. That involved becoming an involuntary target for machine-gun practice at short range, and subsequently the linking up of a few shell holes to connect two trenches (six men employed and five of them were casualties). By the time

we were relieved Savige had established a reputation throughout the brigade as a cool-headed, hard-working soldier, always ready to lend a hand and as reliable as they make them.[252]

While working for several months as the Brigade Intelligence Officer (BIO) during some of the worst battles of the war, the brigadier had made a strong impression on Savige. Savige found Gellibrand to be an introverted, enigmatic fellow in whom there was a nobility and resoluteness of character. Gellibrand commanded the Anzacs at Gallipoli in 1915 on a reputation as the 'keenest selector and finest trainer of young officers in the whole AIF'.[253] There is a wonderful photograph from the early days on the Somme where Gellibrand is crouched around a biscuit crate sharing breakfast with Savige and his staff officers in the middle of a gigantic shell hole at Pozieres. Savige considered it a great honour to serve with the brigadier and they remained friends after the war.

By the end of the Somme Offensive many of Savige's friends had been killed. The I Anzac Corp lost 23,000 officers and men in seven weeks of fighting. The 2nd Division sustained 8,100 casualties, and Gellibrand's 6th Brigade took almost 1,900 casualties in a single fortnight around Mouquet Farm and Sausage Valley.[254] The 24th Battalion diary reads like a Red Cross register with a litany of names and dates of the fallen. General Birdwood presented the remnants of the 6th Brigade with ribbons, and for his exceptional work as BIO, Savige was promoted to captain on 15 September 1916.[255]

It was 18 months since Savige had left Australia and he was showing signs of fatigue.[256] Gellibrand organised an overdue rest, especially because Savige had inhaled the dreaded phosgene gas one night when he couldn't get his mask on quickly enough. He went to London for eight days rest, but when he returned to

Poperinghe he was still medically unfit for duty. Savige went back to London and didn't return to his brigade until early November, by which time unseasonably cold, wet weather blustered over Flanders. The dreaded orders came for the 6th Brigade to return to the Somme Valley and the men retraced their steps through Amiens and St Sauveur like a fretful dream. The whole sector was one vast, boggy wasteland.

At Delville Wood, the 6th Brigade was told to make themselves at home in a putrid boghole of cold mud, branches, tangled wire and human remains. They had no blankets or any hot food, only canvas sheets and their greatcoats. Aside from the incessant artillery fire, there was the noise of mortars, heavy machinery and army vehicles streaming in and out from the lines. It wasn't long before many soldiers succumbed to pneumonia, bronchitis and 'trench foot', forcing them to hobble out of the trenches 'like a procession of lame ducks'.[257] The enemy drilled them with cannon fire night and day without letting up. The month of November was an 'indescribable agony' for the battalion.[258] Over one thousand of the 6th Brigade's officers and men were either killed, wounded, downed by illness or missing in action.[259]

Th winter of 1916 was deeper and colder than most could remember. Captain Savige went down with influenza and was evacuated to an army hospital where he spent Christmas.[260] He rejoined the battalion at Ribemont on 25 January 1917, and took over as adjutant of the 24th Battalion on the 3rd February.[261] Three weeks later the German commanders Ludendorff and Hindenburg withdrew.[262] Along the main Albert-Bapaume arterial route the Anzacs surveyed the scenes of victory—columns of soldiers advancing through silent streets, miserable German prisoners marching under escort, eyes to the ground.

As lovely as spring is in the north of France, it was small consolation for Captain Savige because the 6th Brigade was moved to Noreuil for the First Battle of Bullecourt.²⁶³ He and his comrades laid in wait for 4,000 Prussian guards who swarmed like Visigoths into Noreuil Gully. The battalion took 60 casualties in four days but their war diary is euphemistic about it:

Move forward at night...B and D companies in line. The battle profited them little ground; it was one of those occasions when the cooks and the clerks on Brigade Headquarters took part and the Brigade Commander became a rifleman...One of the battalion's cookers, which was holed by bullets was awarded a gold stripe which it wore for the duration. However the bully beef stew tasted much the same.²⁶⁴

On 25 April 1917, Captain Savige and his mates commemorated the second Anzac Day in the pleasant surrounds of Favreuil Wood. Meanwhile, General Haig hatched plans for the allied Spring Offensive, which was designed to shake the German stranglehold on Belgium, commencing with the Arras Campaign. Captain Savige was in full training mode with the 6th Brigade ready for the Second Battle of Bullecourt, the second attempt by the Australians to pierce the Hindenburg Line. The goal was to wrestle the Germans out of Bullecourt and capture the nearby town of Hendecourt-les-Cagnicourt.²⁶⁵

Under the command of Captains Savige and Lloyd, the 24th Battalion was to spearhead the brigade's assault on the Germans with a series of eight waves using two battalions at a time to encroach over the open ground under a battery of shells at three-minute intervals. It was crucial that they stick to the schedule to prevent men being caught by their own barrage. The attack was timed for 3.45 am on 3 May.

Late on the afternoon of 2 May, the troops fell in for their final inspection before moving to the front. They were due to be in position by nine o'clock, but they arrived a little early in time for one final cigarette. Each soldier was weighed down by 100 pounds of gear—picks, shovels, flares and ammunition were secured to their tunics, rations were stuffed in their sacks, and sandbags were strapped to their legs. The band played them along the road to No-Man's Land. The time had come to crack the crowns of the Württembergers.[266] Just after midnight, Captain Savige ventured out from the embankment with his men to lie down in the grass and wait for the signal. Scouts had been sent forward to stifle any German patrols that might give away their intention to attack.

At ten minutes before zero hour, the German's lost their nerve, sweeping the ground with searchlights and flares. The whole field lit up like day. They dropped a huge barrage on the neighbouring 5th Brigade, followed by machine gun fire. The ground erupted with bombs and mortar shells, instantly making massive craters and confusion. Soldiers scattered and dived for cover, were blown to bits or buried under the dirt. At 3.45 the Australian bombardment started. One lieutenant yelled out, 'When we hit the skyline, go like hell and don't look at the other fellow.'[267] The troops rushed the enemy lines, creating a footbridge over the wire for others to follow. Before the shelling had stopped, some companies had reached the first trenches and were already in a melee, taking prisoners. All around, field artillery felled men to the ground.

Captain Savige and Captain Lloyd bolted ahead of the troops to set up the battalion headquarters in a dugout 'to repel frontal attacks and more easily to regulate and reinforce, as the occasion demanded, whichever flank bombing-party was being pressed by the Germans'. His friend Captain Harriot, the gentle giant, managed to carry forward a huge supply of ammunition across 2,000 yards of exposed slopes. For the first few hours it was almost impossible to make sense of the operation. The 24th watched as the 6th Field Company Engineers and the brigade signals section tried to reach the trench, but the machine gunning overwhelmed them, and they were disoriented by the flares and mortars. Captain Savige could hardly bare to look at his men 'who crowded like sheep in a pen'.[268] It was apparent that Gellibrand's brigade was marooned in No-Man's Land. At that point, Captain Savige thought that it was more or less hopeless:

> The 22nd on our left had been almost annihilated by the German barrage while on their tapes. The survivors had moved forward and we heard them fighting for some time, but they were too weak to maintain their position as isolated parties in the German trenches.[269]

In the smokey daylight Captain Savige searched for his men. Many lay in fragments on the upturned ground. Gellibrand lost 80 per cent of his brigade on that awful day. Savige had departed Favrieul with a fighting force of 586 officers and men; 465 of them never came back. He described a strange stillness that came over him:

> One only remembers from the blur of fighting, when one's head was dizzy, gallant men firing rifles until the barrels were hot and throwing bombs until their arms were numb. The wounded were in a desperate plight, yet one never heard a murmur...Time seemed to be lost. We appeared to have reached an eternity of day without end.[270]

In his tribute to those who died in the Second Battle of Bullecourt, Les Carlyon, the Australian military historian, refers to them as 'Gellibrand's martyrs'.[271] Brigadier Gellibrand remained with his men until they were relieved from the field on 4 May. He later said that his Adjutant, Captain Savige, 'enabled headquarters to size up every factor in the situation' and that 'when many a soldier would have used the word 'critical', Savige's term was 'somewhat serious".[272]

The Red and White Diamond states that Captain Savige remained in the heat of the conflict with his men without rest and, despite their devastating casualties, the battalion achieved their objectives.[273] He was Mentioned in Despatches (MID) for his efforts at Bullecourt. The citation reads:

> For conspicuous gallantry in action at the HINDENBURG Line on 3rd May 1917. After assisting to reorganise a party of broken infantry he acted as Staff Officer to the Senior Officer in the captured position. In this capacity he displayed most commendable coolness, energy and ability, in securing reliable information as to the progress of the action.[274]

Cool, energetic and capable; that was Stanley's character in battle and that became his reputation. One month after the battle Captain Savige retired with his battalion to their favourite village, Warloy-Baillon for a prolonged recuperation. The battalion spent their days at Warloy-Baillon playing foot ball and cricket, and in the evening twilight they promenaded with mademoiselles along the canals and streets, cavorting in the salons and bars.[275] The Warloy cemetery is the final resting place for members of the 24th Battalion who died during the Battle of Pozieres the year before, and the residents of Warloy had marked their graves with red and white diamonds as a symbol of their endearment.

General Birdwood visited Warloy to decorate officers and men for their gallantry at Bullecourt. Their beloved Brigadier Gellibrand was given a sterling send-off to his new training command post in England, and the brigade then shifted camp to an abandoned sugar factory in Le Transloy.[276]

After the summer camp, Captain Savige moved back to Flanders. The battalion chaplains conducted a dedication ceremony for the Somme Battle at the Battalion Memorial erected on the ridge outside Mouquet Farm.[277] As the summer retreated and autumn leaves turned golden, plans were laid for Belgium. The 24th moved again to the Ypres Sector. Captain Savige was transferred to the 6th Brigade HQ as the staff major in-training. He would serve with the brigade for the remaining months of 1917 on other hellish fronts, including Broodseinde Ridge and the Daisy Wood portion of the Battle of Passchendaele.

Captain Stanley Savige was awarded the Distinguished Service Order (DSO) and again Mentioned in Dispatches for his service and gallantry in February and March of 1917. He was the only member of his battalion to be mentioned in dispatches on three occasions, but the bittersweetness of these accolades were not lost on Savige. His dear friend Captain Harriot was killed at Broodseinde. When they had taken leave together in England Savige said that Harriot stood 'six feet five inches high and perfectly proportioned, when he walked through the streets of London the crowds stopped to look at him and marvelled at what manner of men the weird offshoot of empire at the antipodes could produce'.[278] Stanley was to have been Harriot's best man at his wedding.[279]

Captain Savige was also awarded the Military Cross for his daring accomplishments made during the Battle of Bullecourt the previous May, as well as for Broodseinde and Daisy Wood between September and November 1917. The citation reads:

> 'For consistent good work and devotion to duty. Coolness under fire and tenacity of purpose were further exemplified by this officer's work in the heavy and successful operations on the Hindenburg Line. This officer has at all times rendered exceptionally good service in every capacity.'[280]

He was appointed Acting Brigade Major in November, and wrote to tell Lillian that 'some day I may get the job and come back like a parrot, with a flash cap and red band and staff badge, red tabs and blue arm band and a crown. I hope for that at all events, so possibly you will marry a Major'.[281] Slowly but surely the tide of war was turning in the favour of the allied Entente nations but Stanley's dream of reuniting with his family and his fiancé as a fully-fledged major was not yet to be.

Through three years of hard campaigning at Gallipoli and the Western Front, Captain Savige kept his life and soul together. He had worked his way up from digger, sniper, platoon commander, raider, intelligence officer, adjutant and captain to brigade major. His alacrity, courage and resilience were plain for all to see; only now he had the decorations to prove it.

On 15 December 1917, Stanley moved to Broodseinde with the 6th Brigade into the Ploegsteert Sector of Flanders.[282] Further afield, in foreign theatres of the Great War, mammoth struggles of a different kind were unfolding; revolution, jihad and genocide. In a few days it would be Christmas and Captain Savige would be withdrawn from Flanders for good to take part in a perilous, secret mission.

○ ○ ○

Chapter Fourteen
Never a Finer Gathering

On 29 January 1918, Waterloo station bustled with luggage porters, friends, relatives and British War Office representatives, all there to farewell Dunsterforce on their mission. In keeping with his understated manner, Captain Savige stood alone on the platform, regretting that he had asked his relatives not to bother coming to see him off; he tried to put out of mind those whose absence made them feel all the more present that morning.

The train hauled out of the city, past the well-husbanded pastures of England, on schedule to arrive in Cherbourg by morning, headed for an unknown destination 'somewhere east of Suez'.

Colonel Donnan was in charge of Dunsterforce during their transit. His colourful career included a stint as a British Secret Service agent during which he had collected intelligence throughout the Middle East in collaboration with Lawrence of Arabia.[283] His anecdotes were so farfetched that he left others with mixed feelings of both incredulity and inspiration. Donnan was in the habit of packing a German revolver on his hip whilst dining in the mess, even at breakfast. Therefore, it was safer not to question his fantastic stories.

Dunsterforce made the entire overland trip from Cherbourg to Taranto, southern Italy by rail. Stanley managed to keep his correspondence with his little cousin Grace during the long journey and the coming mission. The letters chart his perceptions and feelings, the highs and lows, of his experience during his adventure with Dunsterforce. Stanley enjoyed the journey despite the crammed compartments. In February, he wrote telling Grace that it was delightful trip.

> There were 39 nurses on board and you may guess I had a very good time of it…We have a very long train journey to do tonight and will be at sea again very shortly.

He liked the Russian language lessons, the 'smoke nights' and the bridge parties, and the luxury of hot baths and tinned food.

It was a world away from the tortures of trench warfare. He thought the Rhone Valley was 'the most beautiful' place and one morning took a wash in the river, describing it as 'all sunshine, a glorious day'. He recalled that:

> Each found the true value of the other fellow and it was with high spirits that we all settled down, determined to do the best, one towards the other. Of all the mingling that this world has seen there was never a finer gathering of real men than that party one was privileged to belong.[284]

On 11 February, Dunsterforce embarked on the *Malwa* from the Italian naval base near Taranto, headed for Alexandria.[285] As he walked down the quay at the Port of Suez something caught Stanley's attention. It turned out to be the *Nile*, the very same 'old tub' that had saved the 24th Battalion from enemy submarine attacks during their sea crossing to Gallipoli in 1915.[286] The ship was built in the Glasgow shipyards for the Royal Mail Steam Packet Company. It had two black funnels, three masts, a carrying capacity of nearly four hundred passengers and crew and travelled 15 knots at full tilt.

The *Nile* had left Southampton in 1893 on its maiden voyage to Buenos Aires laden with letters. Later in its long and thankless career, the *Nile* took on military cargo, making two voyages as a Boer War transport ship. For a quarter of a century the ship had been a familiar feature on the eastern trade routes but now it waited wearily at the Suez docks.[287] Initially, the Suez port authority refused to permit accommodation for Dunsterforce on board the steamer due to an outbreak of smallpox amongst the ship's crew and a nasty plague of mice and insects infesting the first- and second-class cabins, which posed a serious health risk to the soldiers. Eventually, the port authority gave the all clear, and Savige boarded with Dunsterforce for the Red Sea crossing to Mesopotamia.

Stanley wrote to Grace again at the end of February when the sea crossing was coming to an end;

> I have a feeling all will be well with me so do not worry on my life… Naturally, there is very little news at sea… I saw the Southern Cross two night ago for the for the first time in nearly three years and gazed at it for hours thinking of all the happy times in the past.

The *Nile* was manned by a boisterous crew of European officers, nervous Goan stewards and Lascars. Lascars were highly regarded sailors who embodied a 500-year-old seafaring tradition and they were recruited in large numbers by the English Royal Navy and the British East India Company.[288] The mixed crew was under the command of the cantankerous Captain Lockett, a seaworthy creature prone to mercurial moods. One of the Australian officers described the captain:

> ...who could be seen pacing the bridge, unshaven, collarless, a faded cap tilted over one ear, constantly chewing a cigar. When he spoke, he unleashed a string of strange oaths with words borrowed from many languages. His real nationality was unknown, although he affected a strong 'Yankee' accent. According to legend, his life had been spent wandering the oceans of the world, sailing into virtually every port in Africa, Asia and the Pacific coasts of North and South America. As master of the Nile for the past fourteen years, he had accepted many a strange cargo in the name of trade.[289]

One evening, as Captain Lockett steered the ship through a heavy swell and the men engaged in a boozy game of cards, the ship's Second Officer, a raucous Russian, stood up from the table, lurched onto the deck and vanished. Some of the passengers presumed he had fallen overboard but when the Second Officer's disappearance remained unresolved, the ship was engulfed in anxious speculation and aspersions. The timid Goanese stewards believed that the superstitious Lascars had tossed the poor officer overboard as a means of appeasing a gigantic shark that had been trailing their ship for over a week. Sea monsters were believed by the Goans to be a portent of death and they held all night prayer vigils asking to be spared an agonising end between the jaws of the sea monster. Two nights after the first mysterious accident, one of the Lascar sailors disappeared over the rails in tranquil waters.[290]

From bow to stern, an atmosphere of malevolence and suspicion permeated the *Nile*. The Goans were too afraid to walk alone on the decks after dark. The Lascars toiled away nervously in the officers' quarters and the ship's galley below. The British officers, who had been sleeping in the open air above deck, shifted their hammocks back to the pox-ridden, vermin-infested cabins below deck without a word of complaint. The shark vanished and there was no further loss of life on the *Nile*. Captain Savige remarked that the *Nile* 'had saved us in my first venture, so I took it to be a good omen that she should be the vessel that would carry me on my last and greatest venture'.[291]

○ ○ ○

Chapter Fifteen
The High Road to Hamedan

No country is so wild and difficult but men will make it a theatre of war.
Ambrose Bierce

Upstream from the delta where the Shat-al-Arab River flows wide and shallow and date palms grow along its marshy banks, Dunsterforce waited for 'a favourable turn of the tide'. On 18 February 1918, the paddle steamer forged the bar. From the railings, Captain Savige watched with delight as the mythical waters of Mesopotamia, the Tigris and the Euphrates Rivers, mingled beneath them. On the horizon, the bustling port of Basrah was a gladdening sight for all after the tedium of the open ocean.

Basrah pulsated with activity both on land and water. Steam tugs towed barges laden with building materials and fresh produce, hospital ships transported sick and wounded men. Dhows, weighed down with passengers and merchandise, were hauled along the river banks by labourers using thick ropes tied around their waists and foreheads. Women and children swam and washed their clothes in the reedy shallows. From Basrah, Stanley describes the city and its people to Grace in colourful detail, especially the bazaars and life on the Shatt-al-Arab. In early March he wrote that

> 'very soon we shall be doing the long trail and then letters will be few and far between... I miss you all so much and every mile further on makes me long to see you.

Basrah had been one of the principle mercantile centres of the East for centuries, owing to its location at the head of the Persian Gulf, protected from the open sea and providing a gateway to the Arabian Peninsula.[292] From the outset of the Great War the Entente Powers had set their sights on securing their strategic interests in the Middle East, and the Germans were planning the terminus of the proposed Berlin–Baghdad railway at Basrah.[293] When Dunsterforce arrived there, the city had been captured and surrendered successively by the British and the Turks since the Mesopotamian Campaign had commenced in 1914. It continued to function as a major supply base for the allied armies in the Middle East.

The allied defeat at Gallipoli in December 1915 had freed a sizeable portion of the Ottoman Army to regroup and swoop eastwards across Caucasia and southwards into Mesopotamia, where they engaged the Russian and British armies respectively. By late 1917, Russia was in turmoil due to widespread civil and industrial unrest which culminated in the revolution. On 6 December 1917, the British Mesopotamian Expeditionary Force learned that Lenin had signed an armistice with Turkey and Germany; hostilities between Russia and Turkey abruptly ceased. The armistice liberated thousands of Austrian and German prisoners of war throughout Trans-Caucasia and the Caspian basin.[294] When the news of the revolution spread, thousands of Russian soldiers dropped their weapons and headed home across the Caspian Sea, leaving the British to fight on by itself.

Despite the armistice with the Central Powers, the British General Maude struck an excellent deal with the Tsarist General Baratov. He convinced Baratov to stay and assist the British forces in the region. Together they could secure the major overland routes through eastern Turkey, the Caucasus Mountains and North West Persia. Whoever had control of these parts would be spared the dangerous march through the mountain passes en route to the Caspian. From then on, General Baratov's Cossacks became an indispensible ally of Dunsterforce in North West Persia until the end of the war.

Dunsterforce made safe passage to Basrah but the men were still a long way from their ultimate destination and their objectives remained a tightly kept secret. At Murkina, their new camp two miles away, they unloaded their stores and kits. Spring rains turned the campsite into a quagmire and Savige wrote that 'when one is camped under canvas at that time of year, a great many of its charms pass away'.[295] Colonel Byron, who was promoted to brigadier, announced an advance party that would depart on 8 March, but Stanley was not on the list. Having travelled some 10,000 kilometres in five weeks, he found it extremely frustrating to stop just before the jump-off point. During this waiting period there was a steady stream of visitors from the Baghdad General HQ, which Stanley found irritating:

> This meant that everybody had to turn out, spick and span, on the parade ground to be reviewed by the All-Highest, when many very nice things were said to each of us, but the unspoken desire of all was that there were fewer Generals on the earth to 'butt in' upon our time which was so urgently needed for training for the great work ahead.[296]

On 17 March, Captain Savige and the other men were on their way up the Tigris River. For days on end they wended their way through desert landscape, past Kut-el-Amara and Ctesiphon, until Baghdad the city of the Caliphs, appeared like a mirage between the palms, the domes and the minarets.[297] He had a bird's-eye view of the exotic surrounds from the deck, writing:

> What old scenes and recollections of Sunday School days these ancient rivers bring back to one's mind, the conquest of Palestine by Cyrus and the deportation of the Jews to the banks of the noble Euphrates. As one looked across the wide waters and winding turns, the cries of the Jews in the days of that bondage seemed to be echoed by the swirl of the passing waters.[298]

He marvelled at the poultice of humanity in Baghdad—Arabs, Armenians, Persians, Abyssinians, Syrians, Jews and Chaldeans. The city's residents were enjoying a semblance of peace since Baghdad had been captured only a few months earlier by General Maude, forcing the retreat of the Ottoman Army. Savige was rattled by the din of hagglers and the pungent smells of spice markets and street food in the bazaars. One evening, as he relaxed at the mess bar with his mate Captain Stewart, a young boy dragged an uncooperative donkey through the kitchen door. Across the back of the donkey hung a fish so large that its head and tail nearly touched the ground on either side. The boy struggled to get both creatures inside. Captain Stewart remarked that 'if the two that fed the five thousand in the desert place, according to the New Testament, were as big, it was not such a miracle after all'.[299]

> His cousin Grace received a letter from Stanley written in early April from their base camp outside Baghdad, where despite some adventurous interludes with his mates, his mood had flattened;

> I feel very lonely at times and very often get fed up on this job... Here one knows nothing o anything tha tis going on and after my job in France where I was the one know all and say this and have that done, it is hard to understand the other side of things, especially when people haven't the brains or tact... What I miss most of all are the letters from England only a few days old. The news from France is not by any means bright... I long to be with the boys and go through it all with them.'

The wait was finally over. At nightfall on 17 April, Dunsterforce set off on their mission, leaving Baghdad through the ancient city gates. Ahead of them lay an 800-kilometre trek across the Persian frontier. They took the ancient caravan route along the Khorasan Highway over the stony Nineveh Plains, into the unknown.

Captain Savige was in the company of British Colonel Keyworth and Captain Kay, Australian captains Hooper, Williams and Scott-Olsen, and the Canadian captains Fisher and Carpenter.[300] Their orders were to push through to Hamedan, a provincial capital in central western Persia, approximately halfway between Baghdad and Teheran, where their headquarters had been established.[301] They carried their stores on pack horses and mules. Apart from their rations, Dunsterforce would subsist on the open country.

Stanley's letter on 19 April states;

My Dear Little Grace,

> I am chosen as one of the Pioneer Party and we push off tonight,... The march will be hard and exceedingly long averaging 16-18 miles a day over high mountain ranges and then deep passes but I feel quite fit for the task and we are quite strong

enough to resist any raid or attack, so please do not worry about my welfare. I shall think of you often…

Persia, although an avowed neutral country during the Great War, was in a state of civil and political pandemonium. And it was into this volatile territory that Dunsterforce ventured forth; soldiers in an unidentifiable foreign uniform, speaking barely a sentence of Farsi or Arabic between them, with their limited resources strapped to the back of their mules. To make matters worse, the whole country was in the grip of famine. The odds of mission success were not in their favour.

Dunsterforce had been on the road for two days when they arrived at the first Persian pitstop Qasr-i-Shirin, lying in the shadow of the Zagros Mountains. The town was built on the ruins of an ancient Sassasian settlement, which was in such a good state of preservation that stone castles and ramparts remained in situ. Qasr-i-Shirin was a drop-off point. The Cossack Colonel Bicherakov agreed to deliver 250 mules to assist Dunsterforce to transport their stores and ammunition through the ranges.[302] They camped there for six days and, as they prepared to leave, Captain Savige was put in charge of an advance party of eight men, in case they encountered any aggression.

From Qasr-i-Shirin Dunsterforce left the featureless Nineveh Plains of Mesopotamia far behind and the forced marches began in earnest. Captain Savige was geared up before dawn and set off with a sturdy group of officers, soldiers, guides, muleteers and pack animals. They marched for nearly 35 kilometres through the razor-backed high country around the Pia-Taq Pass. In early May Captain Savige described the day in a letter to Lillian:

> Most of the journey has been along valleys bounded by tremendous mountains which rise up for thousands of feet on either

side, with cliffs hundreds of feet high. The valleys are covered in beautiful grass, but the mountains are as bare as a board. Our transport is done entirely by pack animals, there being about 300 in the convoy. Each has a number of bells round its neck, varying from big cowbell to tinkling little rattles and the music of these in the valleys is peculiar, but has a charm of its own. They are led by quaintly dressed Persians with big hats...We have hundreds of miles left to travel.[303]

Each muleteer handled about 20 animals and each lead mule had its own bell strung around its neck. Whenever they stopped to rest, the mules wandered off to graze on the slopes. The highland paths were so narrow that the mule train stretched for nearly two miles behind Captain Savige's advance party. It was perfect terrain for an ambush. They marched and climbed from dawn until dusk without anything to eat except for a few bulletproof army biscuits. They camped on the Pia-Taq plateau overlooking the jagged, tumbling ranges and slopes strewn with wild flowers. There Savige observed that 'the wind and rain of centuries had twisted and carved them into wonderful shapes, and to stand on that plateau and gaze for miles across the country was a most wonderful and inspiring sight'.[304]

The heat was unbearable and their boots sank shin-deep into the muddy clay. The animals became stuck and the signal wagons had to be lifted by hand through the churned-up passes. In the evening, the winds picked up and rattled through the gorges, and their cold, wet clothing cleaved to their skin. The overland trek had become a contest against the elements. As they hike through the wilderness, Stanley's letters indicate that they had little idea of their actual location. His letter to Grace in early May entitled 'Persia' explains the conditions;

We have been marching continuously for 10 days now... At present camped in a big plain 5,500 feet above sea level with snow-capped mountains... Cliffs and ridges abound but very few trees...

The only relief was one evening, when a young boy from a nomad family who were camped nearby approached the men offering some tea and eggs and made a fire for them.[305] At Dilkusha they spent the night in the typhus ward of a Russian military hospital; within a few days several of the men had passed away.[306] They struggled on through the Karind Valley onto the Persian Plateau to Kirmanshah.

On the morning of 9 May, Captain Savige stood on a ridge overlooking a spectacular view of Kirmanshah, a citadel surrounded by orchards and ploughed fields, spreading out like a picnic tablecloth on the valley below. The footsore party camped there for three nights. When Captain Savige went into the beautiful town the next morning he found:

> Knots of starving inhabitants...scattered across the valley actually eating grass, and every step in the city brought one face to face with a living skeleton. Those strong enough begged or watched their opportunity to steal. Those too weak to stand, lay dying in the streets. The dead were passed at frequent intervals. Mothers...clung to their dying and in many cases dead children; children crowded round the dead body of a parent.[307]

The War Cabinet does not appear to have prepared Dunsterforce for the famine conditions in Persia. The famine was most likely caused by widespread crop failure over successive seasons, exacerbated by waves of invading and retreating Russians and Turks, who had sacked the villages and burned farms and fields.[308] Weakened by malnutrition, the local people were doubly susceptible to water-borne diseases, such as typhus and cholera, that incubated in the village wells and sewers. Famine and disease created a purgatorial state of affairs doubling the risk for the men of Dunsterforce.[309]

In spite of the famine Kirmanshah market places continued a basic trade, enough for the men to stock their rations; paneet cheese, cannisters of honey with dead bees drifting in suspended animation and nan-i-churatch, the metre long slabs of pebble bread.[310] Stanley and his advance party were somewhat revived by their rest there but they were also disturbed by the plight of the local people. It was a sign of things to come. From Kirmanshah, Dunsterforce were within a few days travel of their destination; Hamedan.

There was no news from home, and there was scarce communications from London. Stanley must have wondered about the fate of his friends in the 24th Battalion. Were they still battling it out at the Western Front, or was the war over? Their families were clueless as to their whereabouts for weeks at a time, not that the information would have been of much comfort. Stanley wrote briefly to Grace in June to ask her to do him a favour regarding his financial affairs. He wrote;

> ...if my luck runs out then I want you to have 10% of what I have sent you and the rest I will get you to send to my brother Dick to help pay for him to go to college... I am feeling quite fit and tomorrow we are off on a stunt, what it is I cannot tell you but I will be alright.

In relation to the Australian members of the mission, primary sources are few and far between, however, one of Stanley's fellow officers, Captain Latchford, wrote a letter to his family whilst on the road out of Kirmanshah:

> I am sorry that I am unable to tell you of our destination or hopes but you can be sure it is very risky, secret and necessary, otherwise the British Government wouldn't have taken us away. It is just sort of thing I like (adventures). A man feels lost when he thinks of his old pals in the Battalion. Goodness knows how many are left standing...France is just like an awful nightmare to me now, especially the last show at Passchendaele when I lost Jim and 95% of my company in about three hours...Up till that show I didn't mind War but that knocked it all out of me. My nerve was going. Now I feel a bit better after a spell and change of scenery.[311]

On the Western Front there was no end in sight to the bloodbath. As difficult as it is to piece together the exact movements and personal experiences of the Dunsterforce men during this part of their journey, the mission was no secret to the Persians. Persia was becoming the backstage for a more complicated, clandestine field of operations, and the political cyclone engulfing the nation provided scant cover for Dunsterforce. The American consul in Baghdad reported the arrival of Dunsterforce in western Persia on 27 April 1918, and a local Persian newspaper, *El Arab*, dated a week earlier, announced the movement of British troops in the vicinity of Kirmanshah by the British consul there:

> His Britannic Majesty's Government is now pressed by the present events to send sufficient troops into Persia, although it had no intention to do so before. The reason for sending this army in Persia is merely to abolish the action of the enemies and to uproot their intrigues...The Persians are doubtless aware of the devastation of their country by the Turks from Hamedan to Qasr-i-Shirin.[312]

Beyond remote mountains and villages of the Persian frontier, Dunsterforce disappeared off the map. They were cut off from the outside world and for all intents and purposes, existed only as names on paper; from the moment they boarded the train in London, they had essentially become the classified property of the British War Cabinet. The dearth of records about their expedition indicates both the exceptionally harsh conditions as well as the secrecy surrounding the mission. Dunsterforce wired occasional reports of their progress via the Wireless Squadron to Hamedan HQ, but their private letters and field diaries are hard to come by. It is possible that some Dunsterforce records originally stored at the Imperial War Museum were destroyed during the Blitz of the Second World War.

Except for the official wires received at the Political Intelligence Department of the British Foreign Office in London from the Baghdad G.H.Q., and an excellent photographic archive of the various units posted throughout the region, most other sources were written retrospectively, including Captain Savige's own account, Stalky's Forlorn Hope based on his private diaries.[313]

Soon the sealed road fanned out of Kirmanshah into a broad, lush valley about ten miles wide, flourishing with spring grass and crops. Then it was uphill again. Looking ahead Stanley noticed a cloud of dust and it was enough to put a lump in his throat. From the dust cloud a large military caravan of soldiers and camels materialised. As they got closer their uniforms could be made out; two battalions of the Shah's army were approaching. Captain Savige and his six guards were hardly a match for the Persian troops, but they had no choice but to stand their ground.

At the head of the camel column rode a golden-trimmed commanding officer seated on a cushion of coloured blankets. He was flanked by his officers and standard bearers who carried the Persian flag. Strapped on either side of each camel was a large, decorated, wooden box with curtains and doors inlaid with mother of pearl. Captain Savige was astonished to see veiled women riding inside the box with their children. Drummers and trumpeters followed in the procession banging out a strident marching tune. Captain Savige wanted to bluff the Persian officers with an air of formal authority so he yelled sharply to his men 'Eyes left!' He could hardly believe that it worked:

> The old Persian commander was so thunderstruck at being greeted by such a salute that he bowed and saluted like the movements of a jumping jack. Each officer was similarly greeted, much to their edification and if their first thoughts were evilly disposed towards us, it was certain that they were well in our favour before we reached the end of the column.[314]

That night Dunsterforce camped near the heaped ruins of the ancient capital built by Darius king of Persia. There are photographs of some of the men standing at the entrance of one of the massive, encrypted gates. Stanley described the dazzling scene:

> After the evening meal, I sat on a piece of broken column, filled my pipe and was soon lost in thought, picturing the old city in its days of power. Here there were scattered dozens of broken columns. I wondered if this was the site of the King's palace...What stories those old stones could tell, if only gifted with speech!...The stars peeped out...until the heavens were a mass of glistening pin pricks of silver. The cliff stood silhouetted in all its grandeur, unconquered by man.[315]

One bright morning, Captain Savige watched a tribe of nomadic families grazing their flocks in a valley. Their tents and poles were roped to the backs of their cattle, children and lambs were tied onto the backs of their sheep and a few chickens dangled around the neck of an old ewe. It struck Savige as a peaceful oasis until a screeching band of Kurdish tribesmen swooped down the hillside, shooting wildly in the air, and scattering the women and cattle. The Kurds drove the sheep up the valley and disappeared into a granite crevasse. After this raid, Captain Savige ensured that a few of his party remained with the nomadic graziers to ward off further trouble, at least until the Dunsterforce column passed.[316]

After 26 days of forced marching, Dunsterforce had covered almost 500 kilometres and had ascended 2,500 metres above sea level, through the jagged terrain of the Zagros Mountains where the snow still lay in piles across their path. Stanley wrote to Grace at the end of the trek;

> ...if one tightens a hole in the belt after each meal it appears as if one has really had a feed... Still I am happy all this is part of the game and will probably last for a couple of years...but what I miss most of all is a civilised cigarette.

Since leaving London, the men had been on the move for nearly four months, and since their departure from Baghdad, numerous officers and NCOs had succumbed to fatigue, dysentery, meningitis, cholera, malaria and typhus. Those who died were buried in shallow roadside graves marked by crosses made of twigs. The men were worn out by the marching and keeping watch, hauling animals and dismantling campsites. Hamedan was close, and they pressed on through the night until sunrise, knowing that the next day they would meet their commander for the first time.

o o o

Chapter Sixteen
An Alliance of Phantoms

The race is not to the swift, nor the battle to the strong...
But time and chance happeneth to them all.

Eccliasiastes ix, 11

On a barren hillside overlooking Hamedan, Captain Savige waited under a shady tree inside the walls of a mud brick compound. A tall, silver-haired figure arrived at the gatehouse and the whole party immediately stood to attention. Major General Dunsterville addressed the officers:

Well men I suppose you want to know why you are here; to begin with, I might as well tell you the truth, and that is the good Shah has just informed me that I must leave Persia with my force immediately. This I do not propose to do and I have notified his Majesty accordingly...I admit that there are less than a hundred of us here even now, but we have an old Russian armoured car, together with a driver, a few machine guns, one or two Ford cars and each of you have a rifle with a few hundred rounds of ammunition. On the other hand there is such a thing as the Persian army. Still we are of the right stuff, even though we hail from the four corners of the earth.[317]

On first impressions, Captain Savige thought the general was a man of rare quality and felt more confident about the success of the mission. Lionel Charles Dunsterville was a shrewd, talented and lordly gentleman. Like his father and grandfather before him, who were both generals during the British Raj, he was a decorated officer. As a boy, he attended the United Services College where he became firm friends with Rudyard Kipling, who believed that Dunsterville was 'destined for glory in the service of the Empire'.[318] Later Kipling used Dunsterville as the model for his character Stalky in his novel, *Stalky & Co*, and the nickname stuck.[319] It became a bestselling adventure story for boys, and Captain Savige found it amusing that the Stalky he had read about in children's books was now his commanding officer, in charge of this prestigious mission.

General Dunsterville served in China from 1884 and with the 1st Infantry Brigade in Peshawar on the Northwest Frontier of India, until the final stages of the Great War. He was fluent in German, Russian, French and Persian, and proficient in several Indian dialects. His diaries, personal papers and the official record of his experiences in Persia are an excellent insight into his remarkable character and career.

Dunsterville was still in love with his wife, Daisie, after 25 years of marriage. With their three children, the family lived a busy life with a constant stream of military functions, house parties and community events.[320] Each summer Dunsterville was menaced by prickly heat and boils; his backside had to be lanced on a seasonal basis with a sharp implement, then doused with carbolic acid. Aside from his brigade duties he was often away on staff tours and army conferences at which he lectured. He loathed the 'artificiality and humbug' of military life but he couldn't extricate himself from it entirely because his cousin was married to the Viceroy of India and the social pressure to play his part in the merry-go-round never let up. Boils and military humbug were the bane of his existence.

Around his thirty-third anniversary of military service, Dunsterville wrote about his malaise: 'things were distinctly dull and one was beginning to feel that one had drifted into a backwater'. He bemoaned his paltry army salary as well as his mounting debts and, towards the end of 1917, he considered a position as aide-de-Camp to the King or retirement. On Christmas Eve, as he celebrated with Daisie and his colleagues at army HQ in Delhi, he received a letter. It was the 'welcome orders' for a new posting 'to do special work with the Russians in the East'. Daisie was aghast, but Dunsterville was thrilled. At age 53, General Dunsterville clutched the 'longed for opportunity of plunging once more into the tide'.[321]

As General Dunsterville prepared for his new command of the Persian Campaign in the East, General Birdwood opened another letter in his headquarters at Broodseinde on the Western Front. Within a few days, Dunsterforce was in the making. Its sole purpose was to shore up His Majesty's Brittanic supremacy in India by thwarting the German-backed, pan-Islamic powerbase in the Near East.

General Dunsterville's orders were to resurrect the battlelines across the Persian frontiers, north and south, to block the onslaught of the Turkish and German armies on their march towards the Caspian coast. To complicate matters further, there was no safe or fast access into Persia, neither by land, air nor sea. Dunsterforce would have to cross into Persia via Baghdad along the Khorasan

Highway and the old Silk Route. From there, once Dunsterforce had got a foothold in the Trans-Caucasian capital Tiflis, they would reorganise the Russian, Caucuses and Armenian forces to defend the oil wells at the Caspian port of Baku.

It was the enormity and complexity of the challenge that appealed to General Dunsterville in the first place, and he set his mind to scheming. He didn't need foot soldiers or cannon fodder. He needed competent, resourceful officers who could survive this dangerous environment with the skills to raise and manage local forces. Despite how much he relished a good contest, the general was no daredevil or cavalier. His approach to the mission was methodical, tactical and instinctive. Every man would be stretched to their utmost capacity.

It was a teary farewell for Lionel and Daisy Dunsterville at Karachi, on 6 January 1918, when he left for the 'beastly rough' voyage across the Arabian Sea. He disembarked at the port of Basrah six days later; the same day that Captain Savige reported for duty at the Tower of London.[322] From Baghdad G.H.Q. the general had two weeks to prepare for the Dunsterforce mission. His men and matériel would start arriving in batches over the coming weeks and months.

While Dunsterville believed that his mission strategy was based on solid, realistic objectives, he was less convinced that the mission itself was achievable. For a start, it was too broad in scope and there were too many contingencies. He was alarmed about the insufficient armaments and supplies, and feared for the safety of his men who would have to make the journey from Baghdad to Hamedan on foot. He had made his concerns clear to the staff at G.H.Q..

Within a fortnight General Dunsterville was ready to leave Baghdad with an advance party of 55 Dunsterforce men, including four touring vans, 36 light armoured motorcars, medical stores, reserve rations, bedding to ward off the winter and a 'considerable weight of Persian silver and English gold'. Their destination was the Persian port of Anzeli on the Caspian coast.[323] From Anzeli, Dunsterforce would ship northwards to Baku and then cross-country to Tiflis where they would stop the Turks and the Germans in their tracks.

Sitting in the Ford motorvan, travelling over the Nineveh Plains, Dunsterville dwelled on the pitfalls ahead of them. There were the obvious physical hardships—the extreme climate, the challenging terrain and the problem of fresh food and fuel sources—all of which would take a toll on the men, their vehicles and their pack animals. However, the political conditions were no less precarious. There was the questionable neutrality of the Persians who resented the intrusion of British soldiers, and the hostility of the Bolsheviks, which arose from Britain's refusal to acknowledge their authority. Furthermore, the presence of the Persian rebel leader Mirza Kuchik Khan and his 5,000-strong Army of Islam were based in the jungles of Gilan province.[324] And that was not the end of his problems.

Three years of war, revolution and rebellion had rendered the Eastern theatres of the Great War unrecognisable. When Dunsterville arrived in Baghdad, the whole region—from the Mediterranean and Caspian to the Red and Arabian Seas—was in strife. While Britain had been funnelling its energy into ousting the Germans from the Western Front, Central Asia and the Middle East had gone into meltdown. Persia had been inundated with foreign forces fighting a European imperial war on their soil.

Three years earlier, in February 1915, the Persian Foreign Minister had protested at the increasing number of German and Turkish consular officials who had been arriving in the country without official permission. Their aim was to induce priests, imams, tribal chiefs, government officials and the general public to agitate the Persian Government to enter the war on the side of the Central Powers.

In May 1915, the Germans had organised the assassination of both the Russian Vice-Consul and the British Consul-General. By September, the situation in Isphahan had become so dangerous that the entire European colony was forced to leave under the protection of British armed guard.[325]

The Persian parliament, the Majlis, was in uproar over how to address these national emergencies. The British Consul in Teheran and the American ambassador both reported on the dire situation developing on Persia's north-eastern frontier cities of Dilman and Urmiah, where the Russians had been driving out the Turkish and Kurdish troops. Thousands of Assyrian Christians had fled the mountains and plains seeking refuge in mission compounds and consular houses in Urmiah. French, Swiss and American missionaries warned authorities of a pending Christian pogrom.[326] The Persian government was no longer able to protect its borders or its own citizens.

One of the most important railway lines in the region connected the Crimea with the Caspian, running between the Black Sea port of Odessa and Tiflis, the capital of the newly formed Republic of Trans-Caucasia. The last station was Baku.[327] With its oil wells oozing black gold, Baku had become the target of every contestant, old and new—Turkish, Russian, Bolshevik, Tartar, Azeri, Azerbaijani, British and German forces were gathering on the Turkish–Persian frontier. The War Cabinet wanted guaranteed access to the Caspian oil to fuel the new Royal Navy fleet, but it would have to beat down the competition.

At the end of 1917, the world reeled from the news of the Russian Revolution and the murder of the Russian imperial family. When Field Marshal Wilson, Chief of the British General Staff, considered the imminent collapse of the Tsar's Army on the Eastern Front, the blood drained from his extremities. The most frightening question was, who would fill the vacuum?

Late at night after dinner, General Dunsterville sat back from his maps and field reports in his headquarters at Hamedan. It seemed to him that a vast alliance of phantoms whirled around the oil wells of Baku. He understood better than most that the Dunsterforce mission was a desperate manoeuvre that was in real danger of being swallowed up in the maelstrom. Regardless, he was determined to take home the booty. And to do it, he had to 'push on with the job' of securing Persia's overland passes to India and the Caspian Sea.[328]

In February, his first attempt to get to Baku from the Caspian port of Anzali had to be aborted when he was threatened by the Military Revolutionary Committee of the East Persian Circle of the Caucasus Front.[329] The Bolshevik commander, Comrade Cheliapin, impressed upon Dunsterville that their situation was hopeless:

> The Committee stated that among all nations (it) mistrusted only Great Britain, as a symbol of Imperialism and the Tiflis people whom we proposed to help, as being anti-Bolshevik. At Enzeli they possessed the telegraph and telephone line, the wireless apparatus and the petrol supply. All shipping was in their hands, and a gunboat lay ready to open fire on any ship endeavouring to leave the port without their permission. They forbade any endeavour on our part to reach Baku. Baku...had already been informed of our arrival by wireless and had replied that the party was to be stopped at all costs. For Russia the war was over and they objected to a mission whose avowed intention was to prolong the war.[330]

Dunsterforce escaped from Anzali on 20 February, loaded with gold and silver bullion and ammunition to run the gauntlet of

Kuchik Kahn's Jangali rebels. Dunsterforce made it back to Qasvin, an inland Persian town, but the hostility was growing. In April, the Germans occupied the port of Odessa. Persian troops arrived at Baku to stabilise the city, but they were overwhelmed and street skirmishes broke out between the Bolsheviks, Tartars, Azeris, Kurds and Armenians, destroying parts of the city.[331] At the end of the month, Baghdad G.H.Q. informed Dunsterville that the Turkish army occupied Tabriz and two Turkish divisions had surrounded Urmiah.[332] Dunsterville was at odds with the War Office authorities in London because he believed that they failed to grasp the dire reality of the operation. His relations with Badgdad G.H.Q. grew tenser as the situation deteriorated. The general wrote in his diary:

> War Office wire absolutely forbidding me to go to the Caucasus at the present time, so the Germans will get the Baku oil, and the Krasnovodsk cotton, the Astrakhan wheat and the Caspian Sea. It is very hard and disappointing. I am to look after Persia only... troubles in Southern Persia make them anxious, then Kuchik Khan at Rasht, the Turks in Tabriz, the hopelessness of the civil war in Baku.[333]

On 2 May, General Dunsterville tried again to warn British Intelligence of the dangers:

> The War Office refuses to give me any more troops. I asked for a Division, then for a Brigade—and all they give me is 1 Cavalry Regiment and 1 Infantry Battalion to run the country against the Germans, Turks, Democrats and Brigands, from Tabriz, Teheran to Kermanshah, an equilateral triangle with the sides of 400 miles, or a bigger area than the British Isles.[334]

At the end of May, as Dunsterforce had mustered to full strength in Hamedan, Dunsterville realised that he had only two options to achieve mission success in Baku—the overland route or the sea route. His best bet was overland, sending Dunsterforce northwards to capture the railhead at Tabriz, then on to Tiflis. The other way was eastwards, back to the port of Anzali, then along the sea lane to Baku. In the front of his mind were the pitfalls—treacherous Bolsheviks, Persian jungle rebels, famine, civil insurrection in Baku, the siege of Urmiah, and the Turkish Army, which was marching to Tiflis. Either way, he dreaded the inevitable causalities and loss of life. Each moment's delay brought Dunsterforce's enemies closer to Baku. The crafty general decided to take both options.

On 1 June, Dunsterville left Brigadier Byron in command at Hamedan while he went to establish a second garrison at Qazvin, a cosmopolitan city of around 50,000 people, held by Colonel Bicherakov and his Cossack troops, who blocked the road to Teheran.[335] At that point, Baghdad G.H.Q. sent Dunsterville 1,000 men of the 4th Hampshires and 2nd Ghurkas, the No. 8 Battery of the Royal Field Artillery, four Martinsyde fighter planes, 50 Ford motor-vans, eight armoured vehicles, as well as pack animals for hauling supplies and heavy field guns. Dunsterville immediately organised the construction of a hangar and landing strips at Zanjan and Mianeh, their farthest northerly post.[336] Their left flank was guarded by patrols and their right flank was in the allied hands of Colonel Bicherakov. Together they would be able to deflect any potential Turkish advances from the north or west. With the overland option covered, the general made a stealthy bid east to Anzali, with the main force to initiate the sea route to Baku.

From Hamedan, Captain Savige had received his orders for the overland manoeuvre. He was second-in-command of an advance guard of 35 men which was divided in two—one of imperial soldiers, and the other of dominion soldiers lead by Major Starnes of the New Zealand Expeditionary Force. Starnes and Savige were ordered to secure the main Teheran–Tabriz inland road to create a safe passage to the coast. From Qazvin they took their train of mules, camels and stores and would rejoin Wagstaff's party in Zanjan, where the landing strips were under construction.

All along the Teheran–Tabriz Captain Savige came across evidence of deadly skirmishes; the upturned, burned-out shells of Russian army vehicles that had been attacked by Persian highlanders. They arrived at Qazvin on 3 June.[337] Three days later, they received news that Turkish forces were advancing southwards through the mountain passes, and they set off to engage them on the road. Captain Savige wrote that;

> We had to undertake the most venturesome task of any of the parties in pushing across the unknown and unmapped country between Zanjan and Bijar. Before leaving Qazvin we were assembled and any man who did not relish the trip was given the chance to remain behind and join the next party that was moving up. Even though the chances of the march ahead, through enemy controlled country was full of dangers, not one man demurred and once again we were all volunteers on a perilous undertaking.[338]

Between Qazvin and Zanjan, about 1,600 metres above sea level, lay a 180-kilometre stretch of hilly tracks twisting through arid countryside, with orchards and vineyards irrigated by subterranean springs.[339] Not long after Stanley's party swung off the Zanjan road, they were confronted by a Persian Army detachment, under escort by Russian officers, taking arms and ammunition from Tabriz to protect the Shah in Teheran. War was everybody's business.

Captain Savige and his party were heading into famine territory. In his field diary he mentioned his hunger pains for the first time. Following several cruel seasons of war and drought, the poor people of Zanjan were living on the brink of death. Captain Savige watched the local women and children walking into the fields each morning to feed on grass like a flock of sheep. Their eyes were sunken, their bodies emaciated and their bellies bloated. Women huddled around their campsite waiting for a morsel to eat; they eagerly took a load of uniforms to the stream for washing in exchange for food. The Persian muleteers and camel drivers refused to go any further into the mountains than Zanjan for fear of a tribal ambush; during the night they absconded.[340] The next stop was Bijar about 170 kilometres away in the untamed high country of North West Persia:

> The nature of the country became rougher, though the view one obtained from the ridges was beyond description. On gaining these heights one could obtain a view of twenty to twenty-five mile of country...forming mountains of most fantastic formation. Not a tree could be seen but on the lower foothills there was plentiful supply of grass, which appeared to be the background for thousands of wild flowers, growing in great profusion.[341]

Upon entering Bijar from the north, the Sidar (Kurdish leader) offered one of his walled residences and the adjoining stables to accommodate Dunsterforce and their animals. Without any sign of the Turkish troops, Major Starnes and Captain Savige waited at Bijar for further instructions from Hamedan. Around this time, at the height of summer and the local famine, Stanley managed to reach the post, writing to Grace from 'Somewhere', about the monotony of the work. At their lodging the men built a big oven and hope to bake bread and a make a few cakes… but do be a good little girl and send me a few cigarettes. In the meantime, General Dunsterville had bought some time at Anzali. As Colonel Bicherakov had delayed his withdrawal from the port, it gave the general an unexpected opportunity to cut a deal with the Cossacks before they left for good. Dunsterville noted that:

> Bicherakov makes rather large financial demands and the War Office asks if he is worth it. He certainly is. I do not consider his demands exorbitant, when you realise the task he is accomplishing and the fact that he alone can do it. We have no alternative.[342]

The two commanders agreed that Cossack officers and partisans would remain in Qazvin to hold back Kuchik Khan and the Jangali militia.

Dunsterville's tactic to secure the sea route to Baku was almost ready to seal when he began to suspect that Colonel Bicherakov might be wavering under the coercive pressure of the Bolsheviks. Bicherakov was running out of ammunition and patience and perhaps his heart was no longer in the game. The Tsar was being held captive by the Red Army, and he himself wore the uniform of an empire that was falling apart in the field. The Cossack wanted to go home to Tiflis; it was only a few days horseride away and he could take off with his troops at any moment. General Dunsterville realised that any deal struck with the Russians was tenuous at best.

Dunsterville wired Baghdad G.H.Q. about the unfolding turmoil. He was emphatic that Baku was, by that stage, a lost cause, and would probably fall to the Turks or the Germans within weeks, if not days. The authorities overruled the general's advice. Instead they wanted to support Bicherakov's advance to Baku and ordered another party of Dunsterforce men to Anzali, despite the dangers.[343] Dunsterville was incredulous. Even if they reached Anzali safely he would have to face the paranoid Bolshevik Comrade Cheliapin a second time, and that was unlikely to end well. Then, if Dunsterforce was to have the slightest chance of reaching the oil wells before the Turks, Germans and Bolsheviks, they would have to somehow commandeer a ship for the sea crossing to Baku. There was the small matter of fuel. Without it, Dunsterforce would be stranded on the docks.

General Dunsterville made it to Anzali on 27 June and spent the next two days stitching up another deal with Bicherakov and Comrade Cheliapin; neither of them were any match for the masterful negotiation skills of the British commander. For every 100 dollars worth of armoured vehicle handed over to the Bolsheviks, Dunsterforce would receive 300 dollars worth of petrol.[344] Dunsterville's hunch about the Cossack was right. When he announced his conversion to Bolshevism in the local newspapers the following day, 'stating his belief that only by means of the Sovietski Vlast (the power of councils) could Russia find redemption', the Bolshevik Committee offered Bicherakov the command of the Red Army of the Caucasus.[345]

For Bicherakov it was a pragmatic ploy for getting home to Tiflis; for Dunsterville it was a lever to be switched. Bicherakov set off with his new force of 10,000 Red Army soldiers to Tiflis, reinforced with British officers and armaments provided by General Dunsterville.[346] Outside the city, encamped along the railway line, was the Turkish Army of Islam with approximately 12,000 troops ready to take on all-comers.

By the end of June, General Dunsterville had shored up both his options. There were two Dunsterforce parties stationed in the mid-north of Persia; Starnes and Savige were settled in Bijar along with Wagstaff's party in Zanjan. The western Mesopotamian border was patrolled between Kermanshah and Senneh. Airfields were ready at Zanjan and Miyaneh. To the south, Brigadier Byron directed operations from Hamedan and the general's party was working from the fishery depot at Anzali. In effect, Dunsterforce blockaded a gigantic frontier stretching from Baghdad to the Caspian Sea.

Just when it seemed that the path was clear, the general received bad news. Many of his men were falling ill and dying of cholera, dysentery and 'sandfly fever'. The inadequate food and the relentless physical strain were taking their toll on his force. And in Bijar, disturbing rumours percolated down through the mountains about bloodshed somewhere in the north. Urmiah was under attack. General Dunsterville learned of the siege and sent an urgent message via aeroplane to the Assyrian Commander General Petros. Dunsterforce and the Assyrian Army would join forces at Sain Qaleh on 23 July and return together to relieve the citizens of Urmiah from the Turkish siege.

o o o

Chapter Seventeen
All the Best in a Fellow

*Where life is more terrible than death,
it is the truest valour to dare to live.*

Sir Thomas Browne

It was insufferably hot even before dawn illuminated the parched hills surrounding Sain Qaleh. Captain Savige had learned the night before what had happened to the Assyrians of Urmiah, who were hiding in the orchard. He woke early to prepare for the trip back to the besieged city only to see thousands upon thousands of men, women and children streaming from the hills into the wide, bone-dry valley. They sat all over the ground and in the nearby orchards, exhausted, dazed and injured. Captain Savige's heart melted like wax at the sight of them:

> In order to subdue their panic Agha Petros, Captain Reid and myself rode out some miles along the road over which they were coming. Terror and despair were deeply written on their faces. Agha Petros was greeted as their father, and we, being in British

uniform, as their deliverers. It was an extremely hard job to make headway through the crowds that constantly surrounded us.[347]

As the day wore on thousands more walked southwards over the mountain tracks, herding cattle and towing wagons full of chattels—chairs, rugs, pots, pans and tools. Captain Savige learned that the Turks and the Kurdish militia were pursuing the Assyrian refugee column, which was defended only by a flimsy rearguard of unarmed American missionaries—seven men and eleven women, led by the elderly Doctor Shedd. He and his wife had devoted their lives to the Assyrian community in Urmiah and had taken charge of the situation when Agha Petros left. Dr Shedd had pleaded with the Armenian and Russian troops to hold the garrison for four more days, but they evacuated as soon as the blockade at Suldaz was broken. Urmiah fell to the 5th Division of the Ottoman IV Army Corps on 31 July.

From their mission compound, the missionaries witnessed the city and its population overcome by mayhem and hysteria. Official accounts of this exodus from Urmiah and the surrounding Salmas Plains provided by the American, British and Spanish Legations in Persia, estimated that between 80,000 and 90,000 Christians fled the area between the end of July and early August 1918. Local Persian newspapers reported much higher numbers in the vicinity of 200,000.[348] Dr Shedd and the missionaries formed a rearguard for the refugee column to protect them against raids by Kurdish militia and usher them out of the city.[349] Even after they escaped and made their way further into the mountains, the Turkish and Kurdish soldiers continued to attack the refugees for several days and nights.

Dunsterforce officers were transfixed by the swarm of refugees. Captain Savige suggested a plan to Agha Petros to help them:

I would take out with me two officers, six sergeants, three Lewis machine guns and sufficient food for six days. He was to collect and hand over to me one hundred men under the command of one his chiefs, a man who was on the spot. On the assurance that he would have the men ready at dawn, we returned to our camp.[350]

Captain Savige took with him Captain Scott Olsen (55th Battalion, A.I.F.), Captain Nicol (Wellington Regiment, NZEF), Sergeants Murphy (28th Battalion, A.I.F.) and Brophy (75th Canadian Battalion), Casey (29th Canadian Battalion), Nimmo (Otago Regiment, NZEF), Place (1/9 Middlesex Regiment) and Cameron (Cameron Highlanders).[351] Before sunrise on 6 August the men geared up. They left with one Armenian officer, a handful of Assyrian mountaineers and an interpreter. The Assyrians soon dispersed into the crowds in search of their own wives and children. For mile after mile, as Captain Savige and his band of nine pressed against the tide of Assyrian refugees, they were greeted as if they were angels:

> The men would shout in tones of great joy, "the English, the English!" and fired their rifles in the air with loud hurrahs. The unfortunate women folk were so overcome at the sight of the first party of the British that they wept aloud. Striking their breasts they would call down upon us the blessings of God and rush across and kiss our hands and boots in very joy.[352]

On their way to the back of the refugee column, Captain Savige and his men saw many wounded, distraught families who were straggling behind:

> The havoc wrought by the raiders on the column was becoming more evident the further we travelled, as time and time again

one of us dismounted in order to bind up the wounds of some unfortunate woman...Another thing was most noticeable, and that was the destruction of property and crops in the towns along the route, caused by the Armenians and the Assyrians. We passed villages in which there was not a single living Persian, but lying in the streets were bodies of the murdered inhabitants... Two wrongs do not make a right.

Captain Savige arranged for some cavalry to move ahead of the refugee column to prevent any further trouble or violence against local Persian inhabitants and to escort the refugees from Bijar to southwards to Hamedan HQ. At four o'clock that afternoon they found Mrs Shedd and some of the Presbyterian missionaries lying down on the back of a bullock wagon. They had been on the move with the refugees for five days since escaping from Urmiah. Dr Shedd was six or so miles behind them, keeping watch over the refugees with 24 men from a post on a nearby hill; they had exchanged fire with a Kurdish band near the last village.

Captain Savige located Dr Shedd and directed them to the British camp site to help General Petros to take care of the sick and injured Assyrians.[353] The doctor estimated that a force of 500 Turkish soldiers and Kurdish irregulars were about eight to ten miles behind them. Captain Savige felt apprehensive; he remembered well the tenacity of the Turkish army at Gallipoli and could not be sure at what moment they might appear from between the hills.[354] The landscape became more jagged and broken as Captain Savige and his men rode on to engage the raiders.

At the edge of a village in a narrow valley the men spied some horses tethered to the ground. Captain Savige didn't like the look of it; they could easily be trapped or ambushed in that rocky amphitheatre. He grabbed a light field gun for the right flank and sent two men ahead to draw the enemy's fire. Shots rang out. The ricochet of machine gun fire gave the Turks an impression of a much larger force than the reality of three officers, six sergeants and a handful of Assyrian mountaineers. Kurdish mountaineers darted backwards and forwards along the hills above, returning their fire, before dispersing. Turkish soldiers ran from their huts and galloped away. The skirmish was over, but Captain Nicol stayed behind to look after their mules and rations, while Savige and the rest of the party retreated to a village six miles back along the road.

Night descended on the valley and they settled inside an abandoned farmhouse screened by a high mudbrick wall.[355] Their rest was broken at two o'clock in the morning by the tinkling sound of cattle bells; the muleteers had guided the whole mule train back to camp in the pitch dark along with their rations and blankets. At daybreak, as the billy boiled and the men scoffed down their breakfast, one of the sentries yelled out. Captain Savige rushed to the rooftop and snatched the field glasses; 150 horsemen had dismounted in the centre of a broad, grassy ditch. Believing they were the Kurdish tribesmen from the previous day's skirmish, he went back to the campfire in the courtyard. A few minutes later the sentry called out again.

This time Captain Savige recognised the uniforms; 200 Turkish soldiers were bearing down on their campsite from both sides. A quick glance up at the high road showed that the last of the refugees were still packing their wagons and hastening out of the village. The men jumped for their weapons and saddled up the horses. Captain Savige sent two sergeants and four Assyrians to load the mules and to mount a Lewis gun on the roof of the house. Captain Nicol took up position on the left flank with the second machine gun, while Captain Savige took the third gun with

Sergeant Brophy and an Assyrian soldier to the right flank above the village.³⁵⁶

They crept through a grove of trees and waited behind a brick wall until they had a clear line of sight. A few hundred metres away the Turkish battalion lit up their cigarettes in the shade and waited for their scout to return. Captain Savige squeezed a volley of fire on the Turks. They scattered in disarray. Sergeant Brophy put a second round into the enemy until the drum was empty. They lay writhing on the ground, others ran up into the hills. While this was happening, Sergeant Murphy struggled to get the mule train clear of the narrow village lanes. Captain Savige described the bedlam:

> Eventually the leading mules got out of the village, yet the gun continued firing in the streets further back. Our position was about seven hundred yards away and from there we say that things were anything but pleasant with the lads as they endeavoured to get the animals clear of the streets. We stood by in order to give them a hand, but devoted most of our energies in preventing the horsemen riding down from the hills on our flanks and thus cutting us off completely.³⁵⁷

Five hundred Kurdish horsemen and mounted Turkish soldiers swooped from the ridgeline into the village. Captain Savige and his men were trapped, outflanked and outgunned. There was nothing left to do but retreat. A furious gun fight ensued for the next eight hours. Sergeant Murphy let go of the mule train and raced out with the machine gun on his saddle to a nearby slope from where he shot down dozens of horsemen. Spooked by the gunfire, the mules scampered across the village square with all their ammunition boxes still strapped to their backs. Captain Nicol bolted into the square to catch the mules but Kurdish felled several of them. Captain Nichol was shot and dropped to the ground.[358]

For a few moments, Captain Savige and the other men watched Captain Nicol, waiting for him to get up or crawl out of harm's way or signal that he was okay but he never moved. They made three separate attempts that afternoon to retrieve Captain Nicol. When their munitions ran out and the boxes were nowhere to be found they had no choice but to leave him there. They were one man down, unable to reach the mule train safely, without food and water, and under constant fire from three flanks. There was no wireless device and therefore no possibility of backup. Savige sent a despatch rider back to Bijar at the gallop requesting urgent cavalry reinforcements.

At that point the only thing Captain Savige could do was to prepare for a battle of withdrawal. The men would hold the Turks at bay from the tail end of the refugee column by falling back on one position after another, until the cavalry backup arrived from Bijar. It was the only way out.

Captain Savige and his band of seven slung their rifles over their shoulders and geared up for a blazing retreat from the village. With horse reins in one hand, four magazines in the other and a Lewis gun lashed to the back of their saddles, the men dug their spurs into their horses' ribs and thundered through the village high street and down the road, their shirts billowing behind them in a pall of dust.[359] The Turks and the Kurds flew up the road at full force, hollering and firing at the last of the refugees.[360]

Nearing the end of the day, just as Captain Savige and his men were on the brink of collapse, there appeared a small unit of mounted British regulars up ahead, calling out cheery greetings, as though on their way to the pub after a day's work. The sergeant had intercepted the despatch rider's message and decided to help

Savige's party in lieu of the requested cavalry. The gunning started up again at the rear of the column. The jarring, deafening sound distressed the refugees even more, who dispersed over the valley in a fit of panic. Captain Savige wrote:

> At this stage we were just about at our last gasp, and separated one from the other, with not more than half a dozen rounds apiece, riding horses that stumbled along in a state of utter exhaustion. As to what had happened to the cavalry, we were at a loss to understand.[361]

Several miles out from the Dunsterforce base at Sain Qaleh, an Assyrian chieftain rode forward with 50 of his tribal mountaineers to bring Captain Savige's party into the camp where they were met with a rapturous welcome by the crowds. They collapsed off their horses, covered in dust, sunburnt and dehydrated.[362] They hadn't eaten since the day before and had had nothing to drink during the retreat. Yet, they were incapable of swallowing food or water because their throats had cleaved shut from parching and yelling and snorting dust all day. They fell asleep on the ground amid the grateful crowd of Assyrian cavaliers and refugees.

By then, those refugees who had survived the exodus from Urmiah were in a wretched state. After only a day's rest, Captain Savige decided to undertake a controlled evacuation of the Assyrian multitude from Sain Qaleh to Hamedan. The refugees would be taken in batches of 800 and 1,000 individuals at a time. General Petros instructed the people to keep moving through the gorges with their wagons and herds and not to stop or rest for any reason until they reached Hamedan.

The evacuation got underway immediately. The first day was a forced march in the insufferable summer heat. Captain Savige's main concern was keeping the people alive long enough to reach the base at Hamedan, where they could be properly treated for their injuries, illness, shock and exposure. He wrote that:

> It was our endeavour to get the people clear of this dangerous piece of country before the enemy or wild tribesmen had time to seize the heights. It would be an easy matter to ambush the column in this dark defile, which would prove a veritable death trap to thousands of unfortunate refugees.[363]

It was around this time that the Assyrians mourned the passing of Dr Shedd, who had been waylaid in the crowds and not seen for a few days. A search party returned with the news that the old doctor had succumbed to choleric fever the night before.[364] Captain Savige felt that much was owed to the great missionary 'who had inspired the Christians during their long weary months of siege warfare. It was he who conceived the idea to work hand in hand with the British forces operating in Northern Persia, in the hope that relief would come to the people whom he so dearly loved'.[365] On sunrise, a band of Kurds attacked the camp but were driven off by machine guns. Each time they raided and attacked the refugees, more lives were lost and their journey was delayed.

The cavalry escort rode at the front to guard the munitions and money, and Dunsterforce rode behind to protect the stragglers and drive the column forward. They had been walking without rest for nearly 15 hours or more. Captain Savige rode passed some young girls huddled together around the body of their father, clutching his clothes, crying and praying over him. They refused to leave their dead father's side for fear of jackals and vultures. After promising to bury him, Captain Savige cajoled the sisters into riding ahead on the mules. Mothers and children and wounded refugees begged the officers for water as they rode past but they could carry only a few of the worst cases on their horses. Near a stream the people bathed their swollen feet, watered their cattle and filled jars and pots with water to give to their children who were dying. Captain Savige described their anguish:

> So with heavy hearts and big lumps in our throats, we were forced to turn a deaf ear to the pleadings of these poor unfortunates, who called upon us to save them. To have drawn our revolvers and shot them would have been more humane, knowing full well how cruelly they would be treated by the foe behind.[366]

Many of the frailest refugees, young and old, succumbed to malaria, cholera and dysentery during the evacuation to Hamedan, and were either abandoned to the elements or buried by the side of the road. Captain Savige watched with concern as his men struggled with heat exhaustion, thirst and fatigue. They were sagging in their saddles, lagging behind on the trail. Eventually a few of his men became so weak that they were no longer able to sit upright on their horses or hold the reins. To prevent them from falling off Captain Savige was forced to lash the men to their horses with ropes and tow them along behind him. Major Moore, the cavalry leader, was struck down by malarial fever and that afternoon, Captain Savige got word that one of the Dunsterforce sergeants had fallen ill:

> Owing to the vagueness of the message and the doctor who would not go for having to look after Captain Kingscote, who was in a critical condition (being ill with pleurisy), I sent Capt. Kay & a Sgt. out to endeavour if possible to bring France in. He returned about 5pm with the body of Sgt. France who died about 2pm from cholera. We buried him that night. I myself

read the burial service from the Bible, a job I never want to do again.³⁶⁷

In only 10 days, Stanley's party had been reduced to half-strength. The men took a reprieve from marching during the heat of the day and rested their horses. At midnight they arrived in a village but their hopes of rest were dashed when they discovered that it had been destroyed by Assyrians at the head of the column; the inhabitants had been murdered, houses and crops razed to the ground. Dunsterforce secured the local Persian villages from the passing crowd of refugees. General Petros hanged the culprits from a tree as a warning to others who might seek vengeance as they passed through Persian towns and villages.³⁶⁸

They stopped near a village early in the evening purchase grain and fodder from outlying villages to cater for the refugees who had amassed around the town. A messenger arrived with news of 400 Kurdish horsemen foraging for food in the vicinity of the town. Agha Petros arranged 50 of his troops in pairs to raise dust along the roadway giving the impression of a much larger force. Dunsterforce lit a chain of grass fires on the hillcrest along which the refugees progressed, singing and clattering their pots and pans, like medieval troubadours, to scare off the raiders.³⁶⁹

Hunted, footsore, injured, wracked by fever, clean of teeth and hollow of eye; this is how the Assyrians ate the bread of suffering, night and day, on their flight through the wilderness during that fateful summer of 1918. Those who could continue the march to safety departed the following morning, while the sick, injured and incapacitated were looked after in the field. Around 8 August, the refugee convoy made it through the Zagros Mountain gorges into the open country, after which there were no further raids by

Kurdish mountaineers. The British Intelligence Office reported on the numbers and movements of Christian refugees and deportees throughout the Ottoman provinces, the Caucasus, Northern Syria, Mesopotamia and Persia in 1918:

> Since the Turkish advance in Turkish Armenia and North-West Persia this summer, such part of the local Armenian and Nestorian (Assyrian) population as could not escape towards the Caucasus fled south-eastwards...in the direction of Hamedan... Sir Percy Cox estimated the number that had arrived at this place at about 60,000. They began to arrive in August and His Majesty's vice-consul at Hamedan proposed that relief should be organised jointly by the British and American Governments.[370]

Captain Savige drew up at the triage camp established at Takkan Teppeh at two o'clock one morning; he and his men had not eaten for more than 24 hours. The camp and the people were in a squalid condition, weakened by malnutrition, midsummer heat and flies. Without sanitation, infectious diseases erupted among the refugees and the soldiers. Those people too indisposed would be carried on stretchers between horses and camels to field hospitals in Bijar and Hamedan. Captain Savige worked furiously to get the refugee camp ready for their arrival, buying corn and flour in local markets, procuring mules and equipment from local farmers, and sending for doctors and any available medical staff.

Stragglers dragged themselves haphazardly into the refugee camp during the ensuing days; invariably Savige found them starving and often without a stitch of clothing. One morning, as Captain Savige organised the camp stoves and provisions, he noticed two young Assyrian girls approaching the canteen for something to eat. They stood at the door in silence, completely naked. Both girls had bullet wounds in their backs and shoulders and were in a great deal of pain. They had been shot by Kurds during a night raid and their wounds had become infested with maggots. Captain Savige searched around for something to cover the girls, wrapping them in long, cotton army tunics. Next, he attended their injuries, tearing up his shirt tails to bandage them.[371]

After getting the majority of the refugees to safety in Takkan Teppeh it was time for Savige and his remaining men to make the dangerous trek back to Bijar, three days ride away. By evening on the first day, Captain Savige was struck down with a high fever. He was unable to muster the energy to lead the party into the strenuous rearguard position. General Petros took over the rearguard instead, while Dunsterforce moved to the front, checking the main body of the refugee convoy and securing their coin and ammunition boxes.[372]

For three days and nights they pressed forward through the highlands. Along the way they saw dozens of naked corpses lying with their heads and faces near streams and springs as though poisoned by the water; they had been butchered and pillaged by brigands while they stopped to drink. On the horizon lay Bijar, but the strain had taken its toll. Captain Savige noted in his diary:

> Within twenty-four hours of arrival every man but one collapsed. The doctors had arrived from Hamedan and were hard at work in the two hospitals established for the refugees...The month's continuous toil, every day of which was spent in the saddle very often sixteen to eighteen hours at a stretch, lack of food, drinking water polluted with the bodies of those who had died, together with hard fighting, had proved too much for the human frame. The last two days on the road, I, for one, have

little recollection of, beyond the fact that I hung to the saddle and endeavoured to direct the work of the advance guard.[373]

Captain Savige was admitted to hospital in Bijar. A number of his men passed away in the ward over the coming days. The soldiers were laid to rest in a tiny cemetery nearby. Savige spent a week recuperating from the torments of their hellish flight through the mountains. He visited the sick and wounded Assyrian children who survived their ordeal, including the two injured girls whose gunshot wounds he had treated at the canteen. As soon as they recognised him they rushed to greet him from the front gates of the hospital grounds.[374] Despite his fragile state, Savige started managing the day-to-day operations of the Bijar camp and feeding the refugees, who were gradually discharged from the field hospitals and camps and then escorted to Hamedan.

On 26 August, Captain Savige fell ill with fever again, but this time it was more serious. His heart was afflicted by a virus and he had developed beri-beri, an extremely painful condition resulting from prolonged dietary deficiency, which caused his ankles and knees to bloat to almost three times their normal size. He was relocated to the army hospital at Hamedan, having no choice but to make an agonising 12-hour road trip in suffocating heat, whilst running a fever at 102 degrees. He was delirious upon arrival and spent the next eight nights under observation, hovering in fevered half-consciousness. During the night he heard other men calling out in agony, and in the morning he watched others being taken away for burial.

Once he was lucid again, Captain Savige heard that there was a library in a local missionary's house a short distance away, so he decided to walk there as a welcome distraction from the morbid ambience of the hospital ward:

Sitting in an easy chair, smoking real cigarettes and reading an interesting book, interrupted only by the arrival of morning and afternoon tea, helped more than one sufferer along the road to recovery.[375]

It was at Hamdedan Hospital that Stanley realised just how close a shave with death he had had in the last phase of the exodus. He wrote to little cousin Grace;

I have not been able to write for some time, as I have been out on the roads. We were sent out on a special mission, of those which did not come off. We were let in for one of those awful things. A nation in flight. I cannot go into the details of that awful time. Imagine 60-80,000 people with all their earthly belongings on the road harassed by Turks and Kurds. Women and children being slaughtered, others dying from starvation and exhaustion.

I went out with a small party to try to prevent this murdering and to a large extent was successful, but it meant some hard and dangerous fighting.

On arrival here I was laid up, as three days out I caught a fever and for 12 days had a very thing time of it. I am better now though dreadfully weak and thin though in a few days hope to be my old self again.

As Captain Savige recuperated at Hamedan, the Turkish Army attacked Bijar. The next morning a British colonel made frantic rounds of the hospital wards to recruit officers as they lay in their beds. He asked Savige to take charge of some of the operations in Bijar, but he was still in bad shape. His feet and ankles were still so swollen that he was unable to put on his boots, let alone mount a horse. Painful as it was, Captain Savige admitted to himself that he was of 'no use for any further service in Persia'.[376]

Lying unattended in the hospital bed at Hamedan, Captain Savige's condition deteriorated rapidly; his heart could no longer withstand the high altitudes and the prognosis was not bright. Perhaps Stanley tried to ignore the fact that he had taken his fair share of mustard gas in the Somme trenches. On 14 September, he was evacuated to Baghdad Military Hospital in an agitated state:

> Left Hamedan about seven o'clock that morning and continued running a fever…until nightfall, by which time I was again running a high temperature. Being in the open wilds, I was forced to look after myself, but fortunately, not feeling inclined to eat, was not compelled to light a fire…That night the wind blew at hurricane rate, and being camped at the entrance of a pass, we got the full force of the elements.[377]

It may have seemed to Captain Savige that night that the Zagros Mountains were making one final attempt to lay hold of his life before he got away, as though infuriated that he should march through hills and valleys unharmed by battle or pestilence, rescue a sea of souls, and then slip away. By morning the storm had relented, but the interminable road trip to Baghdad lay ahead; he was delirious for most of it.

When the fever broke and he was able to sit up, Captain Stanley Savige watched in disbelief from the army motorcar at the pitiful trail of Assyrian refugees straggling over the Persia frontier across the Nineveh Plains of Mesopotamia. He must have wondered what would become of them, scapegoats of an endless war within a greater war that was not of their making.

Savige was admitted to the British Military Hospital in Baghdad on 28 September 1918, more dead than alive. It wasn't until the end of October that he was able to write to Grace from Basra;

> 'I am so sorry to have kept you so long without a letter, but you will forgive me when you know that for the last 10 weeks I have been too ill to write a line to a soul.
>
> I wrote you after my first attack of fever, well I had another so I then got Beri Beri, a swelling in the ankle and knees. This put the wind up the Dr because not many recover. Then my heart went thud and I was pushed off to Hamedan. I shall never forget the awful trip of over 100 miles over rough a road as one could wish for with a temperature of 103 degrees.
>
> I was just about snuffing it when we reached Hamedan. I was not allowed to move off my back for about 14 days and then was pushed further down when I again had another fever... I have drunk enough quinine to float a ship and worse, they injected quinine into the port and starboard sides of my stern...
>
> Really Grace I thought many a time I must hand my check in, but I forced myself when just about out to fight against the awful feeling of snuffing out... A very happy Christmas and a bright Happy New Year.'

The Anzac had given almost four years of distinguished service in the deadliest battles and most notorious campaigns of the Great War. The Dunsterforce mission had been a perilous venture indeed. Of those 350 officers and NCOs who gathered at the Tower of London in January 1918, only four were ever fit enough for active service in the armed forces again.[378] As he lay in his hospital bed, Stanley must have asked himself what life had in store for him when he returned home to his family and fiancé in Australia.

Part Three
HOMELAND

Chapter Eighteen
Conspicuous Gallantry

The Dunsterforce Mission almost cost Captain Stanley Savige his life; it took months for him to recuperate from the malnutrition, fatigue and malarial infection. While still laid up at the military hospital in Baghdad, he was officially 'struck off the strength of the Mesopotamian Expeditionary Force' at the end of October. By then the Central Powers had capitulated on the Western Front, the Entente forces had captured half of Germany's field artillery and a quarter of its soldiers as prisoners. The threat of mutiny rippled through the German High Seas Fleet. Stanley wrote a letter to his beloved Lillian on 10 November 1918: 'I can hardly realise that the war is practically over and home is in sight. What changes I will see in all of you and what you see in me will probably be surprising. Four years make a difference in one's life.'[379]

The very next day the Armistice was declared. Special envoys of the German High Command met with the Supreme Allied War Council in a wooden railway carriage in the Forest of Compiègne, Northern France to negotiate the terms of the peace treaty.[380] Ninety kilometres to the north of the forest, Stanley's other beloved, the

24th Battalion, lay in fragments at Montbrehain, the village where Australians fought their last battle of the Great War on 5 October 1918. It was a harsh fight, and a symbolic one for the AIF.

Although severely depleted by the end of 1918, the 24th Battalion was instrumental in breaching the Hindenburg line in September, and again at Mont St Quentin on 3 October. The 6th Brigade attempted to undermine the remaining sections of the German defence system at Montbrehain. There are many stories from their last battle, but three in particular show why Captain Savige loved his 24th battalion comrades so well.

Captain John Mahony and Captain John Fletcher were best mates who joined up together in Melbourne; their regimental numbers were 1056 and 1057. They trained, sailed and served alongside Captain Savige from Gallipoli onwards. The captains were renowned for their gallantry, sporting prowess and coolness under fire; Mahony never went into the front lines without his wooden walking stick.[381] They were both fatally wounded and died within an hour of each other on the last day of battle. Captain Ingram, who took dozens of German prisoners that day, won the last Victoria Cross of the Great War. Montbrehain cost the 6th Brigade 430 causalities, most of whom were laid to rest at Calvaire Cemetery on the outskirts of the village. When the family received notice of his death, Captain Mahony's aunt wrote to the general in command:

> We are all broken hearted, especially his mother, to think that on the eve of Peace, he was Called Away. But as it was God's Holy Will, and he was such a good true boy, it is pleasing to remember him as never doing an injustice to anyone.[382]

The day after their final battle, the Roll of the Fallen records a total of 3420 casualties from the 24th Battalion between May 1915 and October 1918. The men of the 24th departed the Western Front on 6 October 1918. It was an enormous honour that upon ceasefire, General John Monash chose the 24th Battalion's band to lead the allied celebrations at Amiens. The city erupted in jubilation as the band played the Marsellaise around the battered streets and lanes until they were 'aroused to new life'.[383] The Australians were showered from the balconies with bouquets, and the champagne flowed for days on end.

When peace finally arrived the old imperial regime of Europe fell in a heap.[384] The Hohenzollern dynasty disintegrated following the abdication of the King of Austria–Hungary, and the Supreme War Lord of the Hapsburg line, Kaiser Wilhelm, was exiled to the Netherlands.[385] The Ottoman Sultan became a virtual captive of the Allied authorities in Constantinople. Twenty-nine countries and 60 million people were ensnared in the Great War; at its close there were an estimated 30 million people missing, maimed or slain, and an imponderable mass of bereaved.

The British public were outraged by the human cost and financial mismanagement of the Eastern campaigns. The Mesopotamian Campaign alone claimed 31,000 British Commonwealth officers and men.[386] Following the official enquiry, Churchill declared in the House of Commons that the Eastern theatres had cost Britain 350 million pounds sterling and 100,000 casualties, all for an indeterminate outcome.[387] The bells of peace pealed around the world but behind closed doors there rose a long, quiet lamentation.

Soon after the Armistice, Captain Savige was 'invalided' on a hospital ship to Bombay, India where he required further treatment and extended rest in a soldiers' hospice. Except for a single clue, there is virtually no trace of Captain Savige's movements between his arrival at the army hospital in Baghdad and his repatriation to the British

Army hospital in Bombay. We know only that he embarked on 27 January 1919 for the long voyage back to Australia via Egypt.[388] This clue is alluded to in Captain Savige's own memoir of the secret expedition to Persia, entitled *Stalky's Forlorn Hope*, which he wrote in 1921.

In his account Captain Savige described what happened to the other members of Dunsterforce after they all separated into special units and left Kasvin with the pioneer party and the subsequent rescue of the Assyrians at Sain Qaleh and their exodus to Baqubah. He also states that General Dunsterville was his key informant and that it was Dunsterville who had recounted the missing pieces of the whole episode to him in person at Agra, in December 1918. Dunsterville's diary entry for the month of December 1918 corroborates Stanley's account; Dunsterville had indeed visited his officers at the soldiers' hospice in Agra.[389]

On 9 October 1918, Dunsterville departed from Basra, Mesopotamia for Bombay, where he awaited further orders from British military authoritics in London. In his personal diary, Dunsterville tells how he had fallen out of favour both with senior officers at Baghdad G.H.Q. and the British War Office in London because of his strident criticism of the British War Cabinet strategy in the Caucasus and throughout the Persian Campaign. General Dunsterville was convinced that he would have to face a British court martial for the failure of the Dunsterforce mission, and that his military career was finished, but his fears were allayed when he received official orders on the eve of the Armistice. He was appointed as a brigade commander in Peshawar, India.

Upon return to India, he travelled to various towns for official military and civic functions and speaking engagements, including two visits to Agra in early and mid-December 1918.[390] It would seem that Dunsterville took the opportunity to visit a few of his Dunsterforce officers who were recuperating at the hospice. In the closing stages of the mission, Dunsterville had lost all contact with many of his men from July 1918 onwards. One of the officers he visited was Captain Savige. They were able to share their firsthand accounts with each other regarding what had befallen the various Dunsterforce parties after they had dispersed in the field in July.

As Captain Savige battled his way through the alpine ranges of North West Persia for the rendezvous with the Assyrians, the situation in Baku imploded. Dunsterforce had failed to lure Turkish troops away from the Caspian city due to the unexpected exodus of the Assyrian refugees from Urmiah. General Dunsterville believed that the British had done too little too late to save the oil wells for the purposes of His Majesty's Navy.[391] At the end of July, as the city was encircled by the Ottoman 6th and 9th Divisions under the command of Halil Pasha, there was a coup d'état, during which the governing Bolshevik Council of People's Commissars was overthrown by the pro-British Central Caspian Dictatorship.[392] A month later, Lenin and the Kaiser forged a treaty that gave Germany full command of all Red Navy vessels and facilities on the Caspian Sea.[393]

As soon as the Bolsheviks were ousted from power they evacuated the city along with the majority of the Red Army. They seized 13 ships from the docks onto which they loaded the entire arsenal and headed for Astrakhan. The new Central Caspian Dictatorship launched several gunboats in pursuit of the Red Army fugitives; the ships and matériel were retrieved and kept at anchor in the harbour. The first decree of the new Central Caspian committee was to officially invite General Dunsterville to protect their assets and the citizens of Baku.[394] He believed there was still a slim chance of securing the city and therefore requested infantry reinforcements from Baghdad. The War Office momentarily considered the idea of destroying 2,000 oil wells before they fell into enemy hands. Dunsterville regarded it as madness and the Russians would have regarded it as treachery:

> Each [was] about 500 feet deep and protected by ferro-concrete and asbestos coverings...how many tons of high explosive would have been required to blow them up is a question I do not enter into. The inhabitants of Baku may not have had much stomach to fight against the Turks but one can hardly imagine that they would have looked on with their hands in their pockets, whilst a few British troops went about blowing their means of livelihood sky-high.[395]

At the flashpoint of Captain Savige's rescue mission of the Assyrian refugees on 5 August, General Dunsterville was arresting the leaders of the Russian Revolutionary Committee and dispatching them to G.H.Q. in Baghdad. On 17 August, the 6,000-strong Russo–Armenian force attacked the Turkish Army.[396] At the same time, the requested infantry and naval reinforcements, under the command of Commodore Norris, also began arriving at the docks. Dunsterville and Norris decided to make their move to fortify the city against the oncoming Ottoman Army. Two days later, Dunsterville inspected the battlements:

> Today I visited the whole front line, about 10 miles long, South on Sea to North where right flank is open, enabling Turks to get round and make trouble in our rear in East of peninsula... My car ran along the front for a while within 3000 yards of the Turkish guns, quite in the open, and they never fired a round at us, so I suppose they are pretty short of ammunition.[397]

The Turks commenced a progressive schedule of heavy shelling over the ensuing three weeks which destroyed parts of the port infrastructure, town centre, roads, hotels and public buildings. During the bombardment, Russian steamers busily evacuated scores of thousands of Armenian refugees and civilians from the dockyards to Krasnovodsk, on the other side of the Caspian sea.[398]

On 27 August, Turkish shells blasted holes in the hotel walls where Dunsterforce officers stayed, narrowly missing their general. Dunsterville came to the view that 'the further defence of Baku is a waste of time and life', but he was not quite prepared to leave it unshielded.[399]

The telegraphs for which Dunsterville surmised could be used later as evidence in a court martial, were sent intermittently from this point onwards, declaring his resolute refusal to follow War Office orders to undertake a full and immediate withdrawal from the city. The next day he posted his personal diary back to Hamedan for safekeeping. He wrote:

> London and Baghdad keep on telling me to leave Baku at once and I finally and firmly refuse—so how it will all end I do not know. I have sent the strongest telegrams that have ever been sent, but they contain nothing but what is true and right and what can be substantiated. Both Baghdad and London have been criminal in their outlook on the strategy, and even now they do not seem to realize that the capture of Baku by the Turks is a far bigger thing for them than the capture of Baghdad by us, was for us.[400]

On 1 September, with Baku in total tumult, General Dunsterville summoned the five Central Caspian Dictators, their flotilla and army, and the Armenian National Council to a conference at the Hotel d'Europe. In view of the immanent Turkish invasion, he implored them to arrange a truce with the Ottomans before all hell broke loose. He berated them in unrestrained terms:[401]

> Why study the map and discuss the value of positions when you know from experience that your troops, when ordered to attack, invariably retire? That being the case, why needlessly prolong the agony and risk the lives of all your non-combatants? I will no longer throw away in vain the lives of my brave soldiers. I am about to withdraw my troops entirely and leave Baku to its fate.[402]

Later that evening the Central Caspian Dictators responded to his advice with an ultimatum: 'any attempt at withdrawal on your part will be regarded as treachery and treated as such'. Dunsterville's response was plain; Dunsterforce left the port of Baku under full steam. As all the British sailors, airmen, soldiers and Dunsterforce officers boarded the Kruger, their aeroplanes were set alight at the airfield and their motor vehicles were blown up at the docks.[403] The crew dodged shells from the gunboat that guarded the mouth of the harbour, churning over the dark waters of the Caspian Sea.

On 14 September, the same night that Captain Savige endured the alpine storm outside of Hamedan, the Central Caspian Dictatorship surrendered the city of Baku to the Ottoman Army. The War Cabinet dismissed General Dunsterville from his command for the disastrous failure of the mission. He and his men were summoned to Baghdad G.H.Q. for decommissioning. Dunsterville received a telegram from the commanders in chief, which he fully expected to be the notice for a court martial, but in fact he was awarded the Companion of the Star of India.[404] Soon afterwards, he was reunited with his wife, Daisie, in India. On the day of his departure from Baghdad, General Dunsterville farewelled his force with these words:

> It is with great regret that I sever my connection with the gallant members of the force I have commanded under very peculiar circumstances for the past nine months...I am prouder of my command of the gallant officers and non-commissioned officers of Dunsterforce than of any other command I have ever held, or am likely to hold. Brought together from every corner of the Empire, all have vied with one another to show the absolute unity of our national aspirations, and our determination to win in this great war as the representative of freedom against the powers of autocracy and militarism.[405]

During his journey homewards, Captain Stanley Savige learned that he had been recommended for the Distinguished Service Order for his part with Dunsterforce. The citation reads:

> For conspicuous gallantry and devotion to duty during the retirement of refugees from Sain Qaleh to Tikkan Tappah between the 26th and 28th July 1918 also at Chalkaman on 5th and 6th August, 1918. In command of a small party sent to protect the rear of the column of refugees, he by his energy, resource and able dispositions the hostile troops, many of whom were mounted were kept at a distance although in greatly superior force. He hung onto position after position until nearly surrounded, and on each occasion extricated his command most skilfully. His cool determination and fine example under fire inspired his men, and put heart into the panic of the stricken refugees.[406]

The Australian war correspondent C.W. Bean remarked on the heroic performance of Captain Savige and the men of Dunsterforce in his official history of the First World War:

> The stand made by Savige and his eight companions that evening and during half of the next day against hundreds of the enemy thirsting like wolves to get at the defenceless throng was as fine as any episode known to the present writer in the history of this war.[407]

◦ ◦ ◦

Chapter Nineteen
Defeat is an Orphan

Oh that I had wings like a dove! For then would I fly away, and be at rest, Lo, then would I wander far off and remain in the wilderness.

Psalm 55[408]

That wretched summer of 1918 ended with a legion of Assyrian refugees stumbling into Hamedan with their children, flocks and worldly possessions in tow, but their plight had only just begun.[409] During the 25-day exodus from Urmiah thousands perished in the highlands from disease, exposure and starvation, while others were murdered or taken captive by Turkish troops and Kurdish raiders. Some may have turned back; others were simply never seen again.[410] To this day, there is no account for around 7,000 individuals of the estimated 80,000 to 90,000 refugees who escaped the siege.

British Government and military agencies were ill-equipped to respond to the humanitarian disaster, especially in a region where the Persian authorities struggled to support the local population due to the ravages of famine and war.[411] The British War Office resolved to transfer the Assyrian refugees en masse from the makeshift emergency camp in Hamedan across the western border of Persia to Mesopotamia. In September, the Persian Government granted permission to the British Army to commence the transfer operation of its citizens. Fit and healthy men were formed into four mountaineer battalions under British command to shepherd the families to the border, and defend them against Turkish troops and raiders along the way.

The British War Cabinet documents from the Turkish Foreign Office, dated October 1918, outlined British responsibilities for relief work with Christians in the former Ottoman territories:

> If we take control of Turkey militarily as a result of an armistice, that is, control of communications and of public security, we shall find ourselves morally bound to take measures of relief work, especially among the non-Turkish nationalities…Among these the Armenians will have a special claim. They have been the worst treated by the Turks during the war and His Majesty's Government have committed themselves in a special degree to putting an end to their sufferings.[412]

It took the Assyrian refugees three and a half weeks to make the 600-kilometre journey on foot from Hamedan across the rocky steppes of the Nineveh Plains to Baqubah, where the British Army had established a refugee camp on the upper reaches of the Tigris River.[413] Captain Savige, deathly ill as he was then, observed the endless trail of refugees from the motorcar on his way to the Baghdad Military Hospital.

By the time the armistice was declared in November 1918, 48,927 Assyrians and a contingent of Armenians had arrived at the British Army refugee camp at Baqubah, 48 kilometres north-east of Baghdad on the banks of the Diala River. Three thousand tents housed the refugees, who represented three basic categories of origin—Armenians from Lake Van (Turkish subjects), Assyrians from the Hakkari mountains (Turkish subjects) and Armenians and Assyrians from the Urmiah and the Salmas Plains (Persian subjects).[414] Official camp records show that between Urmiah and Baqubah, approximately 30,000 Assyrian men, women and children were lost without trace, dead or missing.[415]

Baqubah was under the command of British Brigadier Austin and Colonel Cunliffe Owen. As a result of their adept administration, the British military administrators were able to reduce the mortality rate of the refugees from 60 people per day to three per thousand within the first nine months.[416] Life in the Baqubah refugee settlement was hellish. The physical and psychological afflictions suffered by the people were exacerbated by the humid climate to which they were totally unaccustomed.[417] It was another season of lamentation for the Assyrians, as it was during the time of Tamurlane, the Ascension Day massacres and Seyfo, the Year of the Sword.[418]

Despite their various origins and religious traditions, the Assyrians were united in their determination to return home. The Hakkari mountain tribes were especially zealous about reclaiming their ancestral homeland and property from the Kurds.[419] They could not understand why they had to remain at Baqubah when the armistice had been declared and the Turkish Army had been vanquished. In a British Intelligence Eastern Report of 26 December 1918 to the War Cabinet, Major General Sir Percy Cox, who was to become the high commissioner in Iraq two years later, ventured to remind His Majesty's Government that:

> They (the Assyrians) had special claims to our sympathy and support, as their misfortunes were in part due to our having

been obliged to leave them in the lurch after our Caucasian mission (Dunsterforce) had encouraged them to arm themselves to resist the Turks pending our arrival.'[420]

A few days after Cox's remarks were filed, the Paris Peace Conference commenced in January 1919.[421] At the conference American President Wilson presented his 'Fourteen Points' scheme to the representatives of the Great Powers, which included his concept for a League of Nations and his demand that all national minorities in the former Ottoman territories should be granted guaranteed 'security of life' and an 'absolutely unmolested' opportunity for 'autonomous development'.[422]

The Baqubah refugee settlement hummed with speculation and passionate debate about the possibilities of freedom and independence. The community began to formulate their own political ambitions ranging from religious nationhood to sovereign self-determination. Many harboured the dream of a triumphant return to Bethnahrin, where they would establish an independent Assyrian kingdom and take their place among the nations. The Assyrians started to agitate the British civil authorities for permission to send their own representative to the Paris Peace Conference. Their new Patriarch, Mar Paulos Shimmun would not let the opportunity pass. He advocated his people's cause to the British Civil Commissioner in Baghdad in the following terms:

> As head of the Assyrian Millet...I am disappointed at the decision...if that Government could see its way to reconsider that decision in the light of the fact that Armenians, Kurds and Arabs have been allowed someone to plead their cause, it would be a great joy to us all...we accept your decision loyally but we make two requests to you:

...will you write me a letter such as I can show to my people, saying that I did make a request;

...will you allow me to send a telegram to the Archbishop of Canterbury, asking him to secure that these wishes of our nation be put before the Conference in Paris?

That in any arrangement made, we Assyrians may not be confounded with the Armenians;

That all Assyrians may remain permanently under British protection in their own country;

We should ask also that the position of the Mar Shimmun as head of the Millet may be recognised by the Government.[423]

The reply came in July. The Mar Paulos Shimmun was permitted to elect one person to represent their case to British authorities in London, whereafter their attendance at the Paris conference would be considered by the British Government. Lady Surma Khanum was chosen unanimously by the community. She was the influential, eldest sister of the previous patriarch, Mar Binyamin Shimmun.[424] Brigadier Austin described her as 'a highly cultivated and exceptionally intelligent lady' and fluent in English.[425] Lady Khanum departed Baqubah for London in September 1919, carrying her people's hopes with her. She put them before the British bureaucrats in the following terms:

To obtain future security under the protection of the British Government as a united nation in the area of Mosul-Jezirah-Bashkala-Urmiah;

That the Persian Government should be required to guarantee the security of Assyrians who were formerly Persian subjects and to ensure their resettlement in the districts around Urmiah;

To obtain restitution of private and ecclesiastical lands and buildings, forcibly taken from the Assyrians by the Turks and Kurds during the past fifty years;

That the ecclesiastical laws of the nation be recognised by the protecting nation;

That the former grazing grounds from which the mountain Assyrians had been driven by Moslem oppression, should again be made available for their flocks and herds.[426]

Eloquent and sophisticated though she was, Khanum's quest to represent her people in Paris was denied a few days after she arrived in London.[427] Back in the Baqubah camp, the Assyrian community underwent a turbulent time with the passing of the Mar Shimun Paulos XXII, in April 1920, after only two years as their spiritual leader. The Mar Eshai Shimun XXIII was installed as the next patriarch. Aged only 11 years, he remained under the tutelage and protection of his aunt Lady Surma Khanum. They followed the Paris Peace Conference vigilantly as a litany of international treaties and agreements were signed between former allies and enemies. Turkey and Iran maintained their sovereignty whilst arbitrary borders were drawn up across the Middle East; none of which correlated to the ancient circumference of Bethnahrin. As the community became divided about the best way to gain recognition of their plight for autonomy, factional interests 'commenced to lash the exiles' camp into fury'.[428] General Agha Petros approached the British High Commission with a plan to repatriate the Assyrians to a special buffer state in the Hakkari Mountain Vilayet on the Turko–Persian frontier, which

> called for retaking the town of Urmiah, turning West and retaking the abandoned Hakkari mountains in South Eastern Turkey, and from there heading West to the Mediterranean to form a thin stretch of territory to include the Jacobites of Syria—all of this would form a small Assyrian Christian state with access to the sea.[429]

A majority of refugees departed Baqubah in April 1920, with 6,000 Assyrian mountaineers headed for a temporary transit camp at Mindan, 27 miles north of Mosul on the Nineveh Plains.[430] They got as far Mosul when their transit was thwarted by the Great Iraqi Revolution, otherwise known as the Arab Rebellion, which arose in protest against the British Mandate.[431] Despite the commotion, by the end of September, the Baqubah camp had been evacuated; 35,000 Assyrians moved northwards to the Mosul Vilayet (district) and the Armenians were dispatched to Basrah to await transfer to the Mediterranean.[432] The Urmiah Assyrians went back to the camp but the Hakkari tribes stayed in the mountains, in Turkish territory.[433] The attempt to create an Assyrian kingdom ended in failure and despair. The British civil administrator Brigadier Austin wrote:

> It is entirely incomprehensible to these Assyrians that, in spite of their having fought on the ultimately winning side, their ancient defeated enemies should be left virtually in occupation of their beloved homes and lands, which the Assyrians were forced to abandon.[434]

Despite attempts by various Assyrians representatives to argue their case at the Paris Peace Conference and various treaty conferences, such as the Treaty of Sevres, the plight of a small, stateless minority could hardly have trumped the league's pressing task of erecting the British Mandatory Power in Mesopotamia after the collapse of the Ottoman Empire. The new Kingdom of Iraq was decreed in 1921, ruled by the Hashemite King Faisal I bin Hussein under the administration of the British civil and military authorities overseen by the Permanent Mandate High Commissioner Sir Percy Cox. Assyrians' concerns about their treatment under Arab rule mounted. The British Mandatory Power and the Iraqi Government remained saddled with the dilemma of Assyrian repatriation; how to provide a sanctuary for the community near disputed borders with their old enemies, and to circumvent future internal unrest and hostility from Arabs and Kurds.

The contentious peace negotiations continued over the question of the oil-rich Mosul Vilayet, and the Assyrians attempted once more to convince authorities that an independent homeland was a viable solution. General Petros was the official head of the Assyrian–Chaldean delegation to the treaty conferences held in Lausanne, Switzerland in 1923, where he lobbied for an Assyrian autonomous state. According to Turkish Government telegraphs, Ismet Inönü, head of the Turkish delegation cabled the Turkish Prime Minister in January 1923 with details of Petros' proposal:

> 2. He asked for the return [of the Assyrian Nestorians] who lived in Cölemerik and Gavur before the war and who migrated because of the situation; and in addition those Nestorians who are in Iran, Baghdad and other countries, in short all of the Assyrians and Nestorians, to return and live all together and under the facilitation of Turkey.

3. In the event that this condition were accepted, then the Assyrian-Nestorian delegation will declare that they have no claims against [issues with] Turkey. Furthermore, the Chaldeans who live in Mosul would ask for Mosul to be annexed to Turkey and that they would help us to achieve this end.[435]

The Turkish Prime Minister Rauf responded to the proposal three days later:

It is obvious that we would not approve the settlement of Assyrians and Chaldeans in our country. However, as long as we do not make any commitments and if it is beneficial to send Agha Petros away from Lausanne he could be sent to Ankara.[436]

The Treaty of Lausanne, signed in July 1923, ruled out the Assyrian proposal for an autonomous state either in Iraq or Turkey.[437] In May the following year, the League of Nations' Constantinople Conference aimed to resolve the border dispute between the British Mandate Authority of Iraq and the Republic of Turkey. The British High Commissioner prepared to press for an Assyrian territory to be annexed to Iraq, announcing his intentions to Assyrian community leaders:[438]

His Majesty's Government...keeping in view both the services which they rendered to the Allied cause during the war and their future relations with the Iraqi State...have decided to press for a frontier as far north as possible so as to include the greater part of the Assyrian people other than those who belong to districts subject to the Persian Government.[439]

The Turkish Government again opposed the British settlement proposal with spurious arguments that were 'entirely at variance' with Assyrian refugee experience:

The Nestorians (Assyrian Christians) would still find in Turkish territory all the tranquillity and prosperity which they enjoyed there for centuries, provided they did not repeat the errors which they committed, with foreign encouragement, at the beginning of the Great War.[440]

The Iraqi Government had little alternative but to respond favourably to the new settlement policy including the use of frontier lands by the Assyrians and the governance of their own community affairs 'since without the backing of Great Britain, it was almost certain that the whole of the Vilayet of Mosul would be lost to Turkey'.[441] During the three years of insecurity, upheaval and bureaucratic wrangling at various conferences between different layers of authority, the British High Commission permanently relocated 25,000 Assyrian refugees to the Mosul Vilayet, settling them into Zakho, Dohuk and Amadia neighbourhoods, and further north to the Upper and Lower Tiari areas.[442] The sacrifices and loyalty made by the smallest ally during the Great War were repaid with hypocrisy and profligacy, and their mouths shrivelled with the bitter taste of betrayal.

The vexatious dispute between Britain and Turkey over the frontiers of northern Iraq and the Assyrian repatriation, lead to a special League of Nations commission, which investigated the claims of both parties. The Turkish Government massed its troops on the border ready to occupy the Mosul Vilayet (Province) against which the Iraqi Government deployed 2,000 Assyrian Levies to defend it.[443] Once more, the Assyrians found themselves trapped between two giants fighting over oilfields. As tensions mounted in the borderlands around the middle of 1924, there was a so-called Nestorian Uprising of the Hakkari Assyrians, which was viewed by Turkey as an attempt to legitimise Assyrian claims to incorporate the highland region into an independent Assyrian state.

The Republic of Turkey launched a brutal reprisal. According to contemporary research conducted into Turkish military archives, in particular an account of the campaign recorded by the Turkish Army General Staff for internal purposes, Turkish troops of the 62nd Infantry Regiment crushed the Hakkari tribal insurrection and undertook a general ethnic cleansing of Assyrians in the Hakkari Vilayet. Both the Swedish and British Foreign Service archives, including the Gertrude Bell archive, corroborate the ensuing massacres and deportation of Christians by the Turkish Army in 1925.[444]

In June 1925, the special League of Nations commission tabled its recommendations regarding the status of Assyrians in Iraq and Turkey, including that they should be fully compensated for losses incurred during the Great War.[445] It made its final determination in December 1925 to grant the Mosul Vilayet to Iraq and the Hakkari Vilayet to Turkey.[446] It was the coup de grâce for the Assyrian aspiration of independent statehood, sanctioned by the very entity that promised to safeguard their welfare. The Assyrians were all but spent in their struggle for freedom and endured untold hardships and persecutions in the years that followed. By 1930 it became apparent that the permanent Mandates Commission was actually temporary; Assyrians became alarmed about losing the last vestiges of British protection in Iraq. In October, the Patriarch Mar Eshai Shimun wrote a letter from Mosul to the Chairman of the League of Nations Mandates Commission in Geneva, pleading for clemency:

> I beg to convey to Your Excellency the following:
>
> The Assyrian nation which is temporarily living in Iraq, having placed before their eyes the dark future and the miserable

conditions which are undoubtedly awaiting them in Iraq, after the lifting of the mandate, have unanimously held a conference with me in Mosul on 20th October 1931…At the conclusion of lengthy deliberations, it was unanimously decided by all those present that it is quite impossible for us to live in Iraq…Under the circumstances, I, together with the under mentioned signatories being the responsible leaders of the Assyrian Naiton submit before Your Commission our Nation's humble request, which in past centuries numbered millions but reduced to a very small number due to repeated persecutions and massacres that faced us, we have been able to preserve our Language and Faith up to the present time…This being so, it is unnecessary for us to enlarge upon each item, BUT WE ARE POSITIVELY SURE THAT IF WE REMAIN IN IRAQ, we shall be exterminated in the course of a few years.

WE THEREFORE IMPLORE YOUR MERCY TO TAKE CARE OF US, and arrange our emigration to one of the countries under the rule of one of the Western Nations whom you may deem fit. And should this be impossible, we beg you to request the French Government to accept us in Syria and give us shelter under her responsibility FOR WE CAN NO LONGER LIVE IN IRAQ AND WE SHALL LEAVE. Signed Eshai Shimun, By the Grace of God, Catholics Patriarch of the East.

As with the pleas of past patriarchs, the letter fell on deaf ears, but the prophetic words of Mar Eshai rang true. Within 12 months of the Kingdom of Iraq becoming independent in 1932, the Simele Massacre took place. From 1926, the British Mandatory Authority reduced the ranks of the Assyrian Levies from approximately 2,500 active servicemen to 1,500 in 1932 and then to 800 in 1933.[447] At this time, the Assyrian villages in the Mosul Vilayet reported widespread incidences of social, political and religious discrimination. They included damage to property and theft of livestock, breaches in taxation, violent crimes against persons, including murder and sexual assaults on women and girls, attacks on churches. Most incidents were never attended to by police or redressed within the Iraqi legal system.[448]

One of the men who resigned from the Levies, in 1933, was Yaqu Ismail of the Upper Tiyari clan from the Hakkari mountains. He rose to prominence as a rebel leader in the spring and summer of that year during an unexpected chain of events. Ismail travelled around various Assyrian villages to spruik anti-government sentiment and dissuade the villagers from applying for Iraqi citizenship and permanent settlement as a protest against the treatment of Assyrian people by state officialdom.[449]

On 21 July, he led a contingent of 800 armed compatriots across the Tigris River over the border into Syria in order to negotiate a settlement for the Assyrians with the French Mandatory authorities in that country.[450] No such amnesty or accommodation was ever offered by the French to the Assyrians; the clansmen surrendered their rifles and headed back to Iraq. As they attempted to forge the river the Iraqi Army opened fire on them with machine guns.

Thirty-three soldiers were killed in the melee and 40 were wounded while many of Ismail's group escaped into the mountains, some fleeing back to Syria where they were imprisoned indefinitely.[451] The incident was reported in newspapers all over Iraq in exaggerated terms, which exacerbated the existing hostility towards the Assyrian community.[452] An insidious revenge was soon exacted by the Iraqi Army and the Kurdish irregulars.

On 5 August, the Iraqi Army began to track down and execute the Assyrian fugitives. It was recorded that the shooting continued in the Dohuk and Zakho areas over the next few days, leaving around 80 civilians dead. Colonel Stafford recorded that 'the Army had definitely decided that the Assyrians, as far as possible, were to be exterminated. No pretence was made that these operations had any purely military objective'.[453]

Ismail's expedition into Syria, and the subsequent loss and capture of his men, had left their families unprotected and many of them fled to the village of Simele, where they waited for the trouble to die down. On 8 August, the Qaimaqam (Prefect) of Zakho entered the village in a truck with Iraqi Army soldiers and approached the Assyrians, who had sought safety outside the local police station. They were ordered to hand in their weapons. In the moonlight, the villagers watched as local Arab tribes rustled away their flocks and looted their houses.

On the morning of 11 August, as a policeman lowered the Iraqi flag from the roof of the police post, the Assyrians became increasingly agitated and afraid as the soldiers forced them back to their homes. Iraqi troops then began firing on the villagers with machine guns attached to their armoured cars; some were raped or bludgeoned to death. The shooting lasted until sunset. The survivors were left in the heat without food or water for a few days.[454] Official estimates put the death toll of the Simele massacre at over 600, most of whom were 'peaceful cultivators'. In the first few days after the massacre, Lieutenant Colonel Stafford and the Iraq Minister of the Interior, Hikmet Beg Suleiman travelled to Simele on separate visits to conduct inquiries and take evidence from witnesses. The former later wrote:

When I visited Simmel myself...on August 17th few traces could be seen of what had occurred, but the sight of the women and children is one which I shall never forget—and I spent more than three years in the trenches of France!⁴⁵⁵

The Director of Repatriation in the Civil Government of Mesopotamia, Colonel Clifford-Owen, reported that 64 Assyrian villages in the Mosul, Dohuk and Zhako areas were partially or totally destroyed during the brief Assyrian rebellion.⁴⁵⁶ By the end of summer 1933, approximately 5,000 Assyrians were killed by the Iraqi Army and irregulars.⁴⁵⁷ The Crown Prince decorated Brigadier General Bakr Sidqi and the senior Iraqi Army officers who orchestrated the killing spree, parading them as national heroes though the main streets of Mosul, Kirkuk and Baghdad.⁴⁵⁸ No individuals have ever been charged or brought to trial for the atrocity. It was a watershed for the collective life of the Assyrians in the nascent state of Iraq. The date of the massacre is Assyrian Martyrs' Day, their national Day of Mourning.

A few months later a brilliant lawyer named Raphael Lemkin made his salutary presentation on international criminal law to the Legal Council of the League of Nations using the Simele atrocity as the basis for his original concept of 'genocide'.⁴⁵⁹ The debate over Assyrian repatriation by the presiding League of Nations Council became so hidebound and convoluted as to verge on absurdity. The council considered three misanthropic proposals for a new Assyrian territory; one near the Parana River in Southern Brazil, one on a bend of the Niger River downstream from Timbuktu and another on the equatorial pastures of British Guiana.⁴⁶⁰ Clamped between the impregnable walls of international diplomacy and state bureaucracy, it seemed to the majority of the Assyrians that there was little else to do but resign to life as fringe dwellers on the margins of Iraqi society.

Mar Eshai Shimun was summoned to Baghdad for negotiations with the Iraqi Government but upon his refusal to relinquish his authority over the community he was exiled to Cyprus, after which he migrated to Chicago, U.S.A.[461] Without their patriarch to advocate for them, life was not expected to improve:

> The Assyrians in Iraq continued to suffer untold hardships, mental, physical, and spiritual alike – disappointed and disheartened in the extreme by the failure of the British Government to fulfil its promises towards them—and looked upon with great suspicions by the Iraqi Government and constantly attacked by the Iraqi press as a foreign and unwelcome element—they felt uneasy of the dark future facing them.[462]

A cold-blooded peace was brokered in Paris, but justice was not served. The league's minority protection system was later established to enshrine the human rights of minority peoples, and yet, with the flick of a pen, the persecuted indigenous people of Bethnahrin were doomed to a life of poverty, dispossession and exile; stateless pariahs in their ancestral homeland.[463] The promises made in Paris by the Great Powers may as well have been written on dandelion seeds; the Assyrians watched their dream of their own kingdom float away on the breeze.

○ ○ ○

Chapter Twenty
A Knight's Legacy

Only the dead have seen the end of war.

Plato

While the Paris Peace Conference got underway, Captain Stanley Savige was making his way back to Australia. He walked off the gangway at Port Melbourne on 2 March 1919. His family and friends celebrated his homecoming with a high tea at his family home in Carnegie. He married Lillian on 28 June at the church where they had first met, the South Yarra Baptist Church. They lodged at St Kilda while waiting for their new house to be built.

During this vexatious period of readjustment to postwar life, Savige's life became more demanding and fulfilling. The idea of returning to his counter job as a clerk in a drapery store must have seemed to him insulting, if not absurd and he soon found work in the wholesale trading and warehousing business. This gave him the opportunity to travel to mining towns in Victoria, Queensland and Tasmania. Then at 31 years of age, he decided to reinstate his military career, joining the 37th Infantry

Battalion as captain, followed by stints as a staff officer with the 3rd Division.

In 1923, he started work with the Returned Soldiers' Mill in Geelong and was soon promoted as the company's sole Australian agent, which gave him the confidence to start his own trading firm, S.G. Savige, with only an administrative assistant, two desks and a secondhand typewriter.[464] At this time, Savige reconnected with his former commanding officer and mentor, John Gellibrand, who had been appointed as the Chief Commissioner of Police in Victoria in 1920.[465] After the war, Gellibrand had dedicated himself to the welfare of returned soldiers and when he retired to Hobart, Tasmania in early 1923, he established the Remembrance Club to support the professional interests and social concerns of ex-servicemen.[466] Savige visited Gellibrand in Hobart to discuss the club's modus operandi and potential for expansion in Melbourne.

Inspired by Gellibrand, Savige and a few mates from his old 24th Battalion decided to start a new club on 25 September 1923; it was the beginning of Legacy.[467] The new organisation would assist the rehabilitation of returned soldiers whose livelihoods had been diminished due to physical incapacity. However, by 1925 Legacy aspired to a more idealistic purpose. After dinner at Anzac House in Melbourne, one of the members asked, 'Have you fellows thought that the dying wish of any of our cobbers would be that we should look after his missus and kids?'[468] Savige took this to heart, and he was soon on another mission. In the early days of Legacy, Savige addressed the members thus:

> We did an honest job in the A.I.F. We achieved a measure of success. In re-establishing ourselves we need faith in our own ability and a desire to help our fellow soldiers…and an application of

the A.I.F. spirit by supporting each other in seeking a niche in civil life.[469]

Legacy launched into the arena of social support programs with the establishment of the Deceased Soldiers' Children's Welfare Committee in 1929, including boxing, debating, football, gymnastics and health care. Savige undertook a leadership role and even hosted the first annual Legacy Junior Boys' camp at his holiday property at Balnarring on Boxing Day 1926, incurring personal debt to purchase sports equipment and clothing for the children.[470] Savige was president of the Melbourne chapter in 1929–30, when he travelled interstate to promote Legacy's mission and oversaw the establishment of new chapters. The rapid growth and success of Legacy in Australia is indicative of the need amongst war widows and orphans. By 1932, Legacy committees were active in every state across the country.

The Saviges started a family with the birth of their daughter, Gwendolyn, and the adoption of Stanley's two young nephews following his sister's early death in 1924. Gwendolyn was ill for much of her childhood, and Lillian was unwell for many years after the loss of an unborn child. Stanley made a brief tilt at politics when he stood for the seat of Caulfield in the 1930 by-election, owing to the sudden death of a Legacy member who held the Nationalist seat in the House of Representatives, but he was unable to hold the seat and never again showed any inclination towards public office.[471]

Savige's military career continued through the years of the Great Depression, in addition to his family commitments and hectic community service obligations. After a promotion to rank of major, he commanded the 37th Battalion between 1925 and 1928, after which he became lieutenant colonel in command of his old 24th Battalion until 1935. Following a promotion to colonel in 1935 he took command of the 10th Brigade and as brigadier until 1939.[472] He attended the first Command and Staff School for division and brigade commanders at Victoria Barracks in Sydney in the same year.[473] Underneath, Stanley remained a private and reserved man, preferring the simple comforts of home and family. He took great delight in retreating from the demands of public life with his large, extended family to his seaside holiday house, where he could cook, entertain friends and play with his children and pets.[474]

In September 1939, when Prime Minister Menzies declared war against Nazi Germany, Stanley was officially notified of his appointment as Commander of the 17th Brigade, 6th Division of the 2nd Australian Imperial Force on 6 October 1939. He received hundreds of messages of congratulation, including one from General Birdwood:

> Dear Savige…I hope you will have all the same good fortune and success as we had with our old A.I.F in Gallipoli and France. I have heard much of your good service with 'Dunsterforce' and I much look forward to meeting you in due course. Yours sincerely, Birdwood of Anzac.[475]

On 14 April 1940, Stanley Savige sailed once more to war, this time as Brigadier with the 17th Brigade, Egypt Corps. He prepared his men during the summer months for imminent action in the North Africa campaign, starting with a complicated role in the Battle of Bardia, the first battle of the Second World War involving Australian soldiers.[476] He went on to lead the brigade during the Libyan Campaign of January 1941, including the capture of Sidi Barrani, the surrender of Benghazi and the Battles of Tobruk and Derna, for which he was appointed a Commander of the Order of the British Empire. The citation reads:

He showed fine control, organisation and leadership throughout, culminating in an excellent example of initiative and drive which broke the enemy flank west of Derna thus accelerating the enemy retreat and final defeat.[477]

When the German Army invaded northern Greece in early April 1941, Brigadier Savige received orders to block the German 5th and 9th Armoured Divisions, as well as the 73rd Division and the Adolf Hitler S.S. Division, who were advancing through the ranges to take Athens. The 17h Brigade was the last to come ashore at Volos to join General Blamey's headquarters in the nearby foothills of Mt Olympus.[478] To do the job, Savige took command of four infantry battalions, named Savige Force.[479] They were caught in an enemy air raid during the full withdrawal from the area, but Savige returned safely to Palestine on 1 May 1941, after which he was involved in the Battle of Damour in the Syria-Lebanon campaign.[480] In December 1941, he received the Greek Military Cross for his services during the disastrous Battle of Greece.[481]

The Vichy Government of France had permitted the German High Command at this time to use air force facilities in Syria.[482] Brigadier Savige was placed in charge of French army camps in Northern Syria and was instrumental in the arrest of the Chief of the French Air Force, General Jennequin, who was dispatched back to France along with the Vichy Armed Forces.[483] During a brief rest, he went sightseeing in Jerusalem before making preparations for the winter in Damascus. But there was a change of plans.

In November 1941, Stanley learned of his demotion in an unceremonial fashion; his own batman heard a radio announcement of his pending transfer back to Australia as Director of Army Recruiting.[484] The transfer seems to have been based ostensibly on the results of a medical examination, which confirmed General Blamey's concerns about Savige's declining health and his decision to send him home as 'a graceful way of retiring with honour two officers who have done useful work in the Middle East but seemed to him unequal to the severe physical demands of fast-moving modern warfare'.[485]

Stanley departed for Australia with three other brigadiers on 27 December with the news of the Japanese attack on Pearl Harbour ringing in their ears. The men were taken by seaplane from Lake Tiberias, Palestine via Basra, Karachi and Calcutta, landing in Rangoon, which had been devastated by a Japanese air raid only a few days earlier.[486] Flying over the cities and countries of South East Asia on their way home, the three commanders must have shuddered at the trail of destruction left by the Japanese army and air force on the ground below. The gravity of the situation struck home when they flew into Singapore on 5 January 1942 during the devastating Japanese assault on the city, which forced the crew to land in Souribaya where they waited for further orders.

Two days later the commanders walked across the sizzling tarmac in Darwin, where Brigadier Savige was immediately informed of another twist in his military career. Whilst in transit, the army recruiting role was waived in favour of his promotion to Major General in command of the 3rd Australian Division; an indication of the deepening conflict.[487]

As Australian command was left reeling from the Japanese bombing of Darwin in February, Major General Savige prepared the Australian 3rd Division for the war in the Pacific. Due to the aggressive advance of the Japanese in the Pacific, he took on dual responsibilities as both the Divisional and II Corps Commander from October at his divisional headquarters near Brisbane.[488] As the conflict intensified, Allied Forces concentrated their efforts in Bougainville and Papua New Guinea. Major General Savige arrived with the 3rd Division in Port Moresby in March 1943 to relieve General Allen's 7th Division after their terrible battle with Japanese forces on the Kokoda Track.[489]

He began planning for the Salamaua-Lae Campaign after receiving orders to threaten Japanese positions and prevent them using the airfields in that location.[490] Major General Savige reconnoitred the entire area by air, always wearing his scarlet banded general's cap as a gesture of resolute defiance to both his men and the enemy.[491] Owing to the formidable terrain, flights were necessary to get around the mountains and, being no fan of air travel, he was so nervous about flying in a Piper Cub with an American airman that he almost left his fingernails behind in the cockpit dashboard:

> After we had a smoke, we crawled into the cockpit. My pilot settled down into his seat while I sat on a miniature folding stool behind him. As we moved up the valley to Wau the clouds almost touched the ground...At one stage the single engine began to splutter and my good pilot reached down and began a pumping action...I didn't want to come down too far out to sea or come in over enemy occupied country...we came down through a hole in the clouds...He then made the plane do every trick it could...and said, "Buddy, did you hear her gurgling back there?"...I didn't ask any questions as we were gliding in to land on a roughly constructed strip on the beach—and didn't she bump as we landed.[492]

Major General Savige did not see the final capture of Salamaua because he was ordered to hand over command to the 5th Division under acrimonious circumstances on 23 August, prior to the withdrawal of the Japanese 51st Division.[493] Despite the aspersions that were cast over his performance as a tactician, Savige was recommended for the award of Companion of the Order of the Bath for his services to the campaign with fulsome praise:

> Maj-Gen. Savige had control of the Battle for Salamaua from 30 Jun. 43 till his relief on 26 Aug. 43. The battle was finally won on 11 Sep. 43—the credit for victory must rest with Maj-Gen. Savige during whose period of command, the back of the enemy's defence was broken. The nature of the country rendered great assistance to the defender, and careful planning alone enabled the defences to be overcome. The supplying of our forward troops was also a terrific problem.
>
> The success achieved is of the greatest importance to the Allied cause, and Maj-Gen. Savige by his fine leadership has made a very real contribution to the ultimate success of the United Nations. The victories won over the enemy at the battles for MUBO and KOMIATUM were due to his well conceived plans and energetic execution.[494]

Between 6 May and 1 October 1944, General Savige was G.O.C of the New Guinea Force based at the newly established Lae H.Q. at a time when Australian combat operations were winding down. With orders 'to reduce enemy resistance on Bougainville Island as opportunity offers without committing major forces', he concentrated on dismantling military installations and troop repatriations.[495] His sixth and final military campaign took place on Bougainville Island and ended in victory at the cost of 516 Australian soldiers and 8,500 Japanese soldiers. On 8 September 1945, the Commanders Lieutenant General Masetane Kanda and Vice Admiral Samejima of the Japanese Imperial Forces were brought aboard the HMAS *Diamantina* under armed guard to surrender their ceremonial swords to Lieutenant General Savige.[496]

Before his retirement in 1946, Sir Thomas Blamey wrote a letter to General Savige saying:

> Your services during the period of the war years present a remarkable record. It is too, a record of achievement and of success which has been marked by great hardship, and on many occasions, as I well know, you have had to follow a lonely road. This you have done calmly and quietly and on every occasion the event has proved you right. My sense of your personal loyalty and support will always be very great, and our association over many years of soldiering, both in peace and war, will always recur to me with glowing pride and pleasure...As your reward you will have the knowledge of the strong support of those who served under you and the experience of their faith and loyalty in you to treasure all your life.[497]

The respite of peace time did not afford General Savige a tranquil retirement. When his nephew returned to Australia from a German prison camp he mentored him to take over the family business.[498] He was then appointed as the Coordinator of Demobilization and Dispersal until May 1946 after which he served as Chairman of the Central War Gratuity Board until 1951 and subsequently as the Commissioner of the State Savings Bank of Victoria.[499] Field Marshall Sir Blamey made two postwar recommendations for his commanding officer, both of which were denied by the presiding Labor Government.[500] On 8 June 1950, Savige was honoured by King George VI as Knight Commander of the Order of the British Empire, bestowed with His Majesty's hale:[501]

> GEORGE THE SIXTH by the Grace of God of Great Britain, Ireland and the British Dominions beyond the Seas, King,

Defender of the Faith and Sovereign of the Most Excellent Order of the British Empire to Our trusty and well beloved Stanley George Savige Esquire Companion of our Most Honourable Order of the Bath Commander of Our said Most Excellent Order Companion of our Distinguished Service Order on whom have conferred the Decoration of the Military and the Efficiency Decoration Lieutenant-General in our Australian Military Forces, GREETING. [502]

According to his critics he had returned from the war 'a changed man'—bellicose, introspective, hyper-sensitive and with a 'persecution complex'.[503] Warranted as such criticism may have been, it is little wonder that, having survived two world wars and having ascended through the ranks from corporal to brasshood in the most extenuating circumstances, it would take its toll on Savige's persona in one way or another. There were those, however, who remained unconditionally loyal to the end. Lieutenant Colonel Smith, who served under General Savige, wrote a letter to Lady Lillian stating:

> I will never forget his warning to me when I took over the 24th Battalion. He said, "If you waste one man's life unnecessarily, you're OUT!"...Your husband could ask me to go the ends of the earth and I'd say "Right" before asking the reason. I think Sir Stanley spread his kindness in thought for his men right through his command, certainly in all who had long contact with him.[504]

Savige had the honour of leading the 1951 Anzac Day March in Melbourne and, in 1953, he went to London with his daughter to represent Legacy at the coronation of Queen Elizabeth II.[505] He despaired over the petty squabbling that eventually created a schism within Legacy's Melbourne Board and the Coordinating Council, redolent of the many years of interpersonal rancour that he had experienced at the highest echelons of army command.[506]

Some months after spending a fabulous vacation in Europe together, in March 1954 Lillian passed away and Savige's own health went into a steady decline. Savige had crammed in many lives and had died more than one death in his day and now his heart could no longer withstand the demands he had made of it. At age 64 he was diagnosed with coronary heart disease; the mustard gas and cigarettes and malarial fever had finally got the better of him. On the morning of his death, Stanley was found standing by his bed dressed in a formal mess kit 'looking magnificent', ready to fight the Japanese Army, whom he believed had just invaded Darwin. With his loved one gathered around, he yelled, 'Don't you know there's a crisis? I have to see Robertson at eight!'[507]

Stanley fought gallantly in some of the worst battles of both world wars spanning Asia Minor, the Middle East, Europe, North Africa and the South Pacific. He had almost expired during his breathtaking humanitarian rescue mission; he buried friends in shallow graves and took the shirt from his back to cover a child's nakedness. He accepted the swords of enemies without bluster or malice and gave succour to widows and orphans. According to his Christian principles he served his country, his men, his family and the community with distinction and magnanimity, to the end.

On 19 May 1954, the city thronged with mourners paying their respects to General Sir Stanley George Savige, Anzac. His coffin was drawn by gun-carriage from St Paul's Anglican Cathedral along Flinders Street to Kew Cemetery. There it was laid to rest with full military honours, for a true and valiant Australian knight.

○ ○ ○

Chapter Twenty One
Between the Rivers of Paradise

No fears, nor hopes, but one equal possession.

John Donne

On Friday 18 July 2014, international news agencies began reporting that Islamic State militants had seized key locations and assets in northern Iraq and were broadcasting from mosques in Mosul an ultimatum to all Christians; they had until midday Saturday to convert to Islam, pay a protection tax or leave the city. Failure to do so would end at the edge of a sword. For days beforehand the Islamic State in Iraq and Levant (ISIL) terrorists had been branding the houses of Christians with the Arabic letter N, which stands for Nazarene; a sinister threat implying crucifixion.[508] When Kurdish Forces withdrew from the Mosul Governorate, the Assyrian bishops ordered the city's church bells to be rung as an alarm for the Christians to flee. The exodus began at 2.30 am. The UN Assistance Mission in Iraq estimated that 200,000 Christians, Yezidis, Mandeans and Shebaks fled their towns and villages in horror and were trapped in the searing summer heat around Dohuk and the Jabal Sinjar mountains without food, water or shelter.

The Patriarch of the Holy Apostolic Catholic Assyrian Church of the East, Mar Dinkha IV, had written to the Secretary General of the Unitied Nations, Ban Ki-Moon, in July, pleading for the UN to protect local civilians. It was clear from earlier rampages what ISIL intended to do to religious minorities in the northern region. The patriarch warned of further desecration of sacred sites such as the shrine of Jonah, crucifixions of young men, decapitations, sexual torture and enslavement of women and young girls, extortion and destruction of infrastructure. But it was too late. The storm of terror broke and the people fled. On 6 August 2014, Mar Dinkha wrote again:

> The plight of the ancient Christian communities in Mosul, Iraq, and its environs is a situation by now well known to Your Excellency and to all of the member-states of the United Nations...Christianity has been present in the ancient city of Mosul, known formerly as 'Nineveh' the capital of the ancient Assyrian Empire, since the preaching of the very Apostles of our Lord Jesus Christ...Today, not a Christian is present, and what's more, the ancient churches and relics of our faith have been destroyed before the very eyes of the major countries of the modem civilized West-indeed, before the eyes of the world! This is a great travesty...against the ancient patrimony of civilization... the United Nations, cannot stand by with obvious complacency and apathy towards our plight and allow this destruction of these peoples in Iraq. Mere statements of condemnation by the UN, and even of the major countries of the West, are not sufficient! These statements, though taken with gratitude, are not enough

to bring an end to these atrocities and to stop this genocide of a religious nature!...May Almighty God grant His enduring peace throughout the world and among all peoples.[509]

On 7 August 2014, Assyrian Martyrs' Day, the President of the United States announced immanent joint air strikes on ISIL targets in Iraq and Syria. Islamic State jihadists appeared to burst out of their hiding place like demons unleashed; Tamurlane in a different costume. It may have taken the global press by surprise but for the Christians of Iraq it was old news. The persecution and oppression of their community had continued unabated since the Baqubah Refugee settlement and the Simele Massacre. And yet those tumultuous days under the new monarchy, as the nation established itself in the post-mandate era as a Middle Eastern democracy, seemed good in comparison to what came later. Aside from the milder years under Brigadier Abd al-Karim Qasim (1958–1963), during which the Assyrian community stabilised and organised itself politically, the Arab Socialist Ba'athist regime, starting in 1968, 'was nothing short of a nightmare'.[510]

Under the dictatorship of President Saddam Hussein, the victimisation of Iraq's religious minorities—including Shabaks, Yazidis, Mandaeans, Marsh Arab, Jews and Aramaic Christians—intensified.[511] The disappearance of around 1,000 Assyrians and the destruction of religious assets during the 1970s and 1980s can be attributed to the Arabisation policy (1961–1991) and the Anfal campaigns (February to September 1988); an ethnic cleansing strategy aimed at non-Arabs.[512] By the end of the Anfal campaign the northern region of Iraq was shattered. Among an estimated 4,500 villages that were obliterated by state armed forces, 196 were Assyrian villages, as well as 60 historic churches and orphanages in the provinces of Nineveh,

Dohuk and Arbil.[513] During this period, an estimated 100,000 Kurdish civilians were murdered by the regime, including Assyrian men, women and children 'who were taken to unknown destinations and never seen again'.[514] According to Human Rights Watch, a group of 250 Assyrians were known to have disappeared, most likely executed en masse in the desert and buried in mass graves along with their Kurdish neighbours.[515]

A further 40,000 Assyrian male conscripts were killed or went 'missing in action' during the Iran–Iraq War.[516] In March 1988, President Hussein launched a chemical weapons attack on the residents of Halabja by the Iraqi Air Force.[517] Although the victims were predominantly Kurdish civilians, a substantial number of Christians were murdered in the attacks.[518] By the time of the Iraq War in 1991, it was acknowledged that 'Assyrian national identity in Iraq had all but been erased to the point where foreign journalists unfamiliar with Iraqi history completely missed this hidden community and reported instead on the presence of Arab Christians'.[519] The fall of the Ba'athist Dictatorship, the subsequent occupation of Iraq by Multi-National Forces and the capture of Saddam Hussein in March 2003 sparked waves of violence and persecution against ethnic and religious minorities in a 'climate of impunity'.[520] In August 2004, following a spate of deadly church bombings approximately 15,000 Assyrians fled Iraq.[521]

In the lead up to the national elections in 2009, the Iraqi Christian community was subjected to resurgent violence due to their protests and lobbying for better representation at the Iraqi Council of Representatives, which left 40 people dead and prompted 12,000 Assyrians in Mosul to flee their homes.[522] Amnesty International claimed that the violence was experienced most acutely by Iraq's Christian population who had been targeted by Islamic extremists, including al-Qa'ida, affiliated Sunni Islamist groups and Shi'a militia, such as the Mahdi Army.[523] The most heinous crimes have been perpetrated on infants, children, young women and clergy, such as the Chaldean Archbishop of Mosul, who was abducted, dismembered and decapitated by 'unidentified militants' in February 2008.[524] At the end of 2009, nearly 60 per cent of Iraq's Christian population had been internally displaced or had sought asylum in other countries. Of the es of thousand Assyrian Christians who lived in Baghdad there were only 60 families still residing there.[525]

In 2009, the former Arab League Ambassador and Special Envoy to Iraq, Mokhtar Lamani, accompanied by the nation's Prime Minister Barzani, conducted a field study on the condition and status of Iraq's minorities.[526] Lamani reported that although religious minorities constituted only five per cent of the total population, they comprised one-fifth of its displaced persons and since 2003 they had lived in a constant state of crisis under 'exceptional threat' from 'sectarian' conflict and upheaval.[527] Most Christians have fled to Syria and Lebanon or to Western countries if possible. As of 2007, not a single displaced member of an Iraqi minority group has been able to safely return to their homes.[528]

Those Assyrians who remain in the disputed territory of Iraqi Kurdistan under the Kurdistan Regional Government (KRG) face resurgent nationalism, corruption, increased tensions between the KRG and the central government, and human rights abuses committed by Kurdish security forces.[529] The KRG has confiscated Assyrian land and property across the Kurdish territory, in spite of the KRG being supportive of Assyrian agitation for a self-administered province within the Nineveh Governorate.[530]

Reports from both the European Union Parliament and the United States Commission on International Religious Freedom indicated that international aid funds were distributed inequitably and that only a small proportion of foreign reconstruction dollars reached the Assyrian and Chaldean villages.[531]

In January 2010, the mayor of Habbaniya Cece in north-eastern Iraq paid a visit to the last member of the ancient Assyrian Mary Queen of Peace parish; he bewailed the loss of the Christians from his town and implored his friend to stay.[532] Later that year, armed militants affiliated with al-Qa'ida carried out a siege in an Assyrian church in Baghdad during celebration of the Holy Eucharist, killing 40 civilian hostages. Amnesty International declared the attack to be 'nothing less than a war crime'.[533] Not a single person has been brought to trial for this or the innumerable similar crimes.

There is no amnesty for the indigenous Christians of Iraq. The centuries-old pattern of purging and pogroms, the egregious violation of the human and civil rights of Assyrian Christians in their ancestral homeland is tantamount to religious genocide on an international, intergenerational scale. These crimes should be acknowledged as belonging on the continuum of genocidal acts, commencing with Seyfo at the beginning of the Great War. Otherwise, perceived in a historical vacuum, not only is their vulnerability reinforced, but the smokescreen for denial is perpetuated. According to the International Association of Genocide Scholars:

> The denial of genocide is widely recognised as the final stage of genocide, enshrining impunity for the perpetrators of genocide and demonstrably paving the way for future genocides; Be it resolved that it is the conviction of the International Association of Genocide Scholars that the Ottoman campaign against Christian minorities of the Empire between 1914 and 1923

constituted a genocide against Armenians, Assyrians and Pontiac and Anatolian Greeks.[534]

In the fallout of the Arab Spring, there is now talk of a post-conflict future in Iraq and Syria without Christians, as populations dwindle to single figures. If special protections have been afforded to other indigenous minorities against ethnic cleansing or military-based pogroms, such as in Rwanda, Kosovo and East Timor, it seems only just and reasonable that such protections would be provided for the Aramaic Christians in their homeland. And yet, since the first letter of the Patriarch Mar Abraham to the Archbishop of Canterbury written 174 years ago, to the recent letters of Mar Dinkha IV to the head of the United Nations, Assyrians know to expect little else than glib condolences, equivocation and hand-wringing. Perhaps there is a sign of hope in the official recognition of Seyfo by the German Bundestag in May 2016, and a recent resolution of the European Parliament to support the creation of an autonomous safe haven for Christians in northern Iraq; returning full circle to the original petitions by the Assyrian Patriarch to the League of Nations in 1919.

This international humanitarian and human rights calamity has created a haemorrhage of Christians from Iraq who swell the Diaspora in countries where they have sought asylum—Sweden, Denmark, Germany, the Netherlands, Canada, the United States and Australia. Many Assyrians who now live in Diaspora communities are the descendants of those whose lives were spared almost 100 years ago by Captain Stanley Savige and his Dunsterforce comrades. Today, the majority of Iraqi-born migrants and refugees in Australia are Aramaean Christians. The Assyrian community numbers around 60,000, mainly located in Sydney and Melbourne.

In June 2011, the first Assyrian Australian to be elected to state parliament made his inaugural speech in the New South Wales Parliament as the new member for Smithfield. Andrew Rohan, who was born at Habbaniya on the banks of the Euphrates River in Iraq, told the parliament of his family's journey to Australia:

> A journey that started in the summer of 1918 when my father was just a teenager and my mother a young child…They and their families were among 90,000 Assyrian Christian refugees fleeing their ancestral homeland to escape persecution…My parents and the other refugees were fleeing from the Ottoman Empire to escape what would later be known as the "Armenian, Assyrian and Pontic Greek Genocide". By the grace of God my parents survived, for the reason they were protected, and protected by none other than an Australian soldier.
>
> Lieutenant General Sir Stanley George Savige, KBE, CB, DSO, MC, ED, at that time a 28-year-old captain, was selected to join "Dunsterforce", an elite task force assigned to resupplying the Assyrians fighting in Persia…even though he was outnumbered 100 to one, Captain Savige managed to slow the enemy advance long enough for most of the refugees to flee. This act of courage and self-sacrifice was far beyond what was expected of a junior officer in the field…My parents survived the Genocide because of the heroic actions of Sir Stanley George Savige and I, as the newly elected Liberal member for Smithfield, pay tribute to him today in this House.[535]

In spite of generations of brutal subjugation by successive foreign invaders, imperial armies and regimes, the Assyrians have upheld their religious heritage and continued to cultivate their communal life and honour their ancient traditions. But it is far from the legacy that Captain Stanley Savige bequeathed to them when he offered his life in the Persian Alps in August 1918.

Yet, out of Assyria, the nation which imagines itself as a crucifix, two sacred rivers flow, one of prayer and one of tears. They flow over the mountains and across the stony plains into the hermitages, monasteries and churches, built so long ago as sanctuaries of peace and contemplation.[536] May Bethnahrin become a place of sanctuary once again, where weeping turns to joy in the days to come.

Bibliography

Books

Annemasse, *The Assyrian Tragedy*. online book www.aina.org 1934

Baum, W. and Winkler, D.W. *The Church of the East: A Concise History*. London: Routledge Curzon

Austin, Herbert Henry. *The Baqubah Refugee Camp: An Account of Work on Behalf of the Persecuted Assyrian Christians*. London: The Faith Press, 1920

Bryce Viscount, presented to Viscount Grey of Falldoon, *The Treatment of Armenians in the Ottoman Empire 1915-1916., 'The Blue Book'*. London: Hodder and Stoughton, 1916

Buchanan, G. *The Tragedy of Mesopotamia*. London: William Blackwood & Sons, 1938

Burke, Keast., ed. *With Horse and Morse in Mesopotamia: The Story of Anzacs in Asia*. (Sydney: Arthur McQuitty & Co, 1927

Cameron, N. *Barbarians & Mandarins: Thirteen Centuries of Western Travellers in China*. (York: Walker Weatherhill, 1970

Carlyon, Les. *Gallipoli*. (Sydney: Pan Macmillan, 2001

Cleveland, W.L. *A History of the Modern Middle East*. Boulder: Westview Press, 2004

Cooper, John. *Raphael Lemkin and the Struggle for the Genocide Convention.* London: Palgrave Macmillan, 2008

Cunliffe-Owen, Frederick. *British Policy in Assyrian Settlement.* Compiled for the British Colonial Office, formerly the India Office, 1919

Darwin, J. *After Tamerlane, the Rise & Fall of Global Empires, 1400-2000.* London: Penguin Books, 2008

Davis, P.K., *The British Mesopotamian Campaign and Commission.* Toronto: Associate University Presses, 1994

Donef, R. *The Hakkari Massacres: Ethnic Cleansing by Turkey 1924-1925.* (Sydney: Tatavla Publishing, 2014

Dorn Brose, Erik. *A History of the Great War.* (York: Oxford University Press, 2010

Dunsterville, Lionel Charles. *The Adventures of Dunsterforce.* London: Edward Arnold, 1920

Ellis, M.H. *The Torch: A Picture of Legacy.* (Melbourne: Angus and Roberston, 1957

Gilbert, Martin. *The First World War: A Complete History.* (York: Henry Holt & Company, 1994

Gildea, Robert. *Barricades and Borders: Europe 1800-1914.* Oxford: Oxford University Press, 1987

Goldstein, Erik. *The First World War Peace Settlements 1919-1925.* London: Longman Pearson Education, 2002

Hakan Erdem, Y. *Slavery in the Ottoman Empire and Its Demise, 1800–1909.* (York: St. Martin's, 1996

Harvey, W.J. *The Red and White Diamond: Authorised History of the 24th Battalion Australian Imperial Force.* East Sussex: Naval and Military Press, in association with the Imperial War Museum, 1920

Keating, Gavin. *Right Man for the Right Job: Lieutenant General Sir Stanley Savige as a Military Commander.* South (Melbourne: Oxford University Press, 2006

Kriwaczek, P. *Babylon Mesopotamia and the Birth of Civilisation.* (York : Thomas Dunne Books, 2010

Liman von Sanders, Otto., trans. C. Reichmann, *Five Years in Turkey*, Annapolis: United States Naval & Military Press Ltd, 1927

Majd, Mohammad Gholi. *Iraq in World War I: From Ottoman Rule to British Conquest.* Lanham: University Press of America, 2006

Majd, Mohammad Gholi. *Persia in World War I and Its Conquest by Great Britain.* Lanham: University Press of America, 2003

Miles, R. 'The Assyrians: Shock and Awe in Assur' in *Ancient Worlds: the Search for the Origins of Western Civilisation.* London: Penguin Books, 2011

Moberly, Frederick James. *Operations in Persia 1914-1919.* London: HMSO, 1987

Moberly, Frederick James. *The Campaign in Mesopotamia: 1914-18. Historical Section of the Committee of Imperial Defence,* London: His Majesty's Stationery Office, 1927

Nisan, M. *Minorities in the Middle East: A History of Struggle and Self-Expression.* Jefferson McFarland & Co., 1991

Popowski, Jozef. *The Rival Powers in Central Asia: The Struggle Between England and Russia in the East.* A BiblioLife LLC Reproduction, Westminster: Archibald Constable and Company, 1893

Russell, W.E. *There Goes a Man: The Biography of Sir Stanley G. Savige.* (Melbourne: The Dominion Press, 1959

Sabahi, H. *British Policy in Persia 1918-1925.* Portland: Frank Cass Press, 1990

Savige, R.M. *The History of the Savige Family.* Frankston: Verity Hewitt, 1966

Savige, Stanley George. *Stalky's Forlorn Hope.* (Melbourne: Alexander McCubbin, 1920

Sebag Montefiore, Simon. *Titans of History.* London: Quercus, 2012

Serle, Geoffrey. *John Monash: A Biography.* (Melbourne: (Melbourne University Press, 1998

Stafford, R.S. *The Tragedy of the Assyrians.* Assyrian International (s Agency, www.aina.org, 1935

Stephen, Neill. *A History of Christianity in India: The Beginnings to AD 1707.* (York: Cambridge University Press, 1984

Stewart, Alan. *Persian Expedition: The Australians in Dunsterforce.* (Sydney: Australian Military History Publications, 2006, First Published 1938

Sykes, Percy M. *Persia.* Oxford: Clarendon Press, 1922

Toledano, Ehud R. *Slavery and Abolition in the Ottoman Middle East.* Seattle: University of Washington Press, 1996

Travers, Tim. *Gallipoli 1915.* Stroud: Tempus, 2001

Ward, B. Introduction in *The Desert Fathers, Sayings of the Early Christian Monks.* London: Penguin Classics, 2003

Walker Rockwell, William. *The Pitiful Plight of the Assyrian Christians in Persia and Kurdistan.* (York: American Committee for Armenian and Syrian Relief, 1916

Watson, Peter. *The Great Divide: History and Human Nature in the Old World and the (.* London: Phoenix, 2012

Wigram, W.A. *The Cradle of Mankind, Life in Eastern Kurdistan, Second Edition.* London: A & C. Black Ltd, 1922

Wigram, W. A. *Our Smallest Ally: A Brief Account of the Assyrian Nation in the Great War.* London: Macmillan, 1920

Yonan, Gabriele. *Lest We Perish: A Forgotten Holocaust, The Extermination of the Christian Assyrians in Turkey and Persia.* Syriac Studies, online book, 1996

Diaries and Letters

Dwyer, J. Letter to General Paul Pau, 7 December 1918, "John Austin Mahony", (Canberra: National Archives of Australia, Personal Dossier)

Dunsterville, Major General. Lionel Charles, *The Diaries of General Lionel Dunsterville, 1911-1922*

Latchford, E.W. Private Letters, Persia 9 May 1918, State Library Victoria Collections

Savige, Captain Stanley. Personal Diary, Western Front and Dunsterforce Mission, courtesy of Savige Family Private Collection, (Melbourne, 2018)

o o o

Endnotes

1. Stanley George Savige, *Stalky's Forlorn Hope* (Melbourne: Alexander McCubbin, 1920) p5
2. Charles E.W. Bean, *The Australian Imperial Force in France, Volume VI, the Allied Offensive 1918*, First World War Official Histories (Canberra: Australian War Memorial, 1942) pp.750-1
3. Hannibal Travis, *'Resolution on Genocide committed by the Ottoman Empire'* in International Association of Genocide Scholars, Resolutions and Statements, 13th July (2007) http://www.genocidescholars.org/about-us/iags-resolutions-statements (retrieved 15 July 2011)
4. Full Day Hansard Transcript 1 June 2011, Inaugural Speeches, Legislative Assembly, (South Wales Parliament http://www.parliament.nsw.gov.au/Prod/parlment/hanstrans.nsf/V3ByKey/LA20110601 (retrieved 15 July 2011)
5. Savige, *Stalky's Forlorn Hope*, p45
6. Savige, *Stalky's Forlorn Hope*, p47
7. Savige, *Stalky's Forlorn Hope*, p49
8. Savige, *Stalky's Forlorn Hope*, p47
9. Savige, *Stalky's Forlorn Hope*, p47
10. Captain Stanley George Savige, Personal Diary, (Dunsterforce Mission) Entry September 1918, Persia, Savige Family Private Collection, (Melbourne
11. Savige, *Stalky's Forlorn Hope*, p48
12. Savige, *Stalky's Forlorn Hope*, p48

13. Savige, *Stalky's Forlorn Hope*, p52
14. Savige, *Stalky's Forlorn Hope*, p52
15. Savige, *Stalky's Forlorn Hope*, p54
16. Savige, *Stalky's Forlorn Hope*, p54
17. Savige, *Stalky's Forlorn Hope*, p54
18. Savige, *Stalky's Forlorn Hope*, p55
19. Savige, *Stalky's Forlorn Hope*, p54
20. Arianne Ishaya, "History of Assyrians in Urmia", *Journal of Assyrian Academic Studies,* XVI 1 (2002): pp3-4
21. Mohammad Gholi Majd, *Iraq in World War I: From Ottoman Rule to British Conquest* (Lanham: University Press of America, 2006) Caldwell dispatch 419, July 12 1918, p244
22. Mohammad Gholi Majd, *Persia in World War I and Its Conquest by Great Britain* (Lanham: University Press of America, 2003) p31
23. Percy M. Sykes, *Persia* (Oxford: Clarendon Press, 1922) p6-7
24. Rockwell, W.W., 1916 The Pitiful Plight of the Assyrian Christians in Persia and Kurdistan The American Committee for Armenian and Syrian Relief (York p38
25. William Walker Rockwell, *The Pitiful Plight of the Assyrian Christians in Persia and Kurdistan* (York: American Committee for Armenian and Syrian Relief, 1916) pp21-22
26. Rockwell, *The Pitiful Plight of the Assyrian Christians in Persia and Kurdistan,* p38
27. Viscount Bryce presented to Viscount Grey of Falldoon, *The Treatment of Armenians in the Ottoman Empire 1915-1916,* 'The Blue Book' (London: Hodder and Stoughton, 1916) Chapter IV, no. 28
28. Viscount Bryce presented to Viscount Grey of Falldoon, *The Treatment of Armenians in the Ottoman Empire 1915-1916,* 'The Blue Book' (London: Hodder and Stoughton, 1916) Chapter IV, no. 31
29. Savige, *Stalky's Forlorn Hope,* Chapter 33, p53
30. Bryce, *The Treatment of Armenians in the Ottoman Empire 1915-1916*, p105

31. Savige, *Stalky's Forlorn Hope*, Ch.35, p55
32. M. Kenanoglu, *Osmanli Millet Sistemi: Mit ve Gercek* (Istanbul: Klasik Yayinlari, 2007) p5
33. E. and I. Kliszus, *The Assyrian Diaspora a Research Project, 1999* Assyrian International (s Agency, www.aina.org (retrieved 20 June 2011)
34. V. Shumanov, "Mar Binyamin Shimmun", *Zinda Magazine*, vol. X, March 2004
35. Majd, *Iraq in World War I*, p50-54
36. Majd, *Iraq in World War I*, p132
37. Erik Dorn Brose, *A History of the Great War* (York: Oxford University Press, 2010) p103
38. Majd, *Iraq in World War I*, p77-80
39. Dorn Brose, *A History of the Great War*, p160
40. P.K. Davis, *The British Mesopotamian Campaign and Commission* (Toronto: Associate University Presses, 1994) pp18-19
41. W. A. Wigram, *Our Smallest Ally: A Brief Account of the Assyrian Nation in the Great War* (London: Macmillan, 1920) p19
42. Wigram, *Our Smallest Ally*, p20
43. Wigram, *Our Smallest Ally*, p15
44. Rockwell, *The Pitiful Plight of the Assyrian Christians in Persia and Kurdistan*, p38
45. Wigram, *Our Smallest Ally*, p20
46. Wigram, *Our Smallest Ally*, p17
47. Rockwell, *The Pitiful Plight of the Assyrian Christians in Persia and Kurdistan*, p40
48. Rockwell, *The Pitiful Plight of the Assyrian Christians in Persia and Kurdistan*, p41
49. Wigram, *Our Smallest Ally*, p43
50. Wigram, *Our Smallest Ally*, p44
51. Wigram, *Our Smallest Ally*, p26

52. British Parliamentary Debates, House of Lords, 28 November 1933. Vol. 90, No. 4, p142
53. Rockwell, *The Pitiful Plight of the Assyrian Christians in Persia and Kurdistan*, p8
54. Gabriele Yonan, *Lest We Perish: A Forgotten Holocaust, The Extermination of the Christian Assyrians in Turkey and Persia*, 1996 www.syriacstudies.com/2011/04/06/lest-we-perish-a-forgotten-holocaust-the-extermination-of-the-christian-assyrians-in-turkey-and-persiagabriele-yonan, (retrieved 6 April, 2011) p32
55. G. Roper, "George Percy Badger" Bulletin of *British Society for Middle Eastern Studies* vol. 11, No. 2 1984), pp140 -155 Taylor & Francis, http://www.jstor.org/stable/194916 (retrieved 1 August, 2014)
56. Melita Historica, *Journal of the Malta Historical Society* vol.14, 1 (2004) pp67-94 (retrieved 1 August, 2014)
57. George Percy Badger, "Journeying Across Anatolia with Reverend George Percy Badger", Assyrian International (s Agency http://www.aina.org/ata/20091020204546.htm (retrieved 1 August, 2014)
58. R. B. Betts, "The Reverend George Percy Badger and the Syrian Orthodox communities of the Tur Abdin" American Foundation for Syriac Studies; American University of Beirut, www.syriacstudies.com/AFSS/Syriac_Articles_in_ English/Entries/2007 (retrieved 3 June, 2014.)
59. Yonan, *Lest We Perish*, pp23-25
60. Badger, "Journeying Across Anatolia with Reverend George Percy Badger", (retrieved 1 August, 2014)
61. Yonan, *Lest We Perish*, p31
62. Yonan, *Lest We Perish*, Letter from the Nestorian Patriarch to the Archbishop of Canterbury and the Bishop of London after the Massacre of 1843, Mosul, p32.
63. Yonan, *Lest We Perish,* p35
64. Yonan, *Lest We Perish,* Eyewitness Report of British Archaeologist A.H. Layard on the Nestorian Massacre 1843, p37

65. W. Baum and D.W. Winkler, *The Church of the East: A Concise History* (London: Routledge Curzon) p242.
66. Y. Hakan Erdem, *Slavery in the Ottoman Empire and Its Demise, 1800–1909* (York: St. Martin's, 1996) and Ehud R. Toledano, *Slavery and Abolition in the Ottoman Middle East* Seattle: University of Washington Press, 1996)
67. Yonan, *Lest We Perish*, p36
68. Yonan, *Lest We Perish*, pp 38-39
69. Majd, *Iraq in World War I*, p3
70. H. Sabahi, *British Policy in Persia 1918-1925*, (Portland: Frank Cass Press, 1990) p1
71. Baum and Winkler, *The Church of the East*, p242.
72. Yonan, *Lest We Perish*, p37
73. Dorn Brose, *A History of the Great War*, p13
74. Davis, *The British Mesopotamian Campaign and Commission*, p31
75. Yonan, *Lest We Perish*, pp 40-42
76. Wigram, *Our Smallest Ally*, p5
77. H. Travis, "Native Christians Massacred: The Ottoman Genocide of the Assyrians during World War I", *Genocide Studies and Prevention*, vol. 1, no.3 December 2006: p329
78. Dorn Brose, *A History of the Great War*, p31
79. (spaper Documentation of the Assyrian Genocide, *Assyrian Genocide: Assyrian War of Independence* (Memphis: Books LLC, 2010) p37-39
80. Bryce, *The Treatment of the Armenians in the Ottoman Empire*, 1916
81. The National Archives of the United Kingdom, Memorandum CAB/24/48 Colonel Daley-Jones, Political Intelligence Department, October 30, 1918 Turkey, p252
82. Dorn Brose, *A History of the Great War*, p101
83. Jozef Popowski, *The Rival Powers in Central Asia: The Struggle Between England and Russia in the East*, A BiblioLife LLC Reproduction (Westminster: Archibald Constable and Company, 1893) p9-13

84. Robert Gildea, *Barricades and Borders: Europe 1800-1914* (Oxford: Oxford University Press, 1987) p403

85. W.L. Cleveland, *A History of the Modern Middle East* (Boulder: Westview Press, 2004) p144

86. Davis, *The British Mesopotamian Campaign and Commission*, pp35-41

87. "A History of British Petroleum", www.bp.com (retrieved 25 July 2010)

88. M. Abbasov, "The Anglo-American Oil Controversy in Iran 1919-1925", *Journal of Azerbaijani Studies*, vol.1 no.4, (1998) pp1-28 Baku: Khazar University Press

89. Majd, *Iraq in World War I*, p9

90. P.E. McGovern, *Ancient Wine: The Search for the Origins of Viniculture* (Princeton: Princeton University Press, 2013) pp64-84

91. R.S. Stafford, *The Tragedy of the Assyrians*,1935 Assyrian International (s Agency, www.aina.org, (retrieved September 2013) p1-2

92. Sykes, *Persia*, p4

93. Peter Watson, *The Great Divide: History and Human Nature in the Old World and the (* (London: Phoenix, 2012) p271

94. P. Kriwaczek, *Babylon Mesopotamia and the Birth of Civilisation* (York : Thomas Dunne Books,2010) p113

95. Wikipedia. "Aramaeans" http://en.wikipedia.org/wiki/Aramaeans, (retrieved 19 July 2014)

96. Wikipedia. "History of the Assyrian People, http://en.wikipedia.org/wiki/History_of_the_Assyrian_people (retrieved 20 July 2014)

97. R. Miles, 'The Assyrians: Shock and Awe in Assur' in *Ancient Worlds: the Search for the Origins of Western Civilisation* (London: Penguin Books, 2011)

98. R.J. Clifford, *The Cosmic Mountain in Canaan and the Old Testament* (Cambridge: Harvard University Press, 1972)

99. Kriwaczek, *Babylon Mesopotamia and the Birth of Civilisation*, p7

100. Wikipedia. "Ashurbanipal" https://wikipedia.org (retrieved 2 July 2012)

101. Wikipedia. "Ashurbanipal' https://wikipedia.org (retrieved 2 July 2012)

102. Kriwaczek, *Babylon Mesopotamia and the Birth of Civilisation*, p207

103. Neill Stephen, *A History of Christianity in India: The Beginnings to AD 1707* (York: Cambridge University Press, 1984): pp43-45

104. F.L. Cross, ed. *Liturgy of Addai and Mari*, in The Oxford Dictionary of the Christian Church (Oxford: Oxford University Press, 2005)

105. B. Ward, 'Introduction' in *The Desert Fathers, Sayings of the Early Christian Monks* (London: Penguin Classics, 2003)

106. S.A. Millick "Mar Thoma: The Apostolic Foundation of the Assyrian Church and the Christians of St. Thomas in India", *Journal of Assyrian Academic Studies* vol. XIV, no. 2, (2000): p33

107. Yonan, *Lest We Perish*, p12

108. P. Gavrilyuk, "Theopatheia: Nestorius's Main Charge against Cyril of Alexandria", *Scottish Journal of Theology* no.56 (2003): pp190-207

109. N. Cameron, *Barbarians & Mandarins: Thirteen Centuries of Western Travellers in China* (York: Walker/ Weatherhill, 1970) pp 17-27.

110. Yonan, *Lest We Perish*, p14

111. Yonan, *Lest We Perish*, p15-17

112. World Digital Library, "Six Essays from the Book of Commentaries on Euclid", https://www.wdl.org (retrieved June 9th, 2014)

113. Simon Sebag Montefiore, *Titans of History* (London: Quercus, 2012) p154

114. J. Darwin, *After Tamerlane, the Rise & Fall of Global Empires, 1400-2000* (London: Penguin Books, 2008) pp4-5

115. Yonan, *Lest We Perish*, p17

116. Yonan, *Lest We Perish*, p18

117. Wikipedia, "Dioceses of the Church of the East, 1552-1913". www.wikipedia.org (retrieved October 18th, 2014)

118. Yonan, *Lest We Perish*, p18

119. Wigram, *Our Smallest Ally*, p50

120. Wigram, *Our Smallest Ally*, p49

121. W.A. Wigram, *The Cradle of Mankind, Life in Eastern Kurdistan, Second Edition*, (London: A & C. Black Ltd, 1922) pp218-220

122. Keast Burke, ed. *With Horse and Morse in Mesopotamia: The Story of Anzacs in Asia* (Sydney: Arthur McQuitty & Co, 1927) p106

123. Lionel Charles Dunsterville, *The Diaries of General Lionel Dunsterville, 1911-1922*, Entry 18 July 1918

124. Shumanov, "Mar Binyamin Shimmun".

125. Savige, *Stalky's Forlorn Hope*, p45

126. W.J. Harvey, *The Red and White Diamond: Authorised History of the 24th Battalion Australian Imperial Force*, (East Sussex: Naval and Military Press, in association with the Imperial War Museum, 1920) p205

127. AWM Dunsterforce File, Miscellaneous Papers, Series no. AWM224

128. AWM, Dunsterforce File, Series No. AWM224

129. C.E.W. Bean, *The Australian Imperial Force in France in 1917*, (Sydney: Angus and Roberson, 1933)

130. W.E. Russell, *There Goes a Man: The Biography of Sir Stanley G. Savige* (Melbourne: The Dominion Press, 1959) p93

131. Captain Stanley Savige, Personal Diary, (Dunsterforce Mission), Entry January 1918, Savige Family Private Collection, Melbourne, 2011.

132. Savige, *Stalky's Forlorn Hope* ,p5

133. Savige, *Stalky's Forlorn Hope*, p23

134. Bean, *The Australian Imperial Force in France in 1917*, p.729

135. AWM, Dunsterforce File, Series No. AWM224

136. Savige, *Stalky's Forlorn Hope*, p5

137. Dorn Brose, *A History of the Great War*, p342-343

138. Savige, *Stalky's Forlorn Hope*, p5

139. Savige, *Stalky's Forlorn Hope*, p25

140. Savige, *Stalky's Forlorn Hope*, p25

141. C.E.W. Bean, *Official History of Australia in the War of 1914 – 1918, Volume V*, (Brisbane: University of Queensland Press, 1983) p1

142. Savige, *Stalky's Forlorn Hope* p25

143. Savige, *Stalky's Forlorn Hope* p25

144. Savige, *Stalky's Forlorn Hope* p25
145. Alan Stewart, *Persian Expedition: The Australians in Dunsterforce* (Sydney: Australian Military History Publications, 2006, First Published 1938), p18
146. Stewart, *Persian Expedition*, p33
147. Savige, *Stalky's Forlorn Hope*, pp22-23
148. Russell, *There Goes a Man*, p26
149. R.M. Savige, *The History of the Savige Family* (Frankston: Verity Hewitt, 1966) p5
150. Savige, *The History of the Savige Family*, p25-31
151. Savige, *The History of the Savige Family*, p26-29
152. Savige, *The History of the Savige Family*, p29-33
153. Savige, *The History of the Savige Family*, p38
154. Russell, *There Goes a Man*, p16
155. Russell, *There Goes a Man*, p17
156. S.M. Legg, *Heart of the Valley: A History of the Morwell Municipality* Morwell Shire Council, 1992 p121
157. Legg, *Heart of the Valley*, p121
158. Russell, *There Goes a Man*, p19
159. John Hetherington, "Savige, the man's man," in *The Argus*, 17 May 1954
160. Russell, *There Goes a Man*, p24
161. Russell, *There Goes a Man*, p25
162. Russell, *There Goes a Man*, p30
163. Russell, *There Goes a Man*, p31
164. Russell, *There Goes a Man*, p31
165. Russell, *There Goes a Man*, p31
166. Russell, *There Goes a Man*, p33
167. Harvey, *The Red and White Diamond*, p13
168. Russell, *There Goes a Man*, p33
169. Lieutenant General Savige's Service Records and Citations, CARO

170. AWM, Embarkation Record, AIF Nominal Roll, HMAS Euripides, 1915.
171. Harvey, *The Red and White Diamond*, p16
172. Russell, *There Goes a Man*, p34
173. Bean, *Official History of Australia in the War of 1914–1918 vol.1*, Ch. VII Training in the Desert, p116
174. Bean, *Official History of Australia in the War of 1914–1918 vol.1*, Ch. VII Training in the Desert, p118-119
175. Russell, *There Goes a Man*, p36
176. Russell, *There Goes a Man*, p35
177. Russell, *There Goes a Man*, p37
178. Les Carlyon, "Robert Rhodes James", in *Gallipoli*, (Sydney: Pan Macmillan, 2001) p336
179. AWM4-23/41/1, A.I.F. Unit War Diary 1914-18, 24th Infantry Battalion, August 1915
180. AWM4-23/41/2, A.I.F. Unit War Diary 1914-18, 24th Infantry Battalion, September 1915
181. Special Army Corps Orders, in *The ANZAC Book*, (Melbourne: Sun Books, 1975) p153
182. Russell, *There Goes a Man*, p39
183. Psalm 91, The Holy Bible, King James Version (London: Collins Clear Type Press)
184. Harvey, *The Red and White Diamond*, p25
185. Harvey, *The Red and White Diamond*, p26
186. Harvey, *The Red and White Diamond*, p26
187. Bean, *Official History of Australia in the War of 1914–1918 vol. 1*, Chapter VII, p527
188. Geoffrey Serle, *John Monash: A Biography* (Melbourne: Melbourne University Press, 1998) pp219-220
189. Carlyon, *Gallipoli*, p338-39

190. Martin Gilbert, *The First World War: A Complete History* (New York: Henry Holt & Company, 1994) p180-183

191. Tim Travers, *Gallipoli 1915*, (Stroud: Tempus, 2001) p21

192. Travers, *Gallipoli 1915*, p32

193. Dorn Brose, *A History of the Great War*, p164

194. Gilbert, *The First World War*, p152

195. Otto Liman von Sanders, trans. C. Reichmann, *Five Years in Turkey*, (Annapolis: United States Naval & Military Press Ltd, 1927) p58

196. Russell, *There Goes a Man*, Letter to Lillian Stockton 12 September 1915.

197. AWM4-23/41/2, A.I.F. Unit War Diary 1914-18, 24th Infantry Battalion, September 1915

198. Harvey, *The Red and White Diamond*, p25

199. Harvey, *The Red and White Diamond*, p43

200. The Indian Mule Corps by B.R. in The ANZAC Book, written by the Men of ANZAC, (Melbourne: Sun Books, 1915) p50.

201. Harvey,, *The Red and White Diamond*, p42

202. Harvey, *The Red and White Diamond*, p43

203. Harvey, *The Red and White Diamond*, p31

204. Harvey, *The Red and White Diamond*, p36-37

205. Russell, *There Goes a Man*, p49

206. Bean, *Official History of Australia in the War of 1914–1918 – vol.2, Ch. XXIX The Onset of Winter*, p840

207. Harvey, *The Red and White Diamond*, p37

208. Dorn Brose, *A History of the Great War*, p211

209. Bean, *Official History of Australia in the War of 1914–1918 – vol.2, Ch. XXX The Evacuation*, p853

210. Bean, *Official History of Australia in the War of 1914–1918 – vol.2, Ch. XXIX The Onset of Winter*, p843

211. Stanley G. Savige, "Lone Pine Sector", *Reveille*, 1, December, 1932): p8

212. AWM4-23/41/4, A.I.F. Unit War Diary 1914-18, 24th Infantry Battalion, November 1915
213. Bean, *Official History of Australia in the War of 1914–1918 – vol.2, Ch. XXIX The Onset of Winter*, p844
214. Gavin Keating, *Right Man for the Right Job: Lieutenant General Sir Stanley Savige as a Military Commander,* South (Melbourne: Oxford University Press, 2006) p3
215. AWM4-23/41/4, A.I.F. Unit War Diary 1914-18, 24th Infantry Battalion, November 1915
216. Harvey *The Red and White Diamond*, p39
217. Harvey *The Red and White Diamond*, p39
218. Russell, *There Goes a Man*, p49
219. Carlyon, *Gallipoli*, p519
220. Harvey, *The Red and White Diamond*, p50
221. Savige, "Lone Pine Sector", p9
222. Harvey, *The Red and White Diamond*, p57
223. Savige, "Lone Pine Sector", p9
224. Harvey, *The Red and White Diamond*, p51
225. Savige, "Lone Pine Sector", p9
226. Russell, *There Goes a Man*, p52
227. Russell, *There Goes a Man*, p53
228. Savige, "Lone Pine Sector", p8
229. Savige, "Lone Pine Sector", p9
230. AWM4-23/41/5, A.I.F. Unit War Diary 1914-18, 24th Infantry Battalion, December 1915
231. Psalm 91, The Holy Bible
232. Russell, *There Goes a Man*, p56
233. Russell, *There Goes a Man*, p58 Letters to Lillian Stockton, 31 March, 1916 and 11 April, 1916
234. Harvey, *The Red and White Diamond*, p72

235. Bean, *The Australian Imperial Force in France in 1916, vol. 3, Ch. III Move to the Front*, p93
236. Bean, *The Australian Imperial Force in France in 1916, vol. 3, Ch. III Move to the Front*, p94
237. Harvey, *The Red and White Diamond*, p71
238. Bean, *The Australian Imperial Force in France in 1916, vol. 3, Ch. III Move to the Front*, p131
239. Bean, *The Australian Imperial Force in France in 1916, vol. 3, Ch. III Move to the Front*, p95
240. Russell, *There Goes a Man*, p60
241. Harvey, *The Red and White Diamond*, p73
242. Harvey, *The Red and White Diamond*, p75
243. Harvey, *The Red and White Diamond*, p78-79
244. Russell, *There Goes a Man*, pp61-62
245. AWM4-23/41/9, A.I.F. War Diary 1914-18 War 24th Infantry Battalion, June 1916
246. Harvey, *The Red and White Diamond*, p85
247. Harvey, *The Red and White Diamond*, p87
248. Harvey, *The Red and White Diamond*, p91-92
249. Harvey, *The Red and White Diamond*, p95
250. Harvey, *The Red and White Diamond*, p98
251. Harvey, *The Red and White Diamond*, p101
252. Quail John Gellibrand's (nom de plume), "Celebrities of the AIF: Brigadier Savige", in *Reveille*, no. 103, May (1939)
253. Carlyon, *Gallipoli*, p177
254. Bean, *The Australian Imperial Force in France in 1916, vol. 3, Ch. XXIV The effects of Pozieres and The rest at Ypres*, p862
255. AWM4-23/6/12, A.I.F. War Diary 1914-18 War 6th Infantry Brigade, August 1916
256. National Archives of Australia (NAA), Officers List of the Australian Military Forces, War Services Supplement, Issued 1 April 1920.
257. Russell, *There Goes a Man*, p76

258. Harvey, *The Red and White Diamond*, p120-121
259. AWM4-23/6/15, A.I.F. War Diary 1914-18 War 6th Infantry Brigade, November 1916
260. Service Record, 6231496), Casualty Form for Stanley George Savige, NAA.
261. AWM4-23/41/17, A.I.F. War Diary 1914-18 War 24th Infantry Battalion, February 1917
262. Harvey, *The Red and White Diamond*, p140
263. Harvey, *The Red and White Diamond*, p145
264. Russell, *There Goes a Man*, p80
265. Wikipedia, "The Battle of Arras", http://www.wikipedia.org (retrieved 2 November 2010)
266. S. G. Savige, "A soldier's Battle: Second Bullecourt", in *Reveille*, May (1933), p7
267. Savige, "A soldier's Battle: Second Bullecourt", p32
268. Carlyon, *Gallipoli*, p373
269. Savige, "A soldier's Battle: Second Bullecourt", p32
270. Savige, "A soldier's Battle: Second Bullecourt", p32
271. Carlyon, *Gallipoli*, p373- 382
272. Quail, "Celebrities of the A.I.F", p.8
273. Harvey, *The Red and White Diamond*, p160
274. AWM, Stanley George Savige, Mentioned in Dispatches, No. 3121, 1st Anzac Corps, May 11th, 1917
275. Harvey, *The Red and White Diamond*, p162
276. Harvey, *The Red and White Diamond*, p165
277. AWM4-23/41/22, A.I.F. War Diary 1914-18 War 24th Infantry Battalion, July 1917
278. Russell *There Goes a Man*, p91
279. Savige, "A soldier's Battle: Second Bullecourt", p32
280. Service Record, no. 6231496, Army Form W.3121, Stanley George Savige, NAA

281. Russell, *There Goes a Man*, Letter to Lillian Stockton 16 September 1917, p92
282. Harvey, *The Red and White Diamond*, p205
283. Stewart, *Persian Expedition*, p34
284. Savige, *Stalky's Forlorn Hope*, p6
285. Savige, *Stalky's Forlorn Hope*, p6-7
286. Savige, *Stalky's Forlorn Hope*, p6-7
287. The Ship's List. "The Nile" http://www.theshipslist.com (retrieved 05 May 2010)
288. British National Maritime Museum, Royal Museums Greenwich Collections, "Report of the Board of Directors of the Peninsular and Oriental Steam Navigation Company, 1900" www.rmg.co.uk (retrieved 18 June 2011)
289. Stewart, *Persian Expedition*, 39
290. Stewart, *Persian Expedition*, p40
291. Savige, *Stalky's Forlorn Hope*, p6-7
292. Stewart, *Persian Expedition*, p43
293. Frederick James Moberly, *The Campaign in Mesopotamia: 1914-18, Historical Section of the Committee of Imperial Defence* (London: His Majesty's Stationery Office, 1927) p97-98
294. Moberly, *The Campaign in Mesopotamia: 1914-18*, p98
295. Savige, *Stalky's Forlorn Hope*, p7
296. Savige, *Stalky's Forlorn Hope*, p8
297. Savige, *Stalky's Forlorn Hope*, p11
298. Savige, *Stalky's Forlorn Hope*, p9
299. Stewart, *Persian Expedition*, p49
300. Burke, *With Horse and Morse in Mesopotamia*, p105
301. Stanley George Savige, "Epic of Dunsterforce", in *Reveille* vol.5, no.4 December (1931), p3
302. Moberly, *The Campaign in Mesopotamia*, p85
303. Russell, *There Goes a Man*, p96

304. Savige, *Stalky's Forlorn Hope*, p11-12
305. Savige, *Stalky's Forlorn Hope*, p15
306. Burke, *With Horse and Morse in Mesopotamia*, p90
307. Savige, *Stalky's Forlorn Hope*, p16
308. Burke, *With Horse and Morse in Mesopotamia*, p105
309. Majd, *Persia in World War I and Its Conquest by Great Britain*, p150
310. Burke, *With Horse and Morse in Mesopotamia*, p93
311. E.W. Latchford, Private Letters, Persia 9 May 1918, State Library Victoria Collections
312. Majd, *Persia in World War I and Its Conquest by Great Britain*, p193
313. Savige, *Stalky's Forlorn Hope*, p17
314. Savige, *Stalky's Forlorn Hope*, p18
315. Savige, *Stalky's Forlorn Hope*, p19
316. Savige, *Stalky's Forlorn Hope*, p20
317. Savige, *Stalky's Forlorn Hope*, p2
318. Stewart, *Persian Expedition*, p20-22
319. Russell, *There Goes a Man*, p101
320. Lionel Charles Dunsterville, *The Diaries of General Lionel Dunsterville, 1911-1922*, (1917 and 1918) www.gwpda.org (retrieved 3 February 2010)
321. Dunsterville, *The Diaries of General Lionel Dunsterville*, Entry December 1917
322. Lionel Charles Dunsterville, *The Adventures of Dunsterforce*, (London: Edward Arnold, 1920) p9
323. Dunsterville, *The Diaries of General Lionel Dunsterville*, Entry January, 1918
324. Majd, *Persia in World War I and Its Conquest by Great Britain*, p219-22
325. Majd, *Persia in World War I and Its Conquest by Great Britain*, p55-56
326. Majd, *Persia in World War I and Its Conquest by Great Britain*, p244 Caldwell Dispatch 12 July
327. Dunsterville, *The Adventures of Dunsterforce*, p3.
328. Savige, *Stalky's Forlorn Hope*, p3

329. Dunsterville, *The Adventures of Dunsterforce*, p25.
330. Dunsterville, *The Adventures of Dunsterforce*, p29.
331. Dunsterville, *The Adventures of Dunsterforce*, p71
332. Moberley, *The Campaign in Mesopotamia: 1914-18*, p289 - 291
333. Dunsterville, *The Diaries of General Lionel Dunsterville*, Entry 28 May, 1918
334. Dunsterville, *The Diaries of General Lionel Dunsterville*, Entry 2 May, 1918
335. Dorn Brose, *A History of the Great War*, p344
336. Stewart, *Persian Expedition*, p84
337. Savige, *Stalky's Forlorn Hope*, p25
338. Savige, *Stalky's Forlorn Hope*, p25
339. Russell, *There Goes a Man*, p104
340. Stewart, *Persian Expedition*, p 96
341. Savige, *Stalky's Forlorn Hope*, p30
342. Dunsterville, *The Adventures of Dunsterforce*, p75
343. Moberly, *Operations in Persia 1914-1919*, p323
344. Dunsterville, *The Adventures of Dunsterforce*, p101
345. Dunsterville, *The Adventures of Dunsterforce*, p99
346. Dunsterville, *The Adventures of Dunsterforce*, p100
347. Savige, *Stalky's Forlorn Hope*, p55
348. Majd, *Persia in World War I and Its Conquest by Great Britain*, pp248-250
349. Savige, *Stalky's Forlorn Hope*, p55
350. Savige, *Stalky's Forlorn Hope*, p55
351. Stewart, *Persian Expedition*, p106
352. Savige, *Stalky's Forlorn Hope*, p56
353. Savige, *Stalky's Forlorn Hope*, p56
354. Savige, *Stalky's Forlorn Hope*, p57
355. Savige, *Stalky's Forlorn Hope*, p58
356. Savige, *Stalky's Forlorn Hope*, p59

357. Savige, *Stalky's Forlorn Hope*, p60
358. Savige, *Stalky's Forlorn Hope*, p61
359. Savige, *Stalky's Forlorn Hope*, p63
360. Savige, *Stalky's Forlorn Hope*, p62
361. Savige, *Stalky's Forlorn Hope*, p63
362. Savige, *Stalky's Forlorn Hope*, p62
363. Savige, *Stalky's Forlorn Hope*, p64
364. Russell, *There Goes a Man*, p116
365. Savige, *Stalky's Forlorn Hope*, p63
366. Savige, *Stalky's Forlorn Hope*, p64
367. Savige, *Personal Diary*, Sheet 19, Dunsterforce Papers, September 1918
368. Savige, *Stalky's Forlorn Hope*, p66
369. Savige, *Stalky's Forlorn Hope*, p65
370. The National Archives of the United Kingdom, Memorandum CAB/24/48 Colonel Daley-Jones, Political Intelligence Department, October 30, 1918, Turkey p253
371. Savige, *Stalky's Forlorn Hope*, p68
372. Savige, *Stalky's Forlorn Hope*, p68
373. Savige, *Stalky's Forlorn Hope*, p69
374. Savige, *Stalky's Forlorn Hope*, p70
375. Savige, *Stalky's Forlorn Hope*, p72
376. Savige, *Stalky's Forlorn Hope*, p72
377. Savige, *Stalky's Forlorn Hope*, p72
378. Savgie, "Epic of the Dunsterforce", p32
379. Russell, *There Goes a Man*, p120
380. Gilbert, *The First World War*, p497
381. Harvey, *The Red and White Diamond*, p301
382. National Archives of Australia, Letter J Dwyer, Wangaratta, to General Paul Pau, 7 December 1918, John Austin Mahony, personal dossier) http://www.

wwlwesternfront.gov.au/bellenglise/calvaire-cemetery-montbrehain/captains-fletcher-and-mahony.php (retrieved 20 July 2016)

383. Harvey, *The Red and White Diamond*, p309
384. NAA, Service and Casualty Form, 24th Infantry Battalion, 28 October 1918, Basrah, Baghdad G.H.Q.
385. Gilbert, *The First World War*, p493
386. Gilbert, *The First World War*, p488
387. G. Buchanan, *The Tragedy of Mesopotamia* (London: William Blackwood & Sons, 1938) p199-200
388. National Archives of Australia, Service and Casualty Form, 24th Infantry Battalion, 28 October 1918, Basrah, Baghdad G.H.Q.
389. Dunsterville, *The Diaries of General Lionel Dunsterville*, Entry 5 and 8 December, 1918
390. Dunsterville, *The Diaries of General Lionel Dunsterville*, Entry 5 and 8 December, 1918
391. Dunsterville, *The Diaries of General Lionel Dunsterville*, Entry 31 July, 1918
392. B. Gokay, "The Battle for Baku: A peculiar episode in the history of the Caucasus", *Middle Eastern Studies*, vol.34, Issue 1, (1998): p30-50
393. Dorn Brose, *A History of the Great War*, p453
394. Dunsterville, *Adventures of Dunsterforce*, p 124
395. Stewart, *Persian Expedition*, p113
396. Savige, "The Epic of Dunsterforce", p32
397. Dunsterville, *The Diaries of General Lionel Dunsterville*, Entry 19 August, 1918
398. Dunsterville, *Adventures of Dunsterforce*, p151
399. Gokay, "The Battle for Baku: A peculiar episode in the history of the Caucasus", p11
400. Dunsterville, *The Diaries of General Lionel Dunsterville*, Entry 9 September, 1918
401. Dunsterville, *Adventures of Dunsterforce*, p168

402. Dunsterville, *The Diaries of General Lionel Dunsterville*, Entry 1 September, 1918
403. Stewart, *Persian Expedition*, p127
404. Dunsterville, *The Diaries of General Lionel Dunsterville*, Entry 5 December, 1918
405. Savige, *Stalky's Forlorn Hope*, p74-75
406. Lieutenant General Savige's Service Records and Citations, London Gazette Second Supplement no. 31583, 4 October 1919, CARO
407. Bean, *The Australian Imperial Force in France During the Main German Offensive*, 1918, pp.750-1
408. Psalm 55, The Holy Bible, King James Version,
409. The National Archives of the United Kingdom, October 30, 1918 Memorandum CAB/24/48 Colonel Daley-Jones, Political Intelligence Department, Turkey p252
410. Majd, *Persia in World War One*, p249
411. Majd, *Persia in World War One*, p249
412. The National Archives of the United Kingdom, October 30, 1918 Memorandum CAB/24/48 Colonel Daley-Jones, Political Intelligence Department, Turkey p252
413. Wigram, *Our Smallest Ally*, p59
414. Herbert Henry Austin, *The Baqubah Refugee Camp: An Account of Work on Behalf of the Persecuted Assyrian Christians*, (London: The Faith Press, 1920)
415. Majd, *Iraq in World War I From Ottoman Rule to British Conquest*, p317
416. Stafford, *The Tragedy of the Assyrians*, Ch. III Refugees, p15
417. Stafford, *The Tragedy of the Assyrians*, Ch. III Refugees, p15-16
418. Austin, *The Baqubah Refugee Camp*, 1920
419. Annemasse, (Nom de plume) *The Assyrian Tragedy*, February 1934, online book, www.aina.org, Ch.5, points 35-36
420. The National Archives of the United Kingdom, Eastern Report, Memorandum CAB/24/145 Colonel Sykes, Political Intelligence Department, December 26, 1918, Turkey, p4

421. Stafford, *The Tragedy of the Assyrians*, Ch. III Refugees, p16
422. A. Link, ed., *The Papers of Woodrow Wilson, vol. 45, November 11 1917 – January 15, 1918* Princeton, NJ, 1984) pp534-539
423. Stafford, *The Tragedy of the Assyrians*, Chapter IV: The Settlements in Iraq.
424. Rockwell, *The Pitiful Plight of the Assyrian Christians in Persia and Kurdistan*, p60
425. Austin, *The Tragedy of the Assyrians*, Chapter IV: The Settlements in Iraq, p2
426. Stafford, *The Tragedy of the Assyrians*, Chapter VI: The Assyrians and the League, p5
427. Stafford, *The Tragedy of the Assyrians*, Chapter VI: The Assyrians and the League, p3
428. Frederick Cunliffe-Owen, *British Policy in Assyrian Settlement*, compiled for the British Colonial Office formerly the India Office, 1919, p342
429. Robert DeKelaita, "The Origins and Development of Assyrian Nationalism", MA Thesis, University of Chicago, 1964 online document, www.aina.org (retrieved 20 August 2010)
430. Cunliffe-Owen, *British Policy in Assyrian Settlement*, p345
431. Wikipedia. "British Mandate of Mesopotamia", http://en.wikipedia.org (retrieved 30/5/2011
432. Cunliffe-Owen, *British Policy in Assyrian Settlement*, p109
433. Annemasse, *The Assyrian Tragedy*, Chapter 5, point 39
434. Stafford, *The Tragedy of the Assyrians*, Chapter VII: The Mar Shimmun
435. B. Simsir, "Lozan Telegraflari", *Türk Tarih Kurumu*, vol. 1, no.353, January 15, 1923 Ankara, The Turkish Historical Society 1990): http://www.atour.com (retrieved 11 July 2016)
436. B. Simsir, "Lozan Telegraflari", *Türk Tarih Kurumu* vol. 2, no. 368 January 18, 1923, Ankara, The Turkish Historical Society 1994) http://www.atour.com (retrieved 11 July 2016)
437. Erik Goldstein, *The First World War Peace Settlements 1919-1925*, (London: Longman Pearson Education, 2002) p64
438. Stafford, *The Tragedy of the Assyrians*, p8

439. Stafford, *The Tragedy of the Assyrians*, p2
440. Stafford, *The Tragedy of the Assyrians*, p10
441. Stafford, *The Tragedy of the Assyrians*, p3
442. Stafford, *The Tragedy of the Assyrians*, p2
443. Wikipedia, "Assyrian Independence, Constantinople Conference" http://wikipedia.org (retrieved 1 June 2011)
444. R. Donef, *The Hakkari Massacres Ethnic Cleansing by Turkey 1924-1925* (Sydney: Tatavla Publishing, 2014) p23-24
445. League of Nations Documents and Serial Publications 1919-1946 https://www.microformguides.gale.com/Data/Download/3028000R.pdf
446. Goldstein, *The First World War Peace Settlements 1919-1925*, p64
447. Stafford, *The Tragedy of the Assyrians*, p3
448. Cunliffe-Owen, *British Policy in Assyrian Settlement*, p348
449. Stafford, *The Tragedy of the Assyrians*, Chapter IX: The Affair of Yacu, p3
450. Stafford, *The Tragedy of the Assyrians*, Chapter X: The Syrian Adventure, p1
451. Stafford, *The Tragedy of the Assyrians*, Chapter XIV: The Future of the Assyrians, p1
452. Stafford, *The Tragedy of the Assyrians*, Chapter X: The Syrian Adventure, p6
453. Stafford, *The Tragedy of the Assyrians*, Chapter XI: The August Massacres, p6
454. Cunliffe-Owen, *British Policy in Assyrian Settlement*, p308
455. Stafford, *The Tragedy of the Assyrians*, Chapter XI: The August Massacres, p9-12
456. Cunliffe-Owen, *British Policy in Assyrian Settlement*, p313
457. Stafford, *The Tragedy of the Assyrians*, Chapter XI: The August Massacres, p9-12
458. Stafford, *The Tragedy of the Assyrians*, Chapter XII: The Looting of the Villages, p2
459. John Cooper, *Raphael Lemkin and the Struggle for the Genocide Convention* (London: Palgrave Macmillan, 2008)

460. Stafford, *The Tragedy of the Assyrians*, Chapter XIV: The Future of the Assyrians, p6-7
461. Wikipedia. "Shimun XXIII Eshai", https://wikipedia.org (retrieved 30 June 2015)
462. Cunliffe-Owen, *British Policy in Assyrian Settlement*, p347 and League of Nations Document, C 400 M. 147, 1925, VII, p. 490
463. Goldstein, *The First World War Peace Settlements 1919-1925*, p32
464. Russell, *There Goes a Man*, pp 120-122
465. Keating, *The Right Man for the Right Job*, p15
466. Russell, *There Goes a Man*, p123
467. Anderson, "The Origin and Growth of the Legacy Movement in Australia", *The Victorian Historical Magazine*, (1967): p.134
468. Russell, *There Goes a Man*, p131
469. M.H. Ellis, *The Torch: A Picture of Legacy* (Melbourne: Angus and Robertson, 1957) p8
470. Mark Lyons, *Legacy: the first fifty years* (Melbourne: Lothian, 1978) for Legacy Coordinating Council, p17
471. Russell, *There Goes a Man*, p128
472. "The Second AIF, Commanders and Staff", *Reveille*, 1 November 1939): p16
473. AWM, Recommendation for the Award of the Efficiency Decoration, 19 November 1939, CRS P, 1535,748181237
474. Russell, *There Goes a Man*, p145
475. Russell, *There Goes a Man*, p187-188
476. Russell, *There Goes a Man*, p203
477. NAA, Officers Service Record, Item no. 6231496 Stanley George Savige www.awm.gov.au (retrieved 20 May 2011)
478. Russell, *There Goes a Man*, p222
479. Gavin Long, "Greece, Crete and Syria. Australia in the War of 1939–1945." Canberra: AWM, 1954) http://www.awm.gov.au (retrieved 15 May 2011)
480. Keating, *The Right Man for the Right Job*, p166

481. NAA, Officers Service Record, Item no.6231496. Stanley George Savige www.awm.gov.au (retrieved 20/5/11)
482. Russell, *There Goes a Man*, p234
483. Russell, *There Goes a Man*, p246
484. Russell, *There Goes a Man*, p248
485. John Herrington, *Blamey, Controversial Soldier: a Biography of Field Marshal Sir Thomas Blamey* (Canberra: Australian War Memorial, 1973) p193-94
486. Russell, *There Goes a Man*, p249
487. Russell, *There Goes a Man*, p250
488. Keating, *The Right Man for the Right Job*, p86
489. AWM52-8/2/17, 2nd A.I.F. War Diary 1939-45 War, 17th Infantry Brigade, October 1942
490. Keating, *The Right Man for the Right Job*, p100
491. Herrington, *Blamey, Controversial Soldier: a Biography of Field Marshal Sir Thomas Blamey*, p315
492. Russell, *There Goes a Man*, p261-62
493. Keating, *The Right Man for the Right Job*, p125
494. London Gazette: Supplement no. 36251, p. 5061, Stanley George Savige, 18 November 1943.
495. AWM 3DRL 2529 53, Savige Papers, II Corps Report on Operational and Administrative Activities 10 April 1944 – 30 September 1944,
496. Long, "Greece, Crete and Syria. Australia in the War of 1939–1945.", p558 and Russell, *There Goes a Man*, p299
497. Letter, Blamey to Savige, 24th January 1946, AWM 3DRL6643, Item 2/136.45
498. Keating, *The Right Man for the Right Job*, 'The Last Post'
499. Australian Dictionary of Biography. http://adbonline.anu.edu.au and NAA, Service and Casualty Record Form, Item 6231496, (retrieved 20 May 2011)
500. D. Horner, *General Vasey's War*, (Melbourne: Melbourne University Press, 1992) p559

501. *The Argus*, Melbourne, 8th June 1950, National Library of Australia, http://trove.nla.gov.au (retrieved 20 May 2011)

502. Russell, *There Goes a Man*, p304

503. Lyons, *Legacy: the first fifty years*, p144

504. Russell, *There Goes a Man*, p288

505. Lyons, *Legacy: the first fifty years*, p146

506. Keating, *The Right Man for the Right Job, 'The Last Post'*

507. Russell, *There Goes a Man*, p308

508. United Nations News Centre http://www.un.org/apps/ (retrieved August 14, 2014)

509. Letter written by Patriarch Mar Dinkha IV to United Nations Secretary General, 'Unrepresented Nations and Peoples' Organisation', http://unpo.org/article/17414 (retrieved August 2014)

510. J.E. Lewis, "The Barometer of Pluralism" in *Middle East Quarterly* (2003): p54 Middle East Forum, https://scholar.google.com.au (retrieved April 2013)

511. 'Continuous and Silent Ethnic Cleansing', International Federation of Human Rights & Alliance Internationale pour la Justice, Iraq, January 2003, http://www.fidh.org (retrieved March 2014)

512. M. Leezenberg, "The Anfal Operations in Iraqi Kurdistan" in *Century of Genocide: Critical Essays and Eyewitness Accounts*, eds S. Totten, and W. S Parsons, p388

513. 'Continuous and Silent Ethnic Cleansing', International Federation of Human Rights & Alliance Internationale pour la Justice, Iraq. January 2003, http://www.fidh.org (retrieved March 2014)

514. Leezenberg, "The Anfal Operations in Iraqi Kurdistan", p386-388

515. Human Rights Watch, Report, 'Genocide in Iraq: The Anfal Campaign Against the Kurds', p317 and Human Rights Watch, 'Iraq's Crime of Genocide', 1995 p. 209. www.hrw.org

516. M. Nisan, *Minorities in the Middle East: A History of Struggle and Self-Expression* (Jefferson McFarland & Co., 1991) p166

517. Leezenberg, "The Anfal Operations in Iraqi Kurdistan", p388
518. Hannibal Travis, "Native Christians Massacred: The Ottoman Genocide of the Assyrians during World War I" *Genocide Studies and Prevention* 1, 3 December 2006): 327-371, p346 and The British House of Lords Early Day Motion #922 'Halabja Gas Attack and Anfal Campaign Anniversary' 2 March 2009 http://www.parliament.uk/edm/2008-09/922 (retrieved 17 Jun 2011)
519. J.E. Lewis, "The Barometer of Pluralism", p53
520. M. Lalani, "Still Targeted: Continued Persecution of Iraq's Minorities", Minority Rights Group International, 2010 Report, p3
521. Travis, "Native Christians Massacred: The Ottoman Genocide of the Assyrians during World War I", p347
522. Lalani, "Still Targeted: Continued Persecution of Iraq's Minorities", Minority Rights Group International, 2010 Report, p5
523. Amnesty International, "Iraq Civilians Under Fire", April 2010 Report, p5 and p13
524. 'Kidnapped Iraqi Archbishop dead', BBC News, 13 March 2008, http://www.news.bbc.co.uk (retrieved 23 June 2011)
525. Lalani, "Still Targeted: Continued Persecution of Iraq's Minorities", p3
526. Mohktar Lamani, "Minorities in Iraq: the Other Victims", Special Report of the Centre for International Governance Innovation, Ontario, Canada, (2009) www.cigionline.org
527. Lamani, "Minorities in Iraq: the Other Victims", p5
528. Lamani, "Minorities in Iraq: the Other Victims", p5
529. Lydia Khalil, "Stability in Iraqi Kurdistan: reality or mirage?", The Saban Centre for Middle East Policy, the Brookings Institution, Working Paper no.2, 1, 19 June (2009): p25-26
530. Minority Rights Group International, World Directory of Minorities and Indigenous Peoples: Assyrians, April 2008, http://www.minorityrights.org (retrieved 23 June (2011)
531. United States Commission on International Religious Freedom, Annual Report 2005, http://wwwuscirf.gov/countries/publications (retrieved 23 june 2011)

532. "Last Christians Ponder Leaving a hometown in Iraq" *(New York Times*, 19 January 2011 www.nytimes.com (retrieved 23 June 2011)

533. Amnesty International, "Killing of civilian hostages in Iraq church a 'war crime'", Report at www.amnesty.org.au (retrieved 3 November 2010)

534. International Association of Genocide Scholars, Resolutions and Statements, 'Resolution on Genocide committed by the Ottoman Empire', 13 July 2007 www.genocidescholars.org (retrieved 15 July 2011)

535. New South Wales Parliament, Legislative Assembly, Full Day Hansard Transcript, Inaugural Speeches, 1 June 2011 www.parliament.nsw.gov.au (retrieved 15 July 2011)

536. G. Gow, *"Assyrian Community Capacity Building in Fairfield City"*, University of Western Sydney, Centre for Cultural Research (2005): p3

Dunsterforce on the road, Persia, 1918.

Refugees on their way to Baqubah with Dunsterforce.

Captain Stanley George Savige, 24th Battalion, AIF, January 1919.

Assyrian refugees, Urmiah, North West Persia, July 1918.

Captain Savige, top right, with Major Gellibrand, third left, and 6th Brigade staff, Pozieres, 1916.

Funeral of General Sir Stanley Savige at St Paul's Cathedral, Melbourne, Australia, May 1954.

SOUTH CAUCASUS, WESTERN IRAN AND MESOPOTAMIA: July – early October, 1918

Boundaries
— International, as of 1914
— International, as of 2010 if different from 1914

Transportation
— Major railway
— Major road

British disposition and Dunsterforce mission
— Disposition, 10.1918
→ Dunsterforce mission to Baku (08-09.1918)

Territory effectively controlled by:

	Entente and pro-Entente forces	Turks and pro-Turk. forces	Germans and pro-German forces	Neutral or no effective control
07.1918				
10.1918				

Isolated enclaves
① Russian Mughan
② Armenian republic
③ Armenian forces under Andranik
④ Parts of Mountainous

www.ingramcontent.com/pod-product-compliance
Lightning Source LLC
Chambersburg PA
CBHW071902290426
44110CB00013B/1245